Sarah Brown's
VEGETARIAN
COOKBOOK

Sarah Brown's
VEGETARIAN
COOKBOOK

DK

DORLING KINDERSLEY
LONDON

Sarah Brown's Vegetarian Cookbook
was conceived, edited and designed by
Dorling Kindersley Limited,
9 Henrietta Street, London WC2

Editor: Ursula Whyte
Editorial Assistant: Polly Kitzinger

Senior Art Editor: Anne-Marie Bulat
Art Editor: Derek Coombes

Managing Editor: Daphne Razazan

Photography: Philip Dowell

First published in Great Britain
in 1984 by Dorling Kindersley Limited,
9 Henrietta Street, London WC2E 8PS
Second impression 1984
Third impression 1985
Fourth impression 1985
Fifth impression 1985
Sixth impression 1986
Seventh impression 1986

British Library Cataloguing in Publication Data
Brown, Sarah
  Sarah Brown's vegetarian cookbook.
  1. Vegetarian cookery
  I. Title
  641.5'636   TX837
  ISBN 0-86318-042-6

Printed in Italy by Arnoldo Mondadori, Verona

Contents

The RECIPES

MENU AND MEAL PLANNER

Introduction

A vegetarian does not eat fish, meat or poultry and may or may not eat milk, dairy products and eggs. People adopt this way of life for various reasons, of which the main ones are usually humanitarian or to do with ecology or health. Those who do so on humanitarian grounds have a basic respect for life in all its forms and will avoid not only meat but any product obtained by exploiting animals. Some (vegans) extend this to include all dairy products and eggs, however humanely they may be produced, and may also avoid honey. Concern for ecology leads many to prefer plant protein, which is far more economical to produce than animal protein.

From the health point of view, the case for vegetarianism is a strong one. Most of the so-called "diseases of civilisation" including heart disease, high blood pressure, strokes, diabetes, obesity and diverticulitis, are linked with, if not directly attributable to, the conventional western diet, which is high in animal fats, salt and sugar but low in fibre. A vegetarian diet not only replaces animal fats with vegetable ones but often cuts down on the total fat intake, since in the average diet a third of the fats come from meat and another third from dairy products. Eating cereals, pulses, fruit and vegetables will ensure adequate fibre intake. Many vegetarians eat whole foods, avoiding the high levels of added salt and sugar in many processed foods.

All the recipes in this book are vegetarian, and dairy produce and eggs are used, although in some recipes an alternative has been suggested. Whole, unrefined foods are invariably used in preference to processed.

Whatever your basic reasons for being interested in vegetarianism, it is a good idea to analyze your existing diet so that you are aware of the changes that need to be made. You may want to cut out animal products completely or perhaps you'd like to have vegetarian food as an occasional alternative to meat. If you want to give up animal products, your body will adjust better if you don't make too violent a change. Start by eating less meat than you have been used to; or give up red meat first, then chicken and fish. Get into the habit of cooking a different type of pulse or grain once or twice a week. Whether your emphasis is vegetarian or on wholefoods, don't throw out all your existing stores and restock with new ones: gradually substitute vegetable oils for animal cooking fats and vegetable stock for meat stock; try small amounts of brown rice and wholewheat pasta and flour. You could try having one or two vegetarian days a week, building up to more gradually. Eating out and travelling need forethought. If you are invited out for a meal, make sure that your friends know in advance exactly what you can and cannot eat. When booking a holiday state clearly your needs as a vegetarian and make sure they can be catered for. I find it a good idea to travel with some "emergency" rations, such as dried fruit and nuts, to tide me over if necessary. There are vegetarian societies in both Britain and the United States whose purpose is to give information and guidance. I hope that this book and the recipes in it will help you to appreciate and enjoy vegetarianism.

The STORE CUPBOARD

One of the joys of trying out a different style of cookery is undoubtedly discovering a fresh range of dishes with new combinations of tastes and textures. Based as it is on the cuisines of many different countries, vegetarian cookery draws on a wide variety of ingredients, some of which will be familiar, others, such as sea vegetables and soya products, less so. This section is intended as a guide to those that play a central part in vegetarian cookery and that feature in the recipes in this book, from the staples such as cereals and legumes to seasonings and flavourings. Naturally, there's no need to buy every type of bean or cereal product shown here—you can gradually add to your stock as you try out different recipes.

Illustrated, too, is a selection of fresh foods, including less common vegetables and wholefood or vegetarian substitutes for animal products. For further information on buying, storing, preparation and cooking, turn to pages 204-223.

Grains

Centre: **Wholewheat flour** (*left*), **Whole wheat berries** (*centre*), **Couscous** (*right*)

Wheat flakes **Bulgar wheat** **Cracked wheat** **Wheatgerm**

Semolina **Unbleached white flour** **Bran** **Wheatmeal flour**

WHEAT (*Triticum vulgare*) is grown over more of the earth's surface than any other grain, and is available in a wide variety of forms. The **whole wheat grain** or **berry** is the most nutritious form, with none of the germ or outer layers removed: when cooked, it is chewy and substantial.

Cracked or **kibbled wheat** is produced by cracking whole wheat berries between rollers so that they will cook more quickly, in only 20 minutes. If they are then hulled, steamed and roasted they are known as **bulgar wheat** or **burghul** and need little or no cooking. **Wheat flakes** are similar, but rolled flatter and often toasted to a golden brown.

All the above are variants on the whole wheat grain, which is often subjected to further milling to produce lighter, more widely desirable results. In the process two very valuable constituents are lost: **wheatgerm** and **bran**. Wheatgerm is the heart of wheat and contains most of the nutrients. Bran is the outer covering of the wheat grain and is valued particularly for its high fibre content. Both wheatgerm and bran can be bought separately and added to breakfast cereals, breads and cakes or used as toppings.

Wholewheat or **wholemeal flour,** made from the whole grain, is available stone-ground or, more commonly, roller-milled.

Wheatmeal flour retains a lot of the nutrients, but has 15-19 per cent wheat (in practice, the germ and most of the bran) removed to make it lighter. White flour has had all the bran and germ removed; **unbleached white flour** is preferable as it has not been chemically treated.

Semolina is produced from the starchy part of the grain, the endosperm. It is available as medium or coarse meal and used for puddings or gnocchi. Semolina from durum wheat is used for making pasta commercially. Fine semolina grains coated with flour are known as **couscous,** the basis of the North African dish.

Oats (*Avena sativa*) The whole oat grain is known as a groat. It is not often seen in this form as although it can be used—for instance for making porridge—it takes time to cook.

Oatmeal is now generally available in three grades, **coarse, medium** and **fine,** but used to be available in far more. A little added to wheat flour gives taste to bread.

Millet (*Panicum miliaceum*) is prolific and easy to grow but has only recently been considered in the West although it has long been an important crop in Africa and Asia, especially Northern China. It is

Rolled oat flakes (oat flakes; rolled oats; porridge oats), produced from groats that have been broken down by rolling; heat can also be applied to prevent the oil going rancid and thus improve shelf life.

Jumbo oat flakes are similar to rolled oats but, as their name implies, larger. They can also be heat-treated.

related to sorghum, an important crop in Africa, and is the staple food of the Hunzas, the Himalayan tribe famous for their longevity. **Millet flakes** can be used like other flakes in cereals and as toppings.

Grains

RICE (*Oryza sativa*) Brown rice is, like the wheat berry, the whole natural grain, unprocessed. The type most commonly found is **long-grain** or *indica* rice, much grown in India.

Short-grain or *japonica* rice is, as its name indicates, popular in Japan as well as in parts of China. Another type of short-grain rice is grown in Italy and used for risottos.

Basmati rice has the finest flavour of any easily available white rice, although like all white rices it has had a high proportion of nutrients removed by milling.

Rice flakes are processed to be quick-cooking, in about 10 minutes, and can be used to thicken soups and casseroles.

Rice flour is usually made from white rice. Because of its lack of gluten it is useful for those on low-gluten diets.

WILD RICE (*Zizania aquatica*) is not a rice although it looks like one. Its grains are longer and more slender, dark brown when raw, slightly purplish when cooked. Native to North America.

BUCKWHEAT (*Fagopyrum esculentum*) is also sometimes called Saracen corn or wheat (it was supposed to have been introduced to Europe by the Crusaders).

Roasted buckwheat grains are popular for their flavour—roasting is the usual way of preparing the grains for cooking.

Buckwheat flour is strong and savoury, and is often mixed with wheat flour. It is good in pancakes and is used in Japan to make noodles called soba.

Coarse cornmeal

Fine cornmeal

CORN (*Zea mays*), known as maize in Europe, originated in Central America. **Popcorn** is a variety with a very hard endosperm, which explodes when heated.

Another variety is used to produce **cornmeal**, both **coarse** and **fine;** this is sometimes bolted, or sieved, which removes the bran and some of the fibre but makes little difference nutritionally.

Barley flakes

Barley flour

BARLEY (*Hordeum vulgare*) Still important for food in some parts of the world, particularly Japan, although elsewhere it has been superseded as a food crop and is used mainly for brewing. It compares well with other grains nutritionally, and is particularly high in niacin.

Like other cereals, it is available in flakes and as flour. The inclusion of a little flour adds a distinctive sweet taste to bread. It is one of the oldest food crops and was known to the Hebrews, Greeks and Romans, as well as in Tibet.

Rye flakes

Rye flour

RYE (*Secale cereale*) Popular in northern and eastern Europe, and parts of Russia, where its distinctive sour taste is much appreciated, particularly in bread. The groats can be made into dark rye flour, or they can be

partially husked and made into light flour. Although rye contains gluten, it is not the same sort as that in wheat and will not leaven bread, so that most rye bread is in fact made from a mixture of rye and wheat.

Beans, peas and lentils

Lima beans

Butter beans

Lima beans and Butter beans (*Phaseolus lunatus*) Originating from tropical America, these are very similar, but lima beans tend to be smaller and sweeter and are an ingredient of the traditional American Indian dish succotash.

Black beans (*Phaseolus vulgaris*) The shiny black outside contrasts with the white inside. Popular in Latin America. Not the same as the black bean used in China, which is a type of soya bean, fermented, salted and used as flavouring.

Aduki beans (*Phaseolus angularis*) Tiny, round, hard, dark red beans, also known as adzuki beans; very popular in the Far East, especially Japan. Rich in protein, they can also be made into flour.

Red kidney beans (*Phaseolus vulgaris*) Like all kidney beans these are native to the New World. This variety is particularly popular in Mexican cookery. Also called chili bean.

Haricot beans (*Phaseolus vulgaris*) One of the best known varieties, also known as white haricots, navy beans or Great Northern beans. The original bean used in Boston baked beans.

Ful medames (*Lathyrus sativus*) These small dark-brown beans are especially popular in Egypt, where they are combined with hard-boiled eggs to make what is almost the Egyptian national dish.

Pinto beans (*Phaseolus vulgaris*) Another variety of haricot bean, not unlike the speckled Italian borlotti beans. The name means "coloured" They turn pink when cooked.

Flageolet beans (*Phaseolus vulgaris*) Very popular in both France and Italy, with an unusually delicate, subtle taste and an attractive pale green colour.

Cannellini (*Phaseolus vulgaris*) A variety of haricot or kidney bean much appreciated in Italy. A similar bean is widely grown in Argentina.

Whole mung beans

Split mung beans

Broad beans (*Vicia faba*) Once important in Europe, but yielded popularity to the various kidney beans, possibly because broad beans contain substances which, if eaten in quantity, can cause a blood disease known as favism.

Mung beans (*Phaseolus aureus*) Native to tropical Asia and still one of the most widely grown legumes. The seeds are mainly used as a vegetable but are also popular, especially in China and the U.S.A. as an important source of bean sprouts.

Black-eyed beans (*Vigna unguiculata*) Also known as cowpeas and native to Central Africa; taken to the New World in the 16th century. Not only the seeds are eaten: the immature pods can be cooked and the young shoots and leaves can be boiled like spinach or eaten raw in salads.

Soya beans (*Glycine max*) The most nutritious bean of all, containing all the essential amino acids. Originally from China, where their value has been recognized for nearly 5,000 years. Can be made into curd, paste or sauce.

Chick peas (*Cicer arietinum*) Highly popular all over the Mediterranean and the Middle East, as well as in India where they are known as Bengal gram (the Indian word gram means pulse or legume). They are also known as garbanzos or garbanzo peas. High in protein, they are very nutritious, and can be ground into flour.

Split green peas

Whole green peas

Split yellow peas

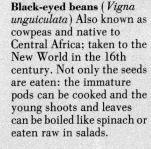

Continental lentils

Brown lentils

Split red lentils

Peas (*Pisum sativum*) Common peas are now mostly eaten fresh, in which form they can be canned or frozen, but were formerly valuable as a dried vegetable. They are available split or whole.

Lentils (*Lens esculenta*) One of the oldest crops, cultivated since prehistoric times; originally from the eastern Mediterranean, now found all over the Middle East and India. Available whole or split and in a variety of colours.

Nuts and seeds

Shelled almond

Blanched almond

Slivered almonds

Whole almond

Almonds (*Prunus amygdalus*) The most popular nut of all. The sweet variety is the kind normally used: bitter almonds are toxic, but the unpleasant taste is a deterrent. Almonds have the highest protein content of any nut and are also rich in minerals, especially calcium.

Ground almonds

Whole hazelnuts   **Shelled hazelnuts**

Hazelnuts, cobs, filberts (*Corylus avellana; C. maxima*) Widely grown in Italy, France and Turkey, they are low in fat and high in vitamins B and E.

Cashews (*Anacardium occidentale*) The unusual fruit looks like an apple with the kidney-shaped nut hanging beneath it. The nutshell contains an acid and is removed before the nuts are sold.

Whole walnut   **Shelled walnuts**

Walnuts (*Juglans regia; J. nigra*) Good sources of protein, vitamins, minerals and unsaturated fats, especially the black or American walnut. Green or unripe walnuts are rich in vitamin C; they are delicious pickled.

Brazil nuts (*Bertholletia excelsa*) From the Amazon basin, the nuts cluster like orange segments inside a woody fruit. They have the highest fat content of any nut and are also rich in minerals.

Shelled Brazil nut

Whole Brazil nut

Shelled pecans

Whole pecans

Pecans (*Carya pecan*) Related to walnuts, but richer, milder and subtler in flavour, they are much appreciated in their native North America. Hickory and bitternut are also related.

Whole chestnut   Shelled chestnut

Shelled and peeled chestnut

Sweet chestnuts (*Castanea sativa*) Native to Southern Europe and unlike most other nuts in that they are very starchy and low in protein. Both the hard shell and the thin inner skin need to be removed. Often also available dried.

Pine kernels (*Pinus pinea*) The seeds of various pines, chiefly the stone pine of the Mediterranean, and also known as pignolias or Indian nuts.

Whole pistachios   Shelled pistachios

Pistachios (*Pistacia vera*) Native to the Mediterranean and Middle East, where they are eaten as a snack. Prized for their bright green colour.

Sunflower seeds (*Helianthus annuus*) Rich in proteins and minerals and containing 40 per cent unsaturated oil, they made an excellent snack.

Chinese water chestnuts (*Eleocharia tuberosa*) are not true nuts, but tubers of a sedge, although with their crisp texture they can be used as nuts.

Whole (unshelled) peanuts   Shelled peanuts, with and without skin

Peanuts (*Arachis hypogaea*) Sometimes called groundnuts or monkeynuts, these are not true nuts but underground legumes.

Pumpkin seeds (*Cucurbita maxima*) Good source of proteins, fats and minerals, especially zinc.

Fresh coconut

Desiccated coconut

Coconut (*Cocus nucifera*) The coconut palm is a source of fibre, soap and animal fodder as well as oil and other edible products. The dried flesh may be compressed into blocks or sold as flakes or powder.

Creamed coconut

Sesame seeds (*Sesamum indicum*) Of African origin, now an important crop in the Middle and Far East as well as in Mexico. Excellent source of oil.

Linseeds (*Linum usitatissimum*) The seeds of the flax plant. The Greeks and Romans used them as food.

Dried fruit

Dried peach

Dried nectarine

Hunza apricot

Whole sulphured apricot

Half sun-dried apricot

Half unsulphured apricot

Peaches and Nectarines (*Prunus persica*) come mainly from Australia, China and California. Some Chinese varieties are preserved in sugar: this will be stated on the box or packet.

Apricots (*Prunus armeniaca*) Mainly grown in the Far East, North Africa and California, dried apricots also come from Turkey and Australia. The best of all are considered to be the wild or Hunza apricots from the Himalayas. Apricots contain more protein than other dried fruits.

Dried apple ring

Apples (*Malus communis*) are usually peeled, cored and cut into rings; occasionally they are cut into segments. The whiter the apple, the more sulphur has been used to preserve it.

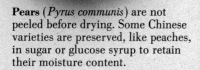

Pears (*Pyrus communis*) are not peeled before drying. Some Chinese varieties are preserved, like peaches, in sugar or glucose syrup to retain their moisture content.

Bananas (*Musa spp.*) dry most successfully when fully ripe with a high sugar content; they may be dried in pieces or slices. Do not confuse with banana chips, thin slices of unripe banana which have been deep-fried.

Figs (*Ficus carica*) are valued according to size, and should be rich brown with a thin skin. The thinner the skin, the more likelihood of sugaring on the surface: this therefore indicates quality. Lerida figs (above) are best.

Dates (*Phoenix dactylifera*) are very high in sugar (66 per cent) and also contain vitamin A and some B vitamins. Dessert dates (above) are sold unpitted; the best variety is "Deglet Nour". Dried dates for cooking are sold in blocks.

Prunes (*Prunus domestica*) The type of plum grown for drying is usually late-ripening and black-skinned. Prunes are sold pitted or unpitted. "Tenderized", or partially cooked, prunes need only 8 minutes further cooking.

Thompson's seedless raisins

Muscatel raisins

Sultanas (*Vitis vinifera*) come from seedless white grapes. Unlike currants, they are often treated chemically—sulphured to preserve colour and sprayed to give them an attractive gloss.

Lexia raisins

Raisins (*Vitis vinifera*) are not chemically treated and darken naturally in the sun. Dessert raisins (the best known variety is the Lexia raisin from Australia) are larger and juicier.

Currants (*Vitis vinifera*) come from small black seedless grapes grown near Corinth (hence their name) and other parts of Greece. They are not chemically treated. Vostizza is considered the best variety.

Seasonings and flavourings

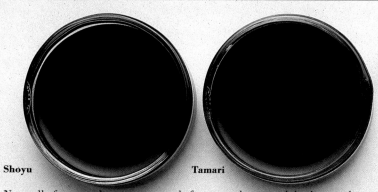

Shoyu　　　　　　　　　　**Tamari**

Naturally fermented soya sauce, made from soya beans with barley or wheat, is known as **shoyu** or **tamari,** and should not be confused with the manufactured soya sauce, which is not the same and usually contains sugar and other additives. True tamari, a liquid from the manufacture of miso, contains no wheat and is therefore suitable for gluten-free diets, but is very difficult to find.

Dried mushrooms are available in several varieties, from the strongly flavoured cep (*Boletus edulis*) to the ordinary cultivated mushroom (*Agaricus bisporus*) shown above. Even this kind makes a valuable contribution of flavour.

Mugi miso

Hatcho miso

Vegetable concentrates, like stock cubes, are a quick way of adding flavour to stocks, soups and casseroles, and for making hot drinks. They can also be spread on toast.

Vegetable stock cubes are quite widely available, but make sure they contain no artificial additives. They should be a concentration of vegetables, yeast and vitamins.

Genmai miso

Grated horseradish, when fresh, is very pungent, and much liked in Germany and Scandinavia as well as Britain. It can be used rather in the same way as mustard.

Miso, like shoyu and tamari, is a product of the fermented soya bean, a little like peanut butter in texture. All misos have quite a high salt content, although lighter coloured miso has slightly less.

Yeast extracts are made from a mixture of brewer's yeast and salt, which produces a highly flavoured brown residue, full of protein, iron, potassium and B vitamins, some with added B_{12}.

Brewer's yeast is exceptionally high in protein as well as in calcium, iron and B vitamins. It can be sprinkled over cereals or used as part of a topping, and adds an interesting flavour as well as nourishment.

Japanese gomashio, or sesame salt, is available from healthfood shops, but it is easy to make your own by grinding 4-5 parts roasted sesame seeds with one part salt. Keep in an airtight container and use instead of salt, not in addition to it.

English mustard powder is made mainly from black mustard seed. Its clean, sharp taste makes it ideal for flavouring sauces, dressings and dips.

Wholegrain mustard, usually from France, contains the whole mustard seed and is often flavoured with herbs such as tarragon. It is used as a relish.

Peanut butter is not only a nutritious spread but can be adapted to other uses, particularly as a flavouring for sauces and dressings.

Rock salt

Salt substitute

Sea salt

Salt (*sodium chloride*) comes from the sea, either as sea salt or as bay salt, which is directly evaporated from sea water, or as rock salt, which is usually found as deposits left by vanished prehistoric seas. Salt substitutes, for those who wish to cut down on sodium, are also available.

Tahini is sesame seed paste, widely used in the Middle East. Strong and nutty, it can be used as a dip on its own or to flavour other dips and sauces.

Sea vegetables

Carrageen (*Chondrus crispus*), also called Irish moss, is still eaten in Ireland, and used to be valued as a cure for bronchial diseases and tuberculosis.

Arame (*Eisenia bicyclis*) has a mild taste that blends well with other flavours, and is a good introduction to sea vegetables. Rich in iron.

Nori (*Porphyra spp.*) is intensively grown in Japan, where it is usually sold in sheets which can be wrapped round rice. Laver, still used in Wales, is similar.

Dulse (*Rhodymenia palmata*) grows in the North Atlantic and is eaten in Ireland and New England as well as Iceland and parts of Canada.

Kombu (*Laminaria spp.*) is much cultivated in Japan and considered suitable for offering as a gift.

Agar (or agar-agar, from a Malay word meaning jelly) is obtained from several different species of sea vegetables. Also called Japanese or Ceylon moss, it is used as a substitute for animal gelatine.

Wakame (*Undaria pinnatifida*) is another Japanese favourite. Softer than kombu, it can be used in many of the same ways, particularly in soup.

Agar flakes

Agar powder

Sweetenings

Muscovado sugar is a dark, moist, partly refined sugar with a strong distinctive flavour, sometimes called Barbados sugar.

Demerara sugar can be white sugar dyed with caramel. If the country of origin is stated on the packet, it is less likely to be dyed.

Light brown sugar As with demerara, check the packet for the country of origin.

Carob powder Carob pods, the size of a banana, but flat and dark brown, contain small black seeds, so uniform in size that the word "carat" as a measure of weight derives from them.

Apple juice concentrate This and other concentrated fruit juices are useful flavourings for fruit salads, sauces and cereals.

Corn syrup, or glucose syrup, is made by heating cornstarch and water with a little sulphuric or hydrochloric acid.

Molasses, sometimes called black treacle, is the residue left when cane sugar is refined. It has some vitamins and minerals.

Maple syrup comes from the sugar maple and black maple. It takes 50 gallons of sap to make one gallon of syrup, so it is a very concentrated form of sweetening.

Malt extract, sometimes also called barley syrup, is not so sweet as sugar; it is used to flavour drinks and malted breads and cakes.

21

Spices

Capers (*Capparis spinosa*)
The buds of a small Mediterranean bush, these are usually sold pickled in vinegar and should not be allowed to dry out. Used mostly in sauces and salads.

Cloves (*Eugenia caryophyllata*)
Buds of an evergreen tree, widely used in curries, marinades, mincemeat, fruit dishes and mulled wine. Use sparingly as the taste is penetrating.

Nutmeg (*Myristica fragrans*)
Always buy whole and grate as required. Ready-ground nutmeg quickly loses it aroma. Sometimes sold coated with lime to repel insects; this is harmless.

Cardamom (*Elettaria cardamomum*) The flavourless pod encloses black aromatic seeds used in curries and pastries and to flavour drinks, including coffee.

Ginger (*Zingiber officinale*)
Fresh root ginger is firm and juicy. It needs peeling before being grated or chopped for use in curries or puddings.

Saffron (*Crocus sativus*)
Always buy the stigmas or "threads" of this extremely expensive spice, as the powder is very easy to adulterate.

Juniper (*Juniperus communis*)
The berries have a pungent, slightly resinous flavour. They go well with cabbage and add a light touch to oily or heavy dishes.

Cinnamon
(*Cinnamomum zeylanicum*)
The "quills" of dried bark can flavour drinks and syrups; the powder is widely used in breads and sweet dishes.

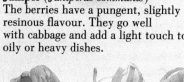

Mace (*Myristica fragrans*)
The dried outer membrane of nutmeg, which it resembles in taste. Sold both in "blades" and ready ground as it is difficult to grind at home.

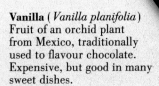

Vanilla (*Vanilla planifolia*)
Fruit of an orchid plant from Mexico, traditionally used to flavour chocolate. Expensive, but good in many sweet dishes.

Allspice (*Pimenta officinalis*)
Also called Jamaica pepper;
the taste combines cloves,
cinnamon and nutmeg.

Aniseed (*Pimpinella asinum*)
Popular in Mexico and all
over the Mediterranean
for its liquorice flavour.

Celery (*Apium graveolens*)
The slightly bitter taste of
celery seeds goes well in
bread, egg dishes and salads.

Chili (*Capsicum frutescens*)
Ripe chili peppers dry and
keep well. "Chili powder"
often includes other spices.

Dill (*Anethum graveolens*)
Popular in Eastern and
Northern Europe, dill seed
is much used in pickles.

Fennel (*Foeniculum vulgare*)
Like the bulb, fennel seeds
have a slight aniseed flavour.
Good with fruit and salads.

Paprika (*Capsicum annuum*)
Made from very mild, sweet
peppers, popular in Hungary
and Spain. Use generously.

Pepper (*Piper nigrum*)
Unripe whole peppercorns
are green. When dried
they turn brown-black.

Caraway (*Carum carvi*)
Looks like cumin seed and
often confused with it, but
the taste is quite different.

Cayenne (*Capsicum
frutescens*) A very hot,
pungent red chili sold ready
ground. Use sparingly.

Coriander (*Coriandrum
sativum*) Mild but aromatic,
coriander seed is important
in Arab and Eastern food.

Cumin (*Cuminum cyminum*)
The pungent seed is often
combined with coriander as
a basic curry mixture.

Fenugreek (*Trigonella
foenum-graecum*) Produces
spicy sprouts. Use the
ground seed sparingly.

Mustard (*Brassica alba;
B. Nigra*) The white (or
yellow) seed is milder than
the black (or brown) seed.

Poppy seed (*Papaver rhoeas;
P. somniferum*) White poppy
seed is much used in curries,
blue in pastries.

Turmeric (*Curcuma longa*)
Always sold ground. Do not
confuse with saffron. The
taste is mustier.

Herbs

Chives (*Allium schoenoprasum*) Mostly eaten raw, but also good in omelettes. Widely used from China and Japan to Europe and America.

Basil (*Ocimum basilicum*) If you cannot find fresh, do not use dried; substitute another herb. A pot of basil in the kitchen will keep flies away.

Lemon balm (*Melissa officinalis*) The crushed leaves give off a wonderful lemony scent. They can be used generously in salads.

Bay leaf (*Laurus nobilis*) Good in milk puddings as well as savoury stews and sauces. A leaf kept in a packet of grains will give them a delicate taste.

Coriander (*Coriandrum sativum*) Also known as Chinese or Japanese parsley, it is used lavishly in the East in the same way as parsley.

Marjoram (*Origanum majorana*) Sweet marjoram, native to the Mediterranean, is very fragrant and can be dried successfully.

Chervil (*Anthriscus cerefolium*) Very popular in France; can be used like parsley but has a more delicate taste with a hint of anise.

Dill (*Anethum graveolens*) The leaves are known as dill weed, one of the most popular herbs in Scandinavia.

Mint (*Menta spp.*) There are many species of this popular herb, from spearmint to the fresh-tasting peppermint used for tisanes.

Oregano (*Origanum vulgare*) This is wild marjoram, which for the best flavour must be grown in strong sun. Luckily it keeps all its aroma when it is dried.

Winter savory (*Satureja montana*) Its German name means "bean-herb", which indicates its traditional use. Summer savory (*S. hortensis*) is similar and even more aromatic.

Rosemary (*Rosmarinus officinalis*) A wonderfully aromatic herb with a strong camphor-like flavour. The spiky needles can be a menace when dried.

Parsley (*Petroselinum crispum*) Available curled (above) or flat (below), parsley is a good source of both vitamin C and iron.

Tarragon (*Artemisia dracunculus*) If possible, make sure that you are getting French tarragon, not Russian which is far less aromatic.

Flat parsley is generally grown in Europe and it is thought to have a finer taste than curled parsley.

Sage (*Salvia officinalis*) There are many varieties. It dries well, but can become musty if kept too long.

Thyme (*Thymus vulgaris*) This popular herb contains an essential oil, thymol, which helps to digest fatty foods.

Vegetables

Pak choi
(*Brassica chinensis*)

Spinach beet
(*Beta vulgaris*)

Chard (*Beta vulgaris*)

Less well known than some other leaf vegetables, **pak choi,** or Chinese cabbage, is crisp and delicate-tasting and needs little or no cooking. **Chard** (Swiss chard or seakale beet) and **spinach beet** are the same species; they resemble spinach, but lack its distinctive flavour. The central spines of **chard** are often cut out and cooked separately.

Batavian endive
(*Cichorium endivia*)

Curly endive
(*Cichorium endivia*)

Chicory
(*Cichorium intybus*)

Radicchio rosso
(*Cichorium endivia*)

Endive and **chicory** have a similar slightly bitter taste.
Both are usually blanched by the grower to reduce this
bitterness to an acceptable level. Chicory can be eaten raw,
braised or stir-fried. Endive is valuable as a salad plant;
the most popular kinds are curly endive (the French
"*frisée*"), the more wavy Batavian endive, or escarole, and
the crisp **radicchio rosso** from Treviso in north Italy.

Salad vegetables and sprouts

Lamb's lettuce (*Valerianella olitoria*) Also known as corn salad and (in France) as *mâche*, this is a very useful winter salad.

Sorrel (*Rumex acetosa*) is high in oxalic acid. This gives it its fresh, sharp taste but also impedes assimilation of minerals, notably calcium and iron. Garden sorrel (*Rumex scutatus*) is less acid.

Dandelion (*Taraxacum officinale*) Dandelion leaves offered for sale have been blanched (like celery and chicory) to reduce their bitterness. If you want to use wild dandelions, pick the young leaves.

Rocket (*Eruca sativa*) is deservedly popular in Italy and parts of France. The young, tender leaves (above) become toothed and taste peppery.

Lovage (*Levisticum officinale*) The young, reddish leaves (above) are good in salads; the older leaves (left) and the stems make powerful flavourings.

Mung beans (*Phaseolus aureus*) **Alfalfa** (*Medicago sativa*) **Wheat** (*Triticum vulgare*)

Cress (*Lepidum sativum*)

Mustard (*Sinapis alba*)

Aduki beans (*Phaseolus angularis*) **Fenugreek** (*Trigonella foenum-graecum*) **Lentils** (*Lens esculenta*)

Sprouts from **wheat** (and other grains such as rye) and from **lentils** are best when grown to about the length of the seeds. **Aduki bean** sprouts should be about 1 cm (½ in) long; **mung beans** can be grown to 2.5 cm (1 in). **Mustard and cress** are eaten at the two-leaf stage, when 3-4 cm (1-1½ in) long; so are **alfalfa** sprouts, which take 5-6 days. **Fenugreek** sprouts are best when not more than 2-3 times the length of the seed, which takes 3-6 days.

Vegetables

Okra (*Hibiscus esculentus*), also known as lady's fingers and gumbo. The edible part is the pod, picked and eaten while still unripe, as when fully ripe it becomes fibrous and indigestible. It is very mucilaginous and when added to soups and casseroles gives them a rich, thick consistency.

Fennel (*Foeniculum vulgare var. dulce*) often known as Florence fennel. The "bulb" is the swollen leaf-base and has a pronounced anise flavour. Usually served raw in salads.

Kohlrabi (*Brassica oleracea*) A variety of cabbage, also called turnip-rooted cabbage, although the apparent root is actually the swollen stem. Both green and purple varieties are good when young, crisp and tender: they can then be eaten raw and have a delicate, slightly turnip-like flavour. Weight for weight they have more vitamin C than oranges.

Daikon (*Raphanus sativus*) A large winter radish, also known as Japanese white radish or mooli. It has a crisp texture and a milder flavour than ordinary winter radishes. It is used like them, in salads and stir-fries. All winter radishes have slightly more nutritional value than spring ones.

Winter radish (*Raphanus sativus*) A useful vegetable for winter salads, much grown in China and Japan. The large roots are crisp, but not quite so tender as spring radishes. Excellent in stir-fries.

Salsify (*Tragopogon porrifolius*) Also called oyster plant or vegetable plant, as its subtle taste is supposed to resemble that of oysters. "Black salsify" is the related scorzonera, similar in appearance but black-skinned.

Sweet potato (*Ipomoea batatas*) This name is also sometimes given to the brown-skinned yam, which is similar in taste but has little nutritive value.

Jerusalem artichoke (*Helianthus tuberosus*) No relation to globe artichokes, but a cousin of the sunflower. Has a sweet, nutty flavour.

Cheeses

All the cheeses on these two pages are made without animal rennet (see page 221). On this page, from top left, clockwise: **Double Gloucester; Botton** (an English farmhouse cheese from Yorkshire) made with chives; **farmhouse** cheese made with celery seeds; **hard goat's** cheese; and **Cheddar.** Other hard cheeses available include Gouda and Munster.

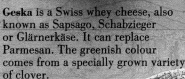

Geska is a Swiss whey cheese, also known as Sapsago, Schabzieger or Glärnerkäse. It can replace Parmesan. The greenish colour comes from a specially grown variety of clover.

Cream cheese is made, as the name indicates, from cream and therefore has a very high fat content. It is valued for its smooth, rich taste and texture.

Chèvre or French goat's cheese is a traditional soft cheese with a distinctive taste. It is usually found in the shape shown here or as a small cylinder.

Coulommiers is a mild French cheese, similar to Brie (it is also called Brie de Coulommiers). Usually eaten unripened, it is often sprinkled with paprika or herbs.

Feta is the best known Greek cheese. with tomato and cucumber, it becomes "Greek salad". Traditionally made from sheep or goat's milk, it is curdled naturally without the addition of rennet.

Cottage cheese is a type of low fat curd cheese made from cooked skimmed cow's milk. It is drained, washed and coated with thin cream and has a granular appearance.

Curd cheese is soft cheese made from whole cow's milk, usually set without using rennet, and sometimes known as lactic curd cheese.

Ricotta is a very low fat cheese made from whey, not from Sometimes available in hard form for grating.

Dairy produce and alternatives

Soya milk can be used as a substitute for dairy milk (for how to make it yourself, see page 220). Commercial soya milk sometimes has added sugar, so do read the packet carefully.

Solid vegetable fat is the only vegetarian alternative to lard or suet. Vegetable oils are hydrogenated to make them solid at room temperature (see page 219).

Buttermilk is the liquid remaining after fresh cream has been churned to make butter. Much of the buttermilk sold today is cultured and soured by adding bacteria to form lactic acid.

Silken tofu

Firm tofu

Soft tofu

Yogurt, one of the most popular fermented milk products, is a natural antibiotic, the acid in it killing almost all harmful organisms. It is easily digested, especially goat's milk yogurt (above).

Tofu, a product of the soya bean, is generally available as silken tofu, made from lightly pressed soya bean curd, and firm tofu, which is more heavily pressed. Soft or regular tofu has a texture in between the two.

Ghee generally denotes clarified butter but a vegetable version (above) made from hydrogenated vegetable oils is also available.

Strained yogurt, popular in Greece, is much smoother, creamier and sweeter than ordinary yogurt, not unlike the French *crème fraîche*. It is an excellent substitute for cream.

The RECIPES

★ *indicates that the dish is suitable for freezing*

STARTERS

Whether you eat a formal meal with separate courses, or whether you follow the example of many vegetarians and combine several dishes at the same time, something to start with is always welcome. This can be simple, perhaps eaten with a drink before the meal—pâté spread on little biscuits, raw vegetables with various dips— or more elaborate, such as a mousse or a savoury water ice.

Vegetarian food lends itself admirably to the occasion and offers endless possibilities. In addition to the recipes given here, you will find many dishes in other sections of the book which can be scaled down to make ideal first courses. Soufflés, quiches or stuffed vegetables are always welcome. For a substantial start to a meal, try pasta, pancakes, risottos or polenta, while for a lighter one, salads are perfect.

Photograph
page 39

Ingredients
350 g (12 oz) button mushrooms
Marinade
60 ml (4 tbsp) sherry
15 ml (1 tbsp) shoyu
2.5 ml (½ tsp) honey
1 tsp grated root ginger
1 clove garlic, crushed
Batter
1 egg white
30 ml (2 tbsp) wholewheat flour
45-60 ml (3-4 tbsp) water

oil for deep-frying
For serving
Chinese leaves, shredded
sprigs of fresh watercress

Serves 4

Tempura mushrooms

Tempura, the technique of cooking vegetables quickly in a light crispy batter, originated in the Far East.

1 Remove the stalks from the mushrooms and chop them finely. Mix with the marinade ingredients, pour this mixture over the mushroom caps and leave for 3-4 hours.

2 Prepare the batter by beating together the egg white and flour, then adding the water gradually, still beating, until the batter has the consistency of double cream.

3 Heat 2.5 cm (1 in) oil in a deep frying pan. Drain the mushrooms, dip them in batter and deep-fry them, about 6 at a time, for 2-3 minutes. Drain on kitchen paper and keep warm while you cook the remaining mushrooms. Serve immediately on a bed of shredded Chinese leaves garnished with watercress.

Artichokes with lemon sauce

A more elaborate variation is to prepare the artichokes as for
Stuffed artichokes on page 63 and partly fill them with sauce.

1 Wash the artichokes thoroughly. Remove the stalks and
trim the bases so that the artichokes will sit flat. Trim the
points off the leaves with scissors.

2 Bring a large pan of water to the boil and cook the artichokes,
covered, for 30-40 minutes or until a leaf pulls out easily.

3 Meanwhile, melt half the butter in a pan. Add the flour and
cook, stirring, over gentle heat for 2-3 minutes. Pour on
the boiling water, stirring vigorously, and as soon as
the mixture is smooth, beat in the remaining butter. Stir in the
lemon juice, grated lemon rind and garlic. Season to taste.
Keep warm, stirring from time to time, on very low heat.

4 Drain the artichokes as soon as they are cooked and arrange
them on a serving dish or on individual plates. Pour the
sauce into a heated sauceboat and sprinkle it with chives.

Ingredients
4 globe artichokes
75 g (3 oz) butter
15 ml (1 tbsp) wheatmeal flour
300 ml (½ pint) boiling water
10 ml (2 tsp) lemon juice
grated rind of ½ lemon
3 cloves garlic, crushed
salt and pepper
1 tbsp snipped chives

Serves 4

Photograph
pages
186-187

Spinach gnocchi

Leftover baked potatoes can be successfully used for this.

1 Put the potatoes on to boil. When they are cooked, peel
them and mash them without adding any more liquid.

2 Meanwhile, wash the spinach and cook it without adding
any extra water. Drain, squeezing out as much liquid as
possible, and chop finely.

3 Mix the potato and spinach with all the other ingredients
except for one tablespoon of the Parmesan and half the butter.
Be generous with the pepper. Chill for 45 minutes.

4 Preheat the oven to gas mark 6, 200°C (400°F) and bring
a large pan of salted water to the boil.

5 To cook the gnocchi, drop teaspoonsful of the mixture into
the pan, a few at a time. Keep the water boiling. The gnocchi
are done when they rise to the surface, after only a couple
of minutes. Remove them with a slotted spoon to an ovenproof
dish and repeat the process until all the gnocchi are cooked.

6 Melt the remaining butter and pour it over the gnocchi.
Sprinkle the rest of the Parmesan over the top and bake for
about 10 minutes or until well browned. Serve very hot.

Ingredients
450 g (1 lb) potatoes
450 g (1 lb) fresh spinach
2 eggs
225 g (8 oz) ricotta *or* cream cheese
100 g (4 oz) butter
25 g (1 oz) freshly grated Parmesan
salt and pepper
¼ tsp grated nutmeg
60-75 ml (4-5 tbsp) semolina

Serves 6-8

Photograph
page 39

★

Chestnut pâté

Ingredients

50 g (2 oz) dried chestnuts
25 g (1 oz) butter
1 small onion, finely chopped
1 clove garlic, crushed
100 g (4 oz) mushrooms, chopped
1 tsp paprika
15 ml (1 tbsp) wholewheat flour
90 ml (6 tbsp) red wine
175 g (6 oz) ground walnuts
25-50 g (1-2 oz) fresh breadcrumbs
2 sticks celery, very finely diced
10 ml (2 tsp) shoyu
salt and pepper

Serves 6-8

This is a rich but not too heavy pâté which makes a splendid start to a dinner party. It can be served warm or cold.

1 Bring a large pan of water to the boil. Put in the chestnuts, remove from the heat and leave them to soak for 1 hour.

2 Return them to the boil in the same water and cook, covered, until tender. This takes 50-60 minutes. Drain, reserving the liquid. Grind or finely chop the chestnuts.

3 Preheat the oven to gas mark 5, 190°C (375°F).

4 Melt the butter in a small frying pan and gently fry the onion and garlic for 3-4 minutes until translucent. Stir in the mushrooms and paprika, cover and continue cooking for 5-8 minutes.

5 Sprinkle on the flour, stir it in and cook for another 2-3 minutes. Pour in 90 ml (6 tbsp) of the chestnut stock and the wine. Stir well, bring to the boil and simmer for another 3 minutes. The sauce should be quite thick.

6 Mix together the walnuts, 25 g (1 oz) of the breadcrumbs, the celery and cooked chestnuts in a large bowl. Add the sauce and season with the shoyu, salt and pepper. Mix very thoroughly. The mixture should be soft but not too wet. Add a few more breadcrumbs if it is too moist.

7 Press into a 450 g (1 lb) loaf tin lined with oiled greaseproof paper. Cover with foil and bake for 50-60 minutes.

★

Photograph
pages
44-45

Lentil and aubergine pâté

Ingredients

100 g (4 oz) whole lentils, green or
    brown
1 medium aubergine
45 ml (3 tbsp) olive oil
100 g (4 oz) mushrooms, chopped
2 cloves garlic, crushed
1 tsp ground coriander
2 tbsp chopped mint
juice of ½ lemon
salt and pepper

Serves 4-6

The texture of lentils is perfect for pâté. Here their earthy flavour marries well with aubergine and mushrooms. An effective way of serving the pâté is in individual ramekins, with melba toast.

1 Preheat the oven to gas mark 4, 180°C (350°F).

2 Bring the lentils to the boil in a large pan of water. Skim off any scum, cover and simmer until soft—about 45 minutes. Leave to cool for 5 to 10 minutes.

3 Meanwhile, split the aubergine in half lengthways, brush the cut faces with oil and bake the halves for 20 minutes or until the pulp is soft. Scrape out all the flesh and chop it finely.

Continued

Clockwise from top: **Tempura mushrooms** (*see p. 36*); **Chestnut pâté**; **Spinach gnocchi** (*see p. 37*)

Lentil and aubergine
paté continued

4 Gently heat 30 ml (2 tbsp) olive oil and sauté the mushrooms and garlic over low heat for 5-6 minutes or until they are soft and well browned.

5 Separately, fry the ground coriander in 5 ml (1 tsp) oil over moderate heat for 3-4 minutes to bring out the aroma.

6 Mix together the lentils, aubergine flesh, mushrooms and garlic. Stir in the coriander, mint, lemon juice and seasoning and blend until smooth. Serve at room temperature.

★

Photograph
pages
44-45

Ingredients
15 ml (1 tbsp) olive oil
1 bunch spring onions, finely
    chopped
2 cloves garlic, crushed
175 g (6 oz) tomatoes, skinned and
    chopped
100 g (4 oz) stoned black olives,
    minced
¼ tsp celery seeds
salt
5 ml (1 tsp) clear honey
175 ml (6 fl oz) red wine

Serves 4

Wine and black olive pâté

This pâté is quite rich, and a little of it goes a long way.

1 Heat the oil and gently fry the spring onions and garlic for 3-4 minutes or until soft.

2 Add the tomatoes, olives and celery seeds, sprinkle with a little salt and stir in the honey. Cook very gently, covered, for 10 minutes.

3 Pour in the red wine, bring to the boil and simmer for another 20 minutes, uncovered.

4 Turn up the heat and stir vigorously for 2-3 minutes or until the mixture has reduced to the consistency of a soft pâté.

5 Turn into a serving dish and allow to cool. This is good with crackers or rye bread, or with blinis and sour cream.

★

Photograph
pages
136-137

Soaking
overnight

Ingredients
50 g (2 oz) wheat berries, soaked
    overnight
100 g (4 oz) cashew nuts, finely
    ground
25 g (1 oz) sunflower seeds
30 ml (2 tbsp) oil, preferably
    sunflower
100 g (4 oz) carrots, grated
1 small onion, minced or grated
1 tbsp finely chopped parsley
30-45 ml (2-3 tbsp) vegetable stock
    (see p. 151)
dash of shoyu
salt and pepper
1 egg, beaten
100 g (4 oz) fine oatmeal

oil for shallow frying

Makes 12 small patties

Cashew patties

1 Drain the wheat berries. Put them in a pan with enough water to cover them by at least 2.5 cm (1 in). Bring to the boil and simmer for about an hour or until the grains burst, adding more water if they dry out.

2 Mix together the ground cashews, sunflower seeds and wheat berries. Add the oil and work it evenly into the mixture.

3 Mix in the carrot, onion and parsley, and enough stock to moisten and bind the mixture.

4 Season with shoyu, salt and pepper. Divide into 12 pieces and shape each one into a patty about 5 cm (2 in) across. Dip into beaten egg and then into oatmeal.

5 Shallow-fry for 5-6 minutes over gentle heat until well browned. Serve hot or cold.

Cucumber mousse

A low fat combination of tofu and curd cheese which gives a lovely creamy consistency and a delicate colour and flavour.

1 Blend together the tofu and curd cheese until smooth.

2 Gently heat the water and agar in a small saucepan until the agar has dissolved and the water boils. Pour this quickly over the tofu mixture and blend again so that the agar is well distributed.

3 Stir in the diced cucumber, spring onions and tarragon and season well.

4 Whisk the egg whites until stiff. Fold one tablespoon of egg white into the tofu mixture, then very carefully fold in the remaining egg white.

5 Pile the mixture into individual ramekins and chill for 3-4 hours before serving.

Ingredients

1 packet silken tofu—approx. 300 g (11 oz)
225 g (8 oz) curd cheese
100 ml (4 fl oz) water
15 ml (1 tbsp) agar powder
½ large cucumber, very finely diced
3 spring onions, finely chopped
1 tbsp finely chopped tarragon
salt and pepper
2 egg whites

Serves 4

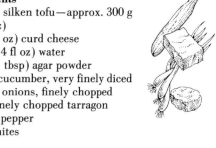

Foreground: **Red pepper ice** (*see p. 42*); behind: **Cucumber mousse**

Red pepper ice

★

Photograph
page 41

Ingredients
4 red peppers
25 g (1 oz) onion, very finely
    chopped
1-1½ tsp salt
1 tsp grated root ginger
2 egg yolks
30 ml (2 tbsp) sunflower oil
15 ml (1 tbsp) brandy
5-10 ml (1-2 tsp) honey

Serves 4

1 Preheat the oven to gas mark 6, 200°C (400°F).

2 Roast the peppers in the oven until the skins are blistered all over. Rub off the skins, cut the peppers in half and remove the seeds and white pith.

3 Put the peppers with all the other ingredients in a liquidizer and blend until smooth. Adjust the seasoning.

4 Turn into a shallow container, cover and freeze for 1 hour. Stir, then freeze again for 2-3 hours or until just firm. If it becomes very hard, stand it in the refrigerator for 20 minutes before serving.

Crudités

Photograph
*pages
44-45*

Broccoli or cauliflower, in tiny florets
Brussels sprouts, quartered
Carrots, in julienne strips
Celeriac, in julienne strips
Celery, in sticks or cut on the
    diagonal
Chicory, in blades
Courgettes or cucumbers, in fingers
Fennel, in thin slices across
Kohlrabi, swede or turnip, in
    julienne strips
Mushrooms, wiped and sliced (or
    quartered)
Peppers, red, green or yellow, in
    rings or sticks
Radish or daikon, in small chunks
Red or white cabbage, shredded
Spring onions, trimmed

Crudités, or raw vegetables, are usually served as part of an hors d'oeuvre, but also make excellent food for a party. Use only top quality really fresh vegetables. Almost any that can be eaten raw are suitable; avoid ones that are too soft, like avocados, or too juicy, like tomatoes. Here are some suggestions. For a party, cut into larger strips and choose vegetables that can be easily picked up. See page 215 for preparation of vegetables.

Arrange a selection on a serving dish, bearing in mind colour, texture and taste. The vegetables can be garnished with olives, lemon wedges, cherry tomatoes or sprigs of fresh herbs. As a starter, allow 100-175 g (4-6 oz) per person. If you provide one dip, allow 200-300 ml (⅓-½ pint) for 4-6 people. If you offer a selection, 150 ml (¼ pint) each of two or three dips should be enough for 6-10.

Caper and olive dip

Photograph
*pages
44-45*

Ingredients
2 tbsp fresh breadcrumbs
15 ml (1 tbsp) lemon juice
2 cloves garlic, crushed
2 tbsp finely chopped parsley
10 g (½ oz) capers
50 g (2 oz) stoned green olives
1 hard-boiled egg yolk
150 ml (¼ pint) olive oil
white wine vinegar to taste

Makes 200-300ml (⅓-½ pint)

1 Soak the breadcrumbs in the lemon juice for 15-20 minutes.

2 Put them in a liquidizer with all the other ingredients except the oil and vinegar and blend until smooth.

3 Add the olive oil, a teaspoon at a time, until 30 ml (2 tbsp) have been added; then pour on the remainder in a thin stream, blending constantly.

4 Thin down the sauce with a little vinegar, turn it into a small bowl or sauceboat and serve with crudités.

Almond dip

1 Preheat the oven to gas mark 4, 180°C (350°F).

2 Put the almonds on a baking sheet and toast them in the centre of the oven for about 7-10 minutes until lightly browned.

3 Put them in a liquidizer with the garlic, cayenne pepper, salt, tomatoes and vinegar and blend to a smooth paste.

4 Now blend in the olive oil, a teaspoon at a time, making sure each teaspoonful is absorbed before adding any more. When about half the oil has been added, pour in the remaining oil in a slow, thin stream, beating constantly, until the sauce becomes thick and creamy.

5 Pour into a small bowl or sauceboat and serve with crudités.

Ingredients
40 g (1½ oz) blanched slivered almonds (see p. 209)
1 clove garlic, crushed
¼-½ tsp cayenne
1 tsp salt
2 small tomatoes, skinned and finely chopped
45 ml (3 tbsp) red wine vinegar
150-200 ml (¼-⅓ pint) olive oil

Makes 200-300 ml (⅓-½ pint)

Photograph
*pages
44-45*

Tofu dip

Blend all the ingredients together until smooth, adding salt and pepper only if you feel it needs it. This gives a light creamy dip. For a peppery version, omit the oil and garlic and add half a teaspoon each of finely ground yellow mustard seeds and black peppercorns, with 10 ml (2 tsp) shoyu.

Ingredients
1 packet silken tofu—approx. 300 g (11 oz)
30 ml (2 tbsp) lemon juice
15-30 ml (1-2 tbsp) sunflower oil
1 clove garlic, crushed

Makes 200-300 ml (⅓-½ pint)

Photograph
*pages
44-45*

Hummus

This version uses less olive oil than the classic recipe.

1 Drain and rinse the chick peas. Put them in a large pan with plenty of fresh water, bring to the boil and boil fiercely for 10 minutes. Reduce the heat, skim off any scum, and simmer, covered, until soft—about 60-90 minutes, depending on the age of the peas.

2 Drain them thoroughly, reserving the liquid, and grind to a fine powder, using the grinder blade of a food processor, a mincer or coffee grinder.

3 Add 150 ml (¼ pint) of the reserved stock and blend to a stiff paste. You may need to add more stock. Add all the other ingredients, mix thoroughly, and leave to stand for at least 2 hours for the flavours to develop. Taste, and add more seasoning and lemon juice if necessary.

4 Turn the hummus into a shallow dish. Just before serving, garnish it with a trickle of oil, lemon slices and parsley. It is traditionally served with pitta bread, but wholewheat bread or toast also goes well.

Ingredients
225 g (8 oz) chick peas, soaked overnight
60-75 ml (4-5 tbsp) tahini
juice of 1½ lemons
30 ml (2 tbsp) olive oil
2-3 cloves garlic, crushed
¼ tsp paprika
½ tsp salt
black pepper
Garnish
extra olive oil *or* sesame oil
lemon slices
sprigs of fresh parsley

Makes about 700 ml (1¼ pints)

Photograph
*pages
44-45*

Soaking
overnight

Cocktails and buffets

Vegetables, cheese and eggs can form the basis for a variety of delicious, easy to eat mouthfuls, suitable for parties or light buffets.

Quiches and other pastry dishes offer plenty of scope: as well as the ones shown here, try the festive pie (page 84) or the flamiche (page 85), cut into small squares or triangles, or serve miniature pizzas or tortillas. Raw vegetables, cut into chunks or slices, go well with savoury dips. As well as olives, nuts and vegetarian cheeses cut into cubes, you could serve little nut patties (page 40) or bean croquettes (page 96), savoury spreads on biscuits, or spicy stuffed vineleaves (page 67). Fill celery and hollowed-out cucumbers with ricotta and chopped walnuts sprinkled with paprika, or with cream cheese mixed with chopped watercress and toasted sunflower seeds.

Kiwi fruit juice with mineral water or carrot and orange are healthy non-alcoholic drinks.

1 Kiwi fruit drink 2 Carrot and orange juice 3 & 10 Lentil and aubergine pâté (*p. 38*) on cheese water biscuits cut into crescents and stars (*p. 135*); wine and olive pâté (*p. 40*) on round oatcakes (*p. 173*) 4 & 6 Tartlets with various fillings: asparagus (*p. 130*), lentil (*p. 92*) and tomato (the pizza topping on *p. 120*); quiche with vegetables (*p. 130*) 5 Peppers with olive, almond and tofu dips (*pp. 42-43*) 7 Cheese puffs with avocado filling (*pp. 134-135*) 8 Cheese dip (*p. 135*) with crudités (*p. 42*) 9 Cucumber and celery "boats" (*see above*); cheese shortbread "straws" (*p. 135*) 11 Hummus (*p. 43*) with crudités.

SOUPS

A pot of lentils or beans, pasta or rice, onions, celery or tomatoes, all simmered in a savoury broth made from fresh vegetables and seasoned with shoyu, herbs and spices—this is more than a welcome hot soup: it is a meal in itself, rich in protein, full of flavour, and with a nutritious balance of beans, grains and vegetables. For summer evenings, light purées of green vegetables such as fresh peas or watercress, or chilled fruit soups, make tempting first courses.

It needs no special skill to produce a splendid home-made soup; nor, in most of these recipes, much preparation. The bulk of the work, including pre-soaking peas and beans, can often be done well in advance; indeed many of the soups benefit from being made the day before and given time to rest and develop their flavour.

★

Soaking
overnight

Ingredients
175 g (6 oz) flageolet beans, soaked
    overnight
225 g (8 oz) leeks, thinly sliced
2 bay leaves
5 juniper berries
2 cloves
15 ml (1 tbsp) olive oil
570-700 ml (1-1¼ pints) water
salt and pepper
1 tbsp finely chopped parsley

Serves 4-6

Flageolet with juniper

The light, delicate flavour of flageolets combines well with the pungency of the juniper berries and leeks.

1 Drain the flageolets and put them in a large pan together with the leeks, bay leaves, juniper berries and cloves.

2 Add the oil and water, bring to the boil and simmer for an hour with the lid on. Remove the bay leaves, juniper berries and cloves and allow to cool for a few minutes.

3 Liquidize two-thirds of the soup, adding a little extra water if it seems too thick, and season to taste.

4 Return all the soup to the pan and reheat gently. Sprinkle with parsley just before serving.

From top: **Cream of split pea** (*see p. 48*); **Flageolet with juniper;**
Spiced lentil with coconut (*see p. 48*)

★

Photograph
page 47

Ingredients

100 g (4 oz) yellow split peas
1 medium onion, finely chopped
1 clove garlic, crushed
15 ml (1 tbsp) sunflower oil
1 large potato, diced
2 sticks celery, diced
1 tsp caraway seed
¼ tsp ground mace
1 bay leaf
700-900 ml (1¼-1½ pints) light
    vegetable stock (see p. 151)
    or water
salt and pepper

Serves 4-6

Cream of split pea

Yellow split peas give this soup a particularly attractive colour, but green split peas or red lentils could be used instead.

1 Steep the split peas in hot water for an hour and drain.

2 Using a large, heavy-based pan, fry the onion and garlic gently in the oil for 3-4 minutes.

3 Add the potato, celery, split peas, caraway and mace. Cook for another 5-6 minutes, stirring occasionally.

4 Put in the bay leaf and most of the stock. Bring to the boil and simmer, covered, for 40 minutes. Remove the bay leaf and leave to cool for a few minutes.

5 Liquidize, adding more stock if you think the soup is too thick. Season generously, reheat in a clean pan, and serve.

Photograph
page 47

Ingredients

100 g (4 oz) red split lentils
15 ml (1 tbsp) peanut oil
1 medium onion, finely chopped
½ tsp chili powder
½ tsp grated root ginger
¼ tsp grated nutmeg
1 medium red pepper, deseeded and
    diced
1 medium green pepper, deseeded
    and diced
300 ml (½ pint) vegetable stock
    (see p. 151) *or* water
570 ml (1 pint) coconut milk
    (see p. 209)
salt and pepper

Serves 4-6

Spiced lentil with coconut

1 Steep the red lentils in hot water for 10 minutes and drain.

2 Heat the oil in a large, heavy-based pan and gently fry the onion and spices for 3-4 minutes.

3 Add the peppers and lentils and continue frying for 4-5 minutes, stirring to distribute the spices evenly among the vegetables.

4 Pour in the stock, bring to the boil and simmer gently, covered, for 10 minutes.

5 Stir in the coconut milk and continue to simmer, covered, for 35-40 minutes. Leave to cool for a few minutes.

6 Liquidize until completely smooth, season to taste and reheat gently before serving.

Photograph
*pages
86-87*

Ingredients

700-900 ml (1¼-1½ pints) water
1 small cauliflower, divided into tiny
    florets
1 medium onion, finely chopped
100 g (4 oz) blanched almonds,
    chopped (see p. 209)
2 sticks celery, chopped
30 ml (2 tbsp) sunflower oil
salt and pepper
grated nutmeg

Serves 4-6

Cream of cauliflower and almond

A subtle and rich soup, made with almonds which have been gently fried to bring out their flavour. It can be prepared a day or so in advance and served hot or chilled, but is not suitable for freezing.

1 Bring the water to the boil and poach the cauliflower in it for 5 minutes or until just tender. Drain, reserving the stock.

2 Using a large, heavy-based pan, fry the onion, almonds and celery in the oil for 5-6 minutes until the almonds are fairly well browned.

3 Add the cauliflower stock, bring to the boil and simmer for 5 minutes. Leave to cool slightly.

4 Liquidize until completely smooth—this will take several minutes in a liquidizer. Season to taste, add the cauliflower florets and reheat gently in a clean pan.

5 Sprinkle with grated nutmeg and serve.

Red bean and vegetable

This can be prepared ahead of time up to the point of cooking the kidney beans. Once the fresh vegetables and macaroni have been added, however, it should not be reheated.

1 In a large, heavy-based pan, cook the onions and garlic for 3-4 minutes in the oil until soft.

2 Add the stock and the drained beans, bring to the boil and boil hard for 10 minutes, then simmer, covered, for 20 minutes. Add the courgettes, French beans and tomatoes, stir in the tomato purée and simmer for another 20 minutes.

3 Season well. Add the basil, 2 tablespoons parsley and the macaroni and cook for a further 15 minutes. Serve hot, sprinkled with the remaining parsley.

Ingredients
1 bunch spring onions, diced
1 medium onion, diced
2 cloves garlic, crushed
30 ml (2 tbsp) olive oil
570 ml (1 pint) light vegetable stock (see p. 151)
100 g (4 oz) red kidney beans, soaked overnight and drained
75 g (3 oz) courgettes, sliced
75 g (3 oz) French beans, sliced
100 g (4 oz) tomatoes, skinned and chopped
15 ml (1 tbsp) tomato purée
salt and pepper
2 tbsp finely chopped basil
3 tbsp finely chopped parsley
25 g (1 oz) short-cut wholewheat macaroni

Serves 4-6

★
Photograph
page 50

Soaking
overnight

Cream of broccoli

Sour cream gives the needed touch of sharpness to this rich, green soup. It is thinned with single cream to make it easier to pour: the exact proportions are a matter of taste.

1 In a large, heavy-based pan sauté the onion and garlic in the oil with the bay leaf until soft—about 3-4 minutes.

2 Add the broccoli and stock, bring to the boil and simmer gently, covered, for 10 minutes, when the broccoli should be tender but still bright green. Remove the bay leaf and let the soup cool a little.

3 Liquidize the soup until it is completely smooth. Season to taste, add the lemon juice and reheat gently in a clean pan.

4 Meanwhile, steam the broccoli florets until tender—about 8-10 minutes. Scatter them over the soup and stir in the cream just before serving.

Ingredients
1 medium onion, chopped
1 clove garlic, crushed
15 ml (1 tbsp) sunflower oil
1 bay leaf
450 g (1 lb) green broccoli, chopped
570 ml (1 pint) light vegetable stock (see p. 151)
salt and pepper
juice of ½ lemon
Garnish
100 g (4 oz) broccoli florets
60 ml (4 tbsp) mixed sour cream and single cream

Serves 4-6

★
Photograph
page 50

Carrot and coriander

These quantities give a very pronounced spicy flavour. You may prefer to use half the amount of coriander and cumin.

1 Melt the butter in a large, heavy-based pan but do not let it brown. Sauté the carrots and celery in it over gentle heat for a minute or two, stirring and turning to coat them with butter.

2 Add the ground coriander and cumin, turn the heat up a little and fry for another 3-4 minutes, stirring fairly vigorously.

3 Pour in the stock, bring to the boil and simmer, covered, for 30 minutes. Leave to cool a little.

4 Liquidize the soup and return it to a clean pan. Season to taste and reheat gently. Add the chopped coriander leaves and serve hot, garnished with a few whole coriander leaves and lemon croûtes.

Lemon croûtes

1 Trim the crusts from the bread and cut into triangles.

2 Heat a little oil (or oil and butter mixed) in a frying pan until it sizzles. Fry the triangles quickly until crisp and brown on both sides. Sprinkle with lemon juice and serve straightaway.

Ingredients
40 g (1½ oz) butter
350 g (12 oz) carrots, diced
100 g (4 oz) celery, diced
2 tsp ground coriander
1 tsp ground cumin
700-900 ml (1¼-1½ pints) light
    vegetable stock (see p. 151)
salt and pepper
1 tbsp finely chopped coriander
    leaves
Garnish
fresh coriander leaves
lemon croûtes (*see below*)
Lemon croûtes
4-6 slices stale bread
oil for frying
lemon juice

Serves 4-6

★

Country vegetable broth

If you do not have the individual grains, peas and lentils readily to hand, a "soup mix", obtainable in many healthfood shops, makes an ideal base.

1 Steep the grains, peas and lentils in hot water for an hour and drain.

2 Gently soften the vegetables in the oil for 10 minutes, using a large, heavy-based pan with a lid. Add the grains, peas and lentils and fry them gently for a further 5 minutes, stirring occasionally.

3 Add the stock and shoyu, bring to the boil and simmer for 50-60 minutes, covered.

4 Stir in the herbs and season to taste. You can serve the soup immediately, just as it is, or blend it briefly in a liquidizer if you prefer a smoother texture, but do not liquidize it completely or it will lose its character.

Ingredients
25 g (1 oz) pot barley
25 g (1 oz) wheat berries
25 g (1 oz) green split peas
25 g (1 oz) red lentils
1 medium onion, finely chopped
1 medium parsnip, diced
1 medium turnip, diced
1 medium potato, diced
30 ml (2 tbsp) sunflower oil
700-900 ml (1¼-1½ pints) vegetable
    stock (see p. 151) *or* water
15 ml (1 tbsp) shoyu
2 tsp finely chopped rosemary
1 tsp finely chopped thyme
salt and pepper

Serves 4-6

★
Photograph
page 52

Onion soup

A vegetarian adaptation of the traditional French onion soup which makes a welcome start to a winter meal.

1 Heat the oil in a large, heavy-based pan and add the onions, garlic, carrot and turnip. Cover the pan and cook the vegetables for 15-20 minutes over very gentle heat. Sprinkle over a little salt to bring out extra juices.

2 Add the bay leaf, celery seeds, mustard powder, stock and shoyu. Stir well, bring to the boil and simmer, covered, for 20 minutes. Remove the bay leaf and carrot (unless you prefer to leave the pieces of carrot in for extra colour).

3 Blend the miso with 15 ml (1 tbsp) of the soup in a small bowl. Stir it back into the soup, mixing well, and season to taste.

4 Simmer gently for another 5 minutes and serve sprinkled with the chopped parsley or chervil and the sesame seeds.

Ingredients ★

22.5 ml (1½ tbsp) sunflower oil
450 g (1 lb) onions, finely chopped
1-2 cloves garlic, crushed
1 medium carrot, roughly chopped
1 small white turnip, grated
1 bay leaf
1 tsp celery seeds
¼ tsp English mustard powder
570 ml (1 pint) dark vegetable
    stock (see p. 152)
10 ml (2 tsp) shoyu
5 ml (1 tsp) miso
salt and pepper
Garnish
2 tbsp finely chopped parsley
    or chervil
1 tbsp sesame seeds

Serves 4-6

Miso julienne

With its strong, salty flavour, miso makes an excellent warming basis for a clear stock. This recipe includes a julienne of carrots and daikon, the subtly flavoured Japanese white radish. The sea vegetable arame contributes a rich mineral content.

1 Soak the arame in hot water for 10 minutes and drain. Either chop it finely or, if you prefer, leave it in strips.

2 In a large, heavy-based pan fry the ginger in the peanut oil for 2-3 minutes over medium heat.

3 Add the sesame oil, carrots, daikon and arame and continue to cook, covered, over gentle heat for 15 minutes.

4 Add the stock and stir in the shoyu and miso. Bring to the boil and simmer, covered, for a further 10 minutes. Serve immediately.

Ingredients ★

5 g (¼ oz) arame
½ tsp sliced ginger root
15 ml (1 tbsp) peanut oil
10 ml (2 tsp) sesame oil
225 g (8 oz) carrots, cut into
    julienne strips (see p. 222)
225 g (8 oz) daikon, cut into
    julienne strips
570 ml (1 pint) dark vegetable
    stock (see p. 152)
30 ml (2 tbsp) shoyu
15 ml (1 tbsp) miso, preferably
    mugi

Serves 4-6

Thanksgiving

Vegetables are the raison d'être of a harvest festival and really come into their own for a Thanksgiving dinner. Here a whole pumpkin takes pride of place, acting as a tureen for its own soup, made with spices and sour cream.

For the main course, serve a raised pie made in an ornamental hinged mould, filled with layers of mushrooms, tomatoes, fennel and aubergines and accompanied by a well-flavoured tomato and orange sauce. More vegetables appear in the two salads—one light, one more substantial—and there are simple jacket potatoes to contrast with the more elaborate dishes. Maize, a traditional American harvest symbol, is represented in the golden cornbread.

Cranberries flavour the light, airy pudding made with egg whites and set with agar. The yolks are used for the sauce, supplying the protein needed to balance a mainly vegetable-based menu, but one that reflects the original purpose of Thanksgiving: to appreciate and give thanks for the home-grown, carefully cultivated, simple but nourishing fruits of the earth.

1 Spiced cranberry soufflé (*p. 160*)
2 Pumpkin soup (*p. 56*) 3 Jacket potatoes
4 Chicory, orange and watercress salad in yogurt and cream cheese dressing (*p. 144*)
5 Raised pie (*p. 89*) 6 Spinach, apple and cauliflower salad in vinaigrette (*p. 142*)
7 Tomato and orange sauce (*p. 154*)
8 Cornbread (*p. 179*)

Photograph
pages
54-55

Ingredients

15 ml (1 tbsp) sunflower oil
1 tsp grated root ginger
1 tsp grated nutmeg
½ tsp ground coriander
1 small onion, chopped
1 medium carrot, chopped
1 medium potato, chopped
2 sticks celery, chopped
700-900 g (1½-2 lb) pumpkin flesh,
    chopped
300-425 ml (½-¾ pint) light
    vegetable stock (see p.151)
salt and pepper
lemon juice *or* apple juice
    concentrate, to taste
sour cream (optional) to taste

Serves 4

Pumpkin soup

For Hallowe'en, this is made with a traditional bright orange pumpkin. When this is not available, any well-flavoured squash with orange or yellow flesh can be substituted.

1 Heat the oil in a large, heavy-based pan and fry the ginger, nutmeg and coriander over medium heat for 4-5 minutes.

2 Add the chopped vegetables and sweat them, covered, over low heat for 20 minutes or until the pumpkin flesh is meltingly soft.

3 Add 300 ml (½ pint) stock, season with salt, pepper and lemon juice (or apple juice concentrate) and stir well. Bring to the boil and simmer, covered, for another 20 minutes. Allow to cool a little.

4 Liquidize, adding more stock if the mixture is too thick. Check the seasoning and reheat gently in a clean pan. If you are using sour cream, stir it in just before serving.

For a really spectacular party dish, use a whole pumpkin and serve the soup in its shell.

Prepare the pumpkin as shown. Dice the flesh, removing the seeds, and weigh it. Adjust the quantities of the other ingredients accordingly. As in the recipe above, fry the spices and then the vegetables. Add the stock and seasonings and liquidize. Pour into the pumpkin and replace its "lid".

Stand the pumpkin on a flan ring or ovenproof dish on which it can be brought to the table and bake at gas mark 5, 190°C (375°F) for 45 minutes or until the pumpkin flesh is completely tender. As you serve the soup, scoop out a few chunks of flesh from the sides of the pumpkin into each bowl.

PREPARING THE PUMPKIN

1 *Slice off the top of the pumpkin about one-third of the way down, making a V-shaped nick to ensure that it can be replaced correctly.*

2 *Scoop out the inside, leaving a thickness of about 2.5 cm (1 in) of flesh in the shell. Season this with a little oil and salt.*

Mushroom with herbs

For extra flavour you can include some dried mushrooms and use their soaking water in the vegetable stock.

1 Heat the oil in a large, heavy-based pan and sauté the onion and herbs gently for about 5 minutes.

2 Add the mushrooms and cook for another 5 minutes or until they are well browned.

3 Stir in the stock, wine, tomato purée and parsley. Bring to the boil, cover and simmer for 30-45 minutes.

4 Remove the bay leaves, season to taste and serve hot. Croûtons or crackers go well with this soup.

Ingredients
45 ml (3 tbsp) sunflower oil
1 medium onion, finely chopped
2 bay leaves
1 tsp chopped marjoram
1 tsp chopped tarragon
225 g (8 oz) mushrooms, chopped
425 ml (¾ pint) dark vegetable
   stock (see p. 152)
50 ml (2 fl oz) red wine
30 ml (2 tbsp) tomato purée
2 tbsp chopped parsley

Serves 4

★
Photograph
pages
188-189

Gumbo

An easy-to-make adaptation of the Creole dish, characterized by the velvety texture of the okra.

1 In a heavy-based pan sauté the onion and garlic gently in the oil until soft—about 3-4 minutes.

2 Add the pepper and okra and fry for another 5 minutes, stirring occasionally.

3 Stir in the tomatoes and tomato purée and add the stock. Bring to the boil, cover and simmer for 20-25 minutes, stirring occasionally. Season to taste and serve immediately.

Ingredients
1 medium onion, finely chopped
1 clove garlic, crushed
15 ml (1 tbsp) sunflower oil
1 medium green pepper, deseeded
   and diced
225 g (8 oz) okra, trimmed and
   chopped
450 g (1 lb) tomatoes, skinned
   and chopped
15 ml (1 tbsp) tomato purée
300 ml (½ pint) dark vegetable
   stock (see p. 152)
salt and pepper

Serves 4-6

★
Photograph
page 58

Avgolemono

A refreshing lemony soup, this is usually made in the Greek way with white rice. Bulgar wheat makes a nutritious alternative.

1 Using a large, heavy-based pan, sauté the onion gently in the oil for 3-4 minutes.

2 Stir in the celery, carrot and spices. Add the lemon juice and water, bring to the boil, cover and simmer for 40 minutes.

3 Strain the stock. Return it to a clean pan and mix in the bulgar wheat. Reheat gently for 5 minutes but do not let it boil.

4 Beat the egg yolks and juice of 1 lemon together in a bowl and mix in a tablespoon or two of the stock. Gradually add this mixture to the pan, heating gently until the soup thickens. It should be single cream consistency. Season to taste and serve immediately.

Ingredients
1 medium onion, finely chopped
30 ml (2 tbsp) olive oil
3 sticks celery, diced
1 small carrot, diced
8 coriander seeds, lightly crushed
12 peppercorns
½ tsp aniseeds
100 ml (4 fl oz) lemon juice
1 litre (1¾ pints) water
50 g (2 oz) bulgar wheat
3 egg yolks
juice of 1 lemon
salt and pepper

Serves 4-6

Photograph
page 58

Cold beetroot rassolnik

The name rassolnik *comes from the Russian for "brine" or "pickle" and is given to fish or meat soups containing pickled cucumber. Here the idea is combined with another Russian speciality, borshch or cold beetroot soup.*

1 Put the beetroot in a pan with the water and apple juice concentrate. Bring to the boil, cover and simmer for 20 minutes. Leave to cool.

2 Liquidize, adding the dill weed, and season well.

3 Pour into a tureen and stir in the minced pickled cucumber, the diced fresh cucumber and all except a tablespoon or two of the sour cream. Chill thoroughly and decorate with the remaining sour cream just before serving.

Ingredients
350 g (12 oz) raw beetroot, peeled and thinly sliced
425 ml (¾ pint) water
15 ml (1 tbsp) apple juice concentrate
1 tsp dried dill weed
salt and pepper
100 g (4 oz) pickled dill cucumber, minced
5 cm (2 in) cucumber, peeled and diced
150 ml (¼ pint) sour cream *or* smetana

Serves 4-6

Fresh pea with mint

This makes a lovely chilled summer soup, but is equally good served hot.

1 Melt the butter in a large, heavy-based pan over gentle heat. Add the Chinese leaves and peas and braise them for 10 minutes with the lid on.

2 Add the stock or water. Bring to the boil, stirring occasionally, and simmer gently, covered, for 20 minutes. Allow to cool a little.

3 Liquidize until completely smooth. Stir in the mint and season to taste.

4 To serve hot, reheat gently, garnish with the cream and sprigs of mint and serve immediately. To serve cold, chill for an hour or two and garnish just before serving.

Ingredients
50 g (2 oz) butter
225 g (8 oz) Chinese leaves, sliced
450 g (1 lb) shelled fresh peas
570 ml (1 pint) light vegetable stock (see p. 151) *or* water
1-2 tbsp finely chopped mint
salt and pepper
Garnish
45-60 ml (3-4 tbsp) single cream (optional)
sprigs of fresh mint

Serves 4-6

★
Photograph
page 61

Watercress

In contrast to many recipes which use onion and stock to soften the taste of watercress, here yogurt and lemon juice are used to bring out its natural sharpness.

1 Chop the watercress finely. Melt the butter and soften the watercress in it for 10 minutes, covered, over gentle heat. Leave until cool.

2 Liquidize with the lemon juice and yogurt. Season to taste and chill thoroughly before serving.

Ingredients
225 g (8 oz) cleaned watercress (approx. 4 bunches)
75 g (3 oz) butter
30 ml (2 tbsp) lemon juice
570 ml (1 pint) yogurt
salt and pepper

Serves 4

Photograph
page 61

From top: **Cold beetroot rassolnik**; Avgolemono (*see p. 57*); **Gumbo** (*see p. 57*)

★

Ingredients
½ small cucumber, peeled and
  coarsely chopped
450 g (1 lb) tomatoes, skinned and
  coarsely chopped
50 g (2 oz) spring onions, diced
1 small green pepper, deseeded
  and diced
2 cloves garlic, crushed
25 g (1 oz) fresh breadcrumbs
15 ml (1 tbsp) red wine vinegar
1 tsp salt
15 ml (1 tbsp) olive oil
15 ml (1 tbsp) tomato purée
Garnish
25 g (1 oz) finely chopped spring
  onions
25 g (1 oz) chopped peeled cucumber
1 small green pepper, deseeded
  and finely chopped

Serves 4-6

Gazpacho

This version uses no water and has a substantial, satisfying consistency. It is worth making an effort to find really well-flavoured ripe tomatoes as they make all the difference to the taste and appearance.

1 Put the cucumber, tomatoes, spring onions, green pepper, garlic and breadcrumbs into a bowl and mix thoroughly. Stir in the vinegar, salt, olive oil and tomato purée.

2 Liquidize for about 1 minute or until you have a smooth purée. Adjust the seasoning and chill the soup thoroughly before serving.

The garnishes can be sprinkled on the soup, or handed round with it, each in a separate bowl.

★

Ingredients
15 ml (1 tbsp) sunflower oil
1 medium onion, finely chopped
2 medium-sized crisp eating apples,
  peeled, cored and chopped
1 large potato, chopped
225 g (8 oz) leeks, sliced
570-700 ml (1-1¼ pints) light
  vegetable stock (see p. 151) *or*
  water
150 ml (¼ pint) yogurt (optional)
salt and pepper
1 tbsp snipped chives

Serves 4-6

Vichyssoise with apple

The unexpected flavour of apple blends very well with the traditional leek and potato Vichyssoise.

1 Heat the oil in a large, heavy-based pan and sweat the onion, apples, potato and leeks for 7-10 minutes over low heat with the lid on.

2 Add the stock or water, bring to the boil and simmer gently, covered, for 20 minutes. Leave until cool.

3 Liquidize until completely smooth, adding a little extra liquid if you think it is too thick.

4 When quite cold, stir or blend in the yogurt and season to taste. Serve chilled, sprinkled with the chives.

★

Photograph
page 62

Ingredients
100 g (4 oz) dried apricots, washed
  and diced
4 oranges, peeled and sliced
570 ml (1 pint) water
6 cloves
300 ml (½ pint) white wine
Garnish
1 orange, peeled and thinly sliced
1 tbsp chopped blanched almonds
  and/or cashews (see p. 209)

Serves 4-6

Chilled apricot and orange

Fresh apricots can be used, but dried ones give more flavour.

1 Put the apricots and oranges in a large pan with the water. Add the cloves, bring to the boil and simmer, covered, for 30 minutes. Leave to cool a little.

2 Remove the cloves. Add the white wine and liquidize to a purée. Chill thoroughly. Garnish just before serving with the orange slices and chopped nuts.

From top: **Watercress** (*see p. 59*); **Vichyssoise with apple**; **Fresh pea with mint** (*see p. 59*); **Gazpacho**

Ingredients
450 g (1 lb) strawberries
570 ml (1 pint) water
2 tbsp dried hibiscus flowers
10 ml (2 tsp) arrowroot
15-30 ml (1-2 tbsp) maple syrup
50 ml (2 fl oz) rosé wine
Garnish
60 ml (4 tbsp) sour cream
1 tbsp slivered almonds

Serves 4-6

Strawberry and hibiscus

Fruit soups are popular in Scandinavia. Hibiscus flowers can be found in some healthfood shops, but you could substitute a sachet of rose hip and hibiscus tea.

1 Slice the strawberries very thinly, reserving 4-6 whole ones for the garnish.

2 Put the sliced strawberries, water and hibiscus flowers into a pan. Bring to the boil and simmer, covered, for 20 minutes or until the strawberries have lost most of their colour. Remove the sachet, if you have used one, and leave for several hours or overnight.

3 Strain the stock and return it to a clean pan. Make a paste with the arrowroot and 15 ml (1 tbsp) of the strained stock. Add this and the maple syrup to the pan and blend well. Bring to the boil and simmer for 5 minutes.

4 Toast the almonds under the grill for 1-2 minutes on each side or until lightly browned.

5 Stir the wine into the soup. Allow to cool and serve slightly warm, garnished with the sour cream, toasted almonds and reserved strawberries.

Left: **Chilled apricot and orange** (*see p. 60*); **Strawberry and hibiscus**

VEGETABLES

Vegetable dishes are very versatile. They can form the centrepiece of a meal or act as a side dish to complement a substantial main course. A recipe for one can usually be adapted for another: for example, the vine leaf stuffing given here also goes well with peppers or courgettes. A simple preparation can be made more elaborate by adding pastry, or a topping of cornbread or nut crumble.

A meal of vegetables alone will be low in protein, so try to have a dish based on grains or beans as well. Some of the recipes here already include high protein ingredients: for example, the nuts in the hazelnut and courgette bake or the broccoli and walnut pie. Wholewheat flour is a nutritious ingredient in a vegetable tart, pie or brioche, all of which are suitable main dishes for a dinner party.

It is difficult to be precise about servings. Most of these recipes serve 4, or 4-6, depending on what else is served.

Stuffed artichokes

Either the lemon sauce on page 37 or one of the tofu dips on page 43 can accompany these artichokes stuffed with a purée of beans and mushrooms.

1 Wash the artichokes thoroughly. Trim the bases so that the artichokes will sit flat, and cut off the sharp tips of the leaves as shown overleaf.

2 Rinse the artichokes and cook them in plenty of boiling water for 35-40 minutes.

3 Simmer the broad beans in plenty of water for about 10 minutes or until quite soft.

Continued

Ingredients
4 globe artichokes
275 g (10 oz) fresh broad beans
30 ml (2 tbsp) olive oil
3 cloves garlic, crushed
1 bunch spring onions, chopped
350 g (12 oz) mushrooms, diced
2 tsp dried dill weed
30 ml (2 tbsp) lemon juice
salt and pepper

Serves 4

★ *(filling)*
Photograph
page 65

Stuffed artichokes continued

4 Heat the oil and gently sauté the garlic, spring onions and mushrooms until soft. Leave to cool a little.

5 Preheat the oven to gas mark 3, 170°C (325°F).

6 Drain the artichokes. Remove the centre leaves and use a teaspoon, as shown, to take out the inedible choke.

7 Purée the mushroom mixture with the cooked beans, dill weed and lemon juice to make a stiff paste. Season well and divide this among the artichokes.

8 Arrange them in a shallow baking dish, cover loosely with foil and bake for 30 minutes. Serve hot.

PREPARING THE ARTICHOKES

1 *Cut off the stalks of the artichokes and use scissors to trim the leaves.*

2 *When the artichokes are cooked and cool enough to handle, pull out the soft inner leaves.*

3 *Carefully scoop out all the fibrous choke with a teaspoon.*

★

Ingredients
2 large aubergines
15 ml (1 tbsp) olive oil
3 medium onions, chopped
3 cloves garlic, crushed
175 g (6 oz) mushrooms, diced
175 g (6 oz) cashew nuts, finely
  ground
15 ml (1 tbsp) tomato purée
1 tbsp finely chopped parsley
salt and pepper
1 bay leaf
550 g (1¼ lb) tomatoes, skinned and
  chopped
45 ml (3 tbsp) red wine

Serves 4

Mushroom-stuffed aubergines

These are served with a rich sauce of tomatoes and red wine. If you cannot get good-quality ripe tomatoes, use canned ones.

1 Bring a large pan of water to the boil and simmer the aubergines, whole, for 10 minutes. Drain, slice them in half lengthways and let them cool completely.

2 Scoop out the centres, leaving the shell intact, and chop the flesh finely.

3 Heat the oil in a frying pan and gently sauté the onions for 3-4 minutes. Add the garlic and mushrooms, cover the pan and cook for a further 10 minutes.

4 Put two-thirds of this mixture into a bowl for the filling. Mix in the chopped aubergine flesh, ground cashews, tomato purée, parsley, salt and pepper.

Continued on page 66

Clockwise from top: **Baked cabbage with chestnuts** (*see p. 66*); **Mushroom-stuffed aubergines**; **Stuffed artichokes** (*see p. 63*)

*Mushroom-stuffed aubergines
continued*

5 To the remaining mixture in the pan add the bay leaf, tomatoes and red wine. Cover and continue cooking for another 20 minutes, stirring from time to time, until you have a thick, smooth sauce. While the sauce is cooking, preheat the oven to gas mark 4, 180°C (350°F).

6 Arrange the aubergine shells in a shallow ovenproof dish and divide the filling between them. Remove the bay leaf from the sauce and pour this over the stuffed aubergines. Bake, covered, for 15 minutes, then remove the lid and bake for a further 5 minutes. Serve hot.

★ *(filling)*
Photograph
page 65

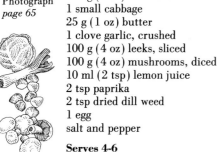

Ingredients
100 g (4 oz) dried chestnuts
1 small cabbage
25 g (1 oz) butter
1 clove garlic, crushed
100 g (4 oz) leeks, sliced
100 g (4 oz) mushrooms, diced
10 ml (2 tsp) lemon juice
2 tsp paprika
2 tsp dried dill weed
1 egg
salt and pepper

Serves 4-6

Baked cabbage with chestnuts

A loosely packed cabbage such as a Savoy is good for this dish. Although fresh chestnuts could be used, dried ones are much easier to handle and have a richer flavour.

1 Soak the chestnuts in hot water for an hour. Cook them in their soaking water for 40 minutes or until soft. Drain and chop finely.

2 While the chestnuts are cooking, detach 8 leaves from the outside of the cabbage, cut out the centre rib of each leaf with a sharp knife and blanch the leaves for 2 minutes in boiling water. Chop the rest of the cabbage finely.

3 Preheat the oven to gas mark 3, 170°C (325°F).

4 Melt the butter in a frying pan and sweat the garlic, leeks, mushrooms and chopped cabbage over low heat for 7-10 minutes or until well softened. Add the chestnuts, lemon juice, paprika and dill weed. Allow to cool a little, then beat in the egg and season well.

5 Line a greased 1.4 litre (2½ pint) pudding basin with some of the blanched cabbage leaves, making sure there are no gaps. Spoon in the filling and cover with the remaining leaves. Put a plate on top to weigh the mixture down and bake for an hour. Turn out before serving. A tomato or a creamy sauce goes well with this.

Spinach darioles

Delicious with most egg dishes, the spinach also complements bakes, roasts or pilafs such as the hazelnut and courgette bake on page 73 or the kasha ring on page 110. This dish looks particularly attractive in the individual moulds.

1 Preheat the oven to gas mark 4, 180°C (350°F) and bring a large pan of water to the boil.

2 Blanch the spinach for a minute in the boiling water so that it becomes slightly wilted. Drain, refresh under cold running water and remove any coarse stems.

3 Lightly grease 8 dariole moulds or an 18 cm (7 in) flan dish. Line with a little over half the spinach leaves, allowing them to overlap the top.

4 Fill with layers of tomato slices, sprinkling each layer with basil, spring onions and pepper. Fold the edges of the spinach over the top and cover with the remaining spinach.

5 Put a small ovenproof plate or weight on top, brush any exposed leaves with a little vegetable oil, and bake for 35-40 minutes. Turn out and serve immediately.

Ingredients
225 g (8 oz) spinach
225 g (8 oz) tomatoes, skinned and sliced
3-4 tsp chopped basil
2-3 spring onions, finely chopped
pepper
a little oil

Serves 4

Photograph
*pages
188-189*

Stuffed vine leaves

A classic Middle Eastern dish which can be eaten hot or cold. Cabbage leaves make an excellent substitute for vine leaves.

1 Heat the oil in a large frying pan and gently fry the onion and garam masala in it over low heat for 5-7 minutes.

2 Add the rice and stir gently for 2-3 minutes or until the grains are lightly fried, then pour over the boiling water and add the saffron, pine nuts and raisins.

3 Bring back to the boil, cover and simmer for about 25-30 minutes or until the rice is tender. Season to taste and stir in the mint and lemon juice. Preheat the oven to gas mark 4, 180°C (350°F).

4 Meanwhile, prepare the vine or cabbage leaves. If using fresh leaves, blanch them, a few at a time, for a minute or two in boiling water; if using vine leaves from a packet, rinse them thoroughly in hot water. For cabbage leaves, trim the centre rib of each leaf as shown overleaf.

Continued

Ingredients
30-45 ml (2-3 tbsp) sunflower oil
1 onion, finely chopped
1 tsp garam masala (see p. 214)
100 g (4 oz) long grain brown rice, washed and drained
300 ml (½ pint) boiling water
large pinch of saffron
50 g (2 oz) pine nuts
50 g (2 oz) dark seedless raisins
salt and pepper
2 tbsp finely chopped mint
juice of ½ lemon
24 vine leaves *or* 12 cabbage leaves
150 ml (¼ pint) vegetable stock (see p. 151)
1 bay leaf
Garnish
slices of lemon
chopped mint

Serves 4

★
Photograph
page 69

Stuffed vine leaves continued

5 Fill each leaf as shown below and arrange them, seam side down, in a lightly oiled ovenproof dish. Pour over the stock, add the bay leaf, cover with a lid or foil and bake for 45 minutes. Remove the bay leaf. Serve garnished.

FILLING THE LEAVES

1 *Remove the stalk by making straight cuts on either side of the base. If the central vein is very thick, remove it as shown for a cabbage leaf, right.*

2 *To prepare a cabbage leaf, carefully remove the thickest part of the central vein by cutting along either side with a sharp knife.*

3 *Put a heaped dessertspoon of filling on the centre of each leaf.*

4 *Starting from the left side of the leaf, fold the base up over the filling.*

5 *Still working on the same part of the leaf, fold the side of the leaf over the filling. Fold in the other side of the leaf.*

6 *Working slowly and carefully, roll the leaf away from you to form a neat cylindrical shape.*

★

Ingredients
4 large courgettes
45 ml (3 tbsp) oil, preferably olive
1 medium onion, finely chopped
2 cloves garlic, crushed
225 g (8 oz) bulgar wheat, washed and drained
2 red peppers, deseeded and diced
1 tsp ground allspice
salt and pepper
up to 300 ml (½ pint) vegetable stock (see p. 151)
Continued

Stuffed courgettes with walnut sauce

Bulgar wheat, a light-textured, partially cooked wheat, provides the perfect base for the different vegetables and spices used in this stuffing.

1 Blanch the courgettes for 3-4 minutes in boiling water. Cut them in half lengthways, scoop out the centres and chop the flesh roughly.

2 Heat 30 ml (2 tbsp) of the oil in a large pan and sauté the onion and garlic gently for 3-4 minutes until transparent.

3 Put in the bulgar wheat, diced red peppers, chopped courgettes and allspice and season well. Add some stock if the mixture seems too dry and cook for 10 minutes over gentle heat, stirring constantly. Preheat the oven to gas mark 4, 180°C (350°F).

4 Fill the courgette shells with the mixture. Arrange them in a lightly oiled ovenproof dish, brush with the remaining oil, cover with a lid or foil and bake for 25 minutes. (Excess filling can be reserved for some other use, or cooked with the stuffed courgettes and presented on a serving dish as a bed for them.) Serve with the walnut and garlic sauce.

Sauce

Put all the ingredients into a liquidizer and blend until smooth. Use 150 ml (¼ pint) water to start with and add more if you prefer not too thick a sauce. Leave to stand for 1 hour. Blend again just before serving and garnish.

Sauce
100 g (4 oz) shelled walnuts, ground
4 cloves garlic, crushed
2 tbsp fresh breadcrumbs
1 tsp salt
30 ml (2 tbsp) olive oil
juice of 1 lemon
water
Garnish
10 g (½ oz) finely chopped walnuts

Serves 4

Left: **Stuffed courgettes with walnut sauce**; right: **Stuffed vine leaves** (*see p. 67*)

Neapolitan peppers

The area around Naples is famous for its mild, sweet yellow peppers. This vegetarian version of a traditional dish includes raisins, hard-boiled eggs and tomato sauce.

1 Make the tomato sauce first. Gently sauté the onion and garlic for 3-4 minutes in the oil until soft. Add the tomatoes and tomato purée and simmer gently, uncovered, for 10-15 minutes, stirring from time to time, until it has reduced to a rich sauce. Season well.

2 Preheat the oven to gas mark 4, 180°C (350°F), and bring a large pan of water to the boil.

3 Blanch the peppers in the boiling water for 5 minutes. Drain them and run cold water over them until they are cool enough to handle. Slice a "lid" off the top of each and reserve. With a teaspoon remove the seeds and any white pith or ribs from the inside, taking care not to puncture the skin.

4 Mix 90 ml (6 tbsp) of olive oil with the breadcrumbs, raisins, olives, eggs, herbs and capers. Season well, adding more oil if the mixture seems a little dry. Stuff the peppers and arrange them in a deep baking dish.

5 Put 30 ml (2 tbsp) of sauce on top of each pepper and cover with its "lid". Cover the dish and bake for 50-60 minutes. Serve hot, accompanied by the remaining sauce.

Ingredients
Tomato Sauce
1 small onion, finely chopped
2 cloves garlic, chopped
15 ml (1 tbsp) olive oil
450 g (1 lb) tomatoes, skinned and chopped
15 ml (1 tbsp) tomato purée
salt and pepper

4 large peppers, yellow or red
90-120 ml (6-8 tbsp) olive oil
8 tbsp fresh breadcrumbs
25 g (1 oz) raisins
12 black olives, stoned and sliced
2 hard-boiled eggs, chopped
2 tsp dried oregano
2 tbsp finely chopped parsley
2 tbsp capers
salt and pepper

Serves 4

★

Broccoli and walnut bake

1 Scrub the potatoes and cook them in their skins until tender in plenty of boiling water. Peel them, mash them with the milk and season to taste.

2 Meanwhile, fry the onion and garlic gently in the oil for 3-4 minutes until soft. Add the broccoli and walnuts, cover the pan and continue cooking for 5 minutes over low heat.

3 Preheat the oven to gas mark 4, 180°C (350°F).

4 In another pan, melt the butter and fry the mushrooms gently for 5 minutes. Sprinkle on the flour and cook for another 2-3 minutes, stirring.

5 Meanwhile, heat the milk to just below boiling point. Pour two-thirds of it over the mushrooms, turn up the heat and bring to the boil, stirring. Reduce the heat and simmer for 2-3 minutes. Season well.

Continued

Ingredients
700 g (1½ lb) potatoes
90 ml (6 tbsp) milk
salt and pepper
1 small onion, very finely chopped
1 clove garlic, crushed
30 ml (2 tbsp) oil, preferably sunflower
225 g (8 oz) broccoli florets
100 g (4 oz) walnuts, chopped
Sauce
50 g (2 oz) butter
225 g (8 oz) mushrooms, chopped
50 g (2 oz) wholewheat flour
425 ml (¾ pint) milk *or* milk and water mixed
salt and pepper

Serves 4

★

Broccoli and walnut bake continued

6 Put half the mashed potato in a lightly greased oven dish. Cover with the walnut and broccoli mixture and pour over half the mushroom sauce. Top with the rest of the mashed potato and bake for 35 minutes or until the potatoes are just browned.

Serve with the remaining half of the mushroom mixture, thinned to a pouring consistency by the rest of the milk and reheated gently.

★

Photograph
page 70

Ingredients
Tomato sauce
450 g (1 lb) tomatoes, skinned
   and coarsely chopped
2 sticks celery, finely chopped
1 medium onion, finely chopped
2 cloves garlic, crushed
1 tsp chopped marjoram
15 ml (1 tbsp) tomato purée

300 ml (½ pint) milk
1 medium cauliflower, divided
   into florets
salt and pepper
Cheese sauce
40 g (1½ oz) butter
25 g (1 oz) wholewheat flour
2 eggs
50 g (2 oz) grated cheese
   (Cheddar, Gruyère or a mixture)

olive oil for frying
350 g (12 oz) aubergines, thickly
   sliced

Serves 4

Cauliflower moussaka

It is difficult to give an exact quantity of oil, as the amount aubergines soak up varies. Start with 30 ml (2 tbsp) and add more as necessary. Olive oil is recommended, but it could be combined with peanut or other oils.

1 Start by preparing the tomato sauce. Put all the ingredients into a pan, cover and simmer over gentle heat for at least 15 minutes or until you have a thick sauce. Stir occasionally. It can cook for 30 minutes or more without coming to harm.

2 Bring the milk to boiling point and poach the cauliflower in it for 5 minutes. Drain, reserving the milk. Add enough water to make it up to 300 ml (½ pint). Chop the cauliflower finely and season well.

3 Heat the butter until it foams. Sprinkle over the flour, stir it in and cook over gentle heat for 2-3 minutes. Add the reserved cauliflower milk gradually, stirring well until thoroughly amalgamated. Let this simmer gently for 5 minutes.

4 Allow to cool a little, then whisk in the eggs and cheese and season well. Preheat the oven to gas mark 4, 180°C (350°F).

5 Meanwhile, heat 30 ml (2 tbsp) oil in a large frying pan and lightly brown the aubergine slices on both sides. Remove and drain on kitchen paper. Only do a few at a time, so that the oil remains hot and less of it is absorbed by the aubergines. When adding more oil, make sure it is well heated before you put in the aubergines.

6 Mix half the cheese sauce with the cauliflower. Lightly grease a 1.7 litre (3 pint) ovenproof dish. Put in a layer of aubergines, then one of cauliflower mixture, and cover with tomato sauce. Continue in this order until you have used all the ingredients, finishing with a layer of aubergines. Cover with the rest of the cheese sauce and bake for 30 minutes. Serve hot.

Baked potatoes with almonds

An easy way to turn a simple baked potato into a special dish.

1 Preheat the oven to gas mark 5, 190°C (375°F).

2 Scrub the potatoes, prick their skins and bake for 1 hour. Cut them in half and remove some of the flesh, leaving enough for a good shell.

3 Mix together the garlic, almonds and lemon juice. Stir in the olive oil by degrees until the mixture has a creamy consistency. Mash in the potato. Add the mushrooms and grated carrot and season well. Pile the mixture generously into the potato skins and bake for 30 minutes.

4 Meanwhile, prepare the sauce. Heat the oil and gently fry the onion and garlic for 3-4 minutes until soft. Add the spices and bay leaf and fry for another 2 minutes. Add the remaining ingredients, bring to the boil and simmer for 30 minutes. Remove the bay leaf. If the sauce still has a grainy appearance, liquidize it before serving.

Ingredients
4 good-sized potatoes
1-2 cloves garlic, crushed
50 g (2 oz) ground almonds
15-30 ml (1-2 tbsp) lemon juice
45 ml (3 tbsp) olive oil
100 g (4 oz) mushrooms, chopped
225 g (8 oz) carrots, grated
salt and pepper
Sauce
15 ml (1 tbsp) oil, preferably
  sunflower
1 medium onion, finely chopped
2 cloves garlic, crushed
½ tbsp paprika
¼ tsp cayenne
1 bay leaf
15 ml (1 tbsp) cider vinegar
75 g (3 oz) ground almonds
425 ml (¾ pint) water
5 ml (1 tsp) honey
5 ml (1 tsp) shoyu

Serves 4

★
Photograph
page 74

Hazelnut and courgette bake

A nutritious combination of nuts, vegetables and oatmeal, this makes a loaf which is satisfying yet not at all heavy.

1 In a large frying pan gently sauté the onion for 3-4 minutes in 30 ml (2 tbsp) oil. Add the hazelnuts and courgettes and cook them over moderate heat for about 10 minutes, until the nuts have browned lightly and the courgettes are soft. You may find you need to add a little extra oil, because although nuts are rich in oil themselves they tend to absorb oil while frying, especially if finely chopped.

2 Preheat the oven to gas mark 4, 180°C (350°F).

3 Heat 10 ml (2 tsp) of oil in a small, heavy-based pan. Mix the sesame, cumin, turmeric and ginger and fry over medium heat, stirring, for 2-3 minutes or until they darken.

4 Away from the heat, mix the hazelnuts and courgettes with the spices, oatmeal, ground nuts, coconut and cayenne and work everything together thoroughly. Season well and stir in the puréed tomatoes.

5 Grease a 450 g (1 lb) loaf tin or deep pâté dish and press the mixture in well. Bake for 35-40 minutes or until the top is well browned and firm to the touch. Serve hot.

Ingredients
1 medium onion, finely chopped
45-60 ml (3-4 tbsp) oil, preferably
  sunflower
100 g (4 oz) shelled hazelnuts,
  roughly chopped
550 g (1¼ lb) courgettes, diced
½ tbsp sesame seeds
½ tbsp cumin seeds
½ tsp turmeric
¼ tsp grated root ginger
75 g (3 oz) medium oatmeal *or*
  rolled oat flakes
75 g (3 oz) ground nuts (peanuts,
  cashews or almonds)
50 g (2 oz) creamed coconut, grated
pinch of cayenne
salt and pepper
150 g (5 oz) canned tomatoes,
  puréed

Serves 4

★
Photograph
page 74

Casserole amandine

*Small new potatoes look best in this robust casserole. It takes
its name from the ground almonds, which give a subtle flavour to
the sauce.*

1 In a large, heavy pan, ideally one with a matching
lid, cook the onions gently in the oil for 3-4 minutes, stirring
frequently, until they are soft and transparent but not brown.

2 Add the potatoes and carrots, cover and cook for a further
5 minutes.

3 Add the parsley, garlic, white wine and water and season
well. Cover and continue cooking for another 10 minutes.

4 Meanwhile, mash the ground almonds, egg yolks and
turmeric to a smooth paste, using a pestle and mortar
or a wooden spoon and a bowl. Thin with 45 ml (3 tbsp)
of the cooking liquid and stir this mixture gradually back
into the pan until thoroughly incorporated.

5 Add the peas, cover, and simmer for a further 10 minutes
or until the vegetables are tender. Adjust the seasoning
and serve hot, sprinkled with parsley and the finely chopped
egg white.

Ingredients
2 large onions, finely chopped
22.5 ml (1½ tbsp) olive oil
450 g (1 lb) new potatoes, scrubbed
450 g (1 lb) carrots, diced
2 tbsp finely chopped parsley
6 cloves garlic, peeled and left whole
180 ml (12 tbsp) white wine
300 ml (½ pint) water
salt and pepper
75 g (3 oz) ground almonds
2 hard-boiled egg yolks
½ tsp turmeric
100 g (4 oz) peas
Garnish
extra chopped parsley
hard-boiled egg white

Serves 4

★

Vegetable cobbler

*Broccoli and corn make a simple yet effective colour combination,
but almost any vegetables could be used. If you want to cut
down the fat content, use half milk and half vegetable stock.*

1 Put the milk in a pan with the onion, bay leaf and
peppercorns. Bring slowly to boiling point, turn off the heat,
cover and leave to infuse for 10 minutes. Strain.

2 Melt the butter, stir in the flour and cook for 2-3 minutes
over gentle heat. Gradually add the milk, stirring constantly.
Bring to the boil and simmer for 4 minutes.

3 While the milk is infusing, prepare the vegetables, starting
with the celery. Put it in a large steamer over boiling water
and cook for 2-3 minutes. Add the broccoli and beans and
continue steaming for another 8 minutes.

4 Cook the corn cob in boiling water for 4-8 minutes. (The
fresher it is, the less time it will take to cook.) Drain it and
use a very sharp knife to scrape off the kernels.
Continued

Ingredients
425 ml (¾ pint) milk
1 small onion
1 bay leaf
6 peppercorns
50 g (2 oz) butter
40 g (1½ oz) wholewheat flour
4 sticks celery, chopped
350 g (12 oz) broccoli florets
225 g (8 oz) French beans, sliced
1 corn on the cob
salt and pepper
Cobbler topping
75 g (3 oz) wholewheat flour
75 g (3 oz) cornmeal
1½ tsp baking powder
½ tsp salt
1 egg
50 ml (2 fl oz) milk
15 ml (1 tbsp) olive oil
75 g (3 oz) grated cheese (Cheddar,
     Gruyère or a mixture)
sesame seeds

Serves 4

★
Photograph
page 77

From top: **Casserole amandine; Baked potatoes with almonds** (*see p. 73*);
Hazelnut and courgette bake (*see p. 73*)

75

Vegetable cobbler continued

5 Mix the vegetables with the white sauce and season well. Preheat the oven to gas mark 6, 200°C (400°F).

6 Mix the flour, cornmeal, baking powder and salt together in a bowl. In another bowl, beat the egg thoroughly and stir in the milk and olive oil. Beat again, pour this over the flour mixture and stir in gently, adding a little extra milk if necessary, until you have a mixture resembling a soft scone dough.

7 Mix in the grated cheese and roll the dough out 1 cm (½ in) thick on a lightly floured board. Cut the dough into 3.5 cm (1½ in) circles.

8 Pour the sauce and vegetables into a greased dish and arrange the dough circles in an attractive pattern on top. Sprinkle with sesame seeds and bake for 25 minutes or until the top is golden brown. Serve immediately.

★

Ingredients
15 ml (1 tbsp) olive oil
2 medium onions, chopped
3 cloves garlic, crushed
1 tsp dried thyme
1 tsp dried marjoram
½ tsp chopped fresh rosemary
2 carrots, diced
225 g (8 oz) potatoes, diced
175 g (6 oz) swede *or* kohlrabi, diced
175 g (6 oz) mushrooms, sliced
175 g (6 oz) leeks, sliced
450 g (1 lb) tomatoes, skinned
   and chopped
15 ml (1 tbsp) tomato purée
2 bay leaves
150 ml (¼ pint) red wine
salt and pepper
Crumble topping
75 g (3 oz) butter
75 g (3 oz) wholewheat flour
75 g (3 oz) flakes—oats, wheat,
   rye or barley
2 tbsp sunflower *or* sesame seeds
   (optional)
salt and pepper

Serves 4

Winter hotpot

A crunchy, savoury crumble topping transforms this simple stew into a substantial main dish.

1 Heat the oil in a heavy pan and gently fry the onion and garlic for 3-4 minutes until soft.

2 Add the herbs, carrots, potatoes, swede, mushrooms and leeks, cover the pan and sweat over low heat for another 3-4 minutes.

3 Now add the tomatoes, tomato purée, bay leaves and red wine. Simmer for 40 minutes with the lid on. Then season to taste.

4 Preheat the oven to gas mark 4, 180°C (350°F).

5 To make the crumble topping, rub the butter into the flour until the mixture resembles coarse breadcrumbs. Mix in the flakes and seeds (if used) and season well. Sprinkle this over the vegetables and bake for 25-30 minutes.

Clockwise from top: **Vegetable cobbler** (*see p. 75*); **Winter hotpot; Samosas** (*see p. 81*); **Broccoli and mushroom gratin** (*see p. 79*); **Peas and pak-choi au gratin** (*see p. 78*)

SIDE VEGETABLES

If you are serving vegetables as an accompaniment, a simple presentation is often the best. Cook them lightly and serve straightaway to preserve as much goodness as possible.

For most vegetables, allow 100-225 g (4-8 oz) per person. Almost all are suitable for boiling or steaming, except some of the fruit vegetables: aubergines benefit from being lightly fried, and tomatoes can be grilled. Carrots, parsnips, potatoes and sweet potatoes are suitable for baking. Braising is a good method for coarse leaves such as kale, Swiss chard or red cabbage as well as for celery and fennel. Marrows, squashes and pumpkins can be roasted. Stir-frying is suitable for nearly all vegetables, except for potatoes and woody root vegetables such as parsnips.

Even with a simple presentation, it is worth sparing a moment or two to make it look attractive. Sprinkle with fresh herbs, chopped toasted nuts or grated orange and lemon rind. For extra flavour, toss the cooked vegetables in a little fruit juice or shoyu, or a mixture of shoyu and tahini.

Two rather more elaborate methods of preparing vegetables are cooking them *au gratin* and stir-frying. These can be served either as a main course or as an accompaniment to a substantial dish of grains or beans.

Ingredients
450 g (1 lb) shelled fresh peas
450 g (1 lb) pak-choi, shredded
40 g (1½ oz) butter
25 g (1 oz) wholewheat flour
100 g (4 oz) Cheddar, grated
Topping
50 g (2 oz) Cheddar, grated *or*
  2 tbsp fresh breadcrumbs

Serves 4-6

Peas and pak-choi au gratin

Gratins do not necessarily involve cheese. Gratin is a term used when a crust forms on a dish during cooking. Breadcrumbs can be used, or a mixture of breadcrumbs and cheese. A secret of success is to undercook the vegetables. Steam green vegetables until barely tender; boil root vegetables in water or milk. Use the steaming or boiling liquid as stock for the sauce. More elaborate versions can be made with two or three different vegetables, perhaps steaming one and lightly sautéing another for a contrast of texture.

1 Steam the vegetables together for 5-7 minutes until just tender. Measure out 570 ml (1 pint) of the steaming water.

2 Melt the butter. Add the flour and stir until smooth. Add the water, which should be hot but not boiling, return to a low heat and stir until thoroughly blended. Leave to simmer for 5-6 minutes.

3 Beat the cheese into the sauce. Mix the sauce with
the vegetables, turn into a lightly greased gratin dish, sprinkle
with the topping and put under a hot grill for 3-4 minutes
until brown. Serve hot.

Broccoli and mushroom gratin

*As in the previous recipe, the vegetables should be undercooked.
This is a lighter dish, made by baking them in an egg custard.
Other possible combinations are: steamed leek with sliced
tomato, seasoned with basil; blanched fennel and celery; boiled
potato and shredded cabbage sautéed and flavoured with garlic
and caraway.*

1 Preheat the oven to gas mark 6, 200°C (400°F).

2 Steam the broccoli for 5-7 minutes until barely tender.

3 Heat the oil and gently sauté the garlic and mushrooms for
5 minutes. Mix together the broccoli and mushrooms and
turn into a lightly greased ovenproof dish.

4 Beat the eggs thoroughly and stir in the milk. Season well
and pour over the vegetables. Sprinkle with the cheese and
bake for 40-45 minutes or until the custard has set.

Ingredients
450 g (1 lb) broccoli florets
15 ml (1 tbsp) olive oil
1 clove garlic, chopped
225 g (8 oz) mushrooms, diced
4 eggs
570 ml (1 pint) milk *or* milk and
   water mixed
salt and pepper
50-75 g (2-3 oz) Cheddar, grated

Serves 4-6

Photograph
page 77

STIR-FRYING

Also known as quick-frying, this is a method of frying
vegetables rapidly, using the minimum amount of oil, so that
they retain all their flavour and freshness and the texture
is light and crisp. To achieve this, the oil must be very
hot and the vegetables cut into similarly sized small pieces so
that they cook as quickly and evenly as possible.

The traditional cooking vessel is a wok. It is usually made
of thin metal, so the oil heats up quickly, and its shallow,
rounded shape means far less oil is needed than in conventional
Western frying while still providing a large area for cooking.

Peanut oil is the most popular, as it can be heated to high
temperatures without any loss of flavour. Sunflower oil and
soya oil are also widely used. All vegetables must be prepared
beforehand, as once you start frying there is no time to do
anything else.
Continued

Stir-frying continued

The basic process is as follows: spices, often garlic and ginger, are fried over medium heat to flavour the oil. Then the vegetable pieces are put in, those that will take longer to cook going first, and stirred over high heat. Finally any liquid—for example, shoyu or sherry—is added and cooked a little longer to reduce and concentrate the flavouring.

You need roughly 1 kilo (2-2½ lb) of vegetables to serve 4-6 people, depending on what else you are having.

Photograph
page 70

Ingredients
Marinade
1 small onion, very finely chopped
60 ml (4 tbsp) peanut oil
60 ml (4 tbsp) lemon juice
45 ml (3 tbsp) shoyu
30 ml (2 tbsp) dry sherry
10 ml (2 tsp) honey
1 tbsp grated root ginger
3 cloves garlic, crushed

225 g (8 oz) firm tofu
15 ml (1 tbsp) peanut oil
1 tsp grated root ginger
175 g (6 oz) beansprouts
175 g (6 oz) spring onions, chopped
175 g (6 oz) green pepper, diced
175 g (6 oz) mushrooms, sliced
175 g (6 oz) Chinese leaves, shredded

Serves 4-6

Stir-fried vegetables with tofu

1 Mix all the marinade ingredients together. Cut the tofu into small chunks, pour the marinade over and leave for several hours.

2 Drain the tofu, straining the marinade into a small saucepan. Set this to heat gently while you stir-fry the tofu and vegetables as shown. Serve immediately, with the rest of the marinade handed round separately.

STIR-FRYING IN A WOK

1 *Heat the oil until it begins to smoke. Add ginger and fry, stirring, over medium heat for a minute or two.*

2 *Turn the heat up, put in the tofu chunks and stir-fry for 2-3 minutes until just beginning to brown.*

3 *Move the tofu to the side of the wok, add all the prepared vegetables and fry, stirring constantly, for 2-3 minutes, keeping the heat high.*

4 *Add 30 ml (2 tbsp) of the warmed marinade and continue cooking for another 3 minutes.*

Stir-fried Chinese leaves with green beans

1 Mix together the miso, hot water and shoyu. Blend the sherry and arrowroot and stir them into the miso stock.

2 Heat the oil in a wok and stir-fry the spring onions, garlic, ginger and aniseeds for 1 minute over brisk heat.

3 Put in the green beans and Chinese leaves, turn the heat up high and fry for a further minute.

4 Pour the stock over the vegetables. Add the beansprouts and continue to stir-fry for 3-4 minutes or until the liquid has evaporated. Serve immediately, sprinkled with a little sesame oil.

Ingredients
10 ml (2 tsp) miso
90 ml (6 tbsp) hot water
60 ml (4 tbsp) shoyu
60 ml (4 tbsp) dry sherry
20 ml (4 tsp) arrowroot
60 ml (4 tbsp) peanut oil
8 spring onions, chopped
4 cloves garlic, finely chopped
2.5 cm (1 in) root ginger, diced
1 tsp aniseeds
225 g (8 oz) green beans, sliced into 2.5 cm (1 in) lengths
450 g (1 lb) Chinese leaves, sliced
225 g (8 oz) beansprouts
a few drops sesame oil

Serves 4-6

Photograph
page 83

Samosas

Traditional Indian savoury snacks, with a spicy filling of potatoes and mung beans.

1 Sift the flour and salt into a bowl. Add the oil and work it in with your fingers until the mixture resembles coarse breadcrumbs. Gradually add about 60 ml (4 tbsp) water and gather the dough into a stiff ball.

2 Turn the dough out on a clean surface and knead it for 3-4 minutes or until it is quite smooth. Rub the surface lightly with a little oil, put it in a polythene bag and leave to rest for 30 minutes.

3 Drain the mung beans and bring them to the boil in a pan of fresh water. Boil fast for 10 minutes, then reduce the heat and simmer, covered, for 20-30 minutes until soft.

4 Meanwhile, boil the potatoes until they are just cooked. When they are cool enough to handle cut them into dice.

5 Heat the oil in a heavy-based pan. Put in the spices and fry over brisk heat until the seeds start to pop. Reduce the heat, add the onion and garlic and continue cooking over medium heat for 3-4 minutes until the onion just begins to turn brown.

6 Add the mung beans, potatoes and lemon juice. Cook over low heat for 4-5 minutes, stirring gently. Add salt to taste and let the mixture cool.

Continued

Ingredients
Pastry
225 g (8 oz) wholewheat pastry flour
½ tsp salt
60 ml (4 tbsp) oil, preferably sunflower
60 ml (4 tbsp) water
a little extra oil
Stuffing
50 g (2 oz) mung beans, soaked overnight
225 g (8 oz) potatoes, peeled
15 ml (1 tbsp) soya oil
¼ tsp turmeric
½ tsp ground cumin
½ tsp cumin seeds
1½ tsp coriander seeds
½ tsp mustard seeds
pinch of cayenne
¼ tsp grated root ginger
1 small onion, finely chopped
1 clove garlic, crushed
juice of ½ lemon
salt

oil for deep frying

Makes 16 samosas

Photograph
page 77

Soaking
overnight

Samosas continued

7 Knead the dough again and divide it into 8 balls. Roll each one into a 12.5 cm (5 in) round. Cut each round in half, shape it into a cone and fill it as shown.

FILLING THE DOUGH

1 Coil each half circle around your thumb to shape it into a cone. Wet the edges and pinch them together to seal.

2 Fill each cone with a tablespoon or so of the bean and potato mixture. Do not fill it too full.

3 Fold the free end up over the stuffing, moisten it and press together to close firmly.

8 Heat 5 cm (2 in) oil in a deep pan over medium heat and deep fry the samosas, a few at a time. Fry slowly for 4-5 minutes, turning frequently, until they are crisp and golden brown. Drain on kitchen paper. They are best eaten hot or warm.

Ingredients
Choux pastry
150 ml (¼ pint) water
50 g (2 oz) butter
50 g (2 oz) wheatmeal flour
2 eggs
50 g (2 oz) Gruyère, grated
pinch of mustard powder
pepper
Filling
1 medium onion, finely chopped
25 g (1 oz) butter
2 cloves garlic, crushed
1 green pepper, deseeded and diced
450 g (1 lb) courgettes, diced
20 g (¾ oz) wholewheat flour
150 ml (¼ pint) milk
½ tsp grated nutmeg
1 tsp dried oregano
salt and pepper
25 g (1 oz) Gruyère, grated

Serves 4

Gougère with courgettes

In its native Burgundy, a gougère is served on its own, without embellishment, and can be eaten hot or cold. It also goes very well with vegetables: apart from courgettes, try cauliflower or broccoli, Brussels sprouts, mushrooms or a mixture of carrots and celery.

1 Preheat the oven to gas mark 7, 220°C (425°F).

2 Bring the water and butter to the boil in a heavy pan.

3 Sieve the flour. When the water and butter are boiling, take the pan off the heat, shoot in the flour all at once and beat very well until glossy.

4 Mix in one of the eggs, beating thoroughly until it is completely amalgamated. There should be no trace of egg left. Repeat with the second egg.

5 Stir in the grated cheese, mustard and pepper. Spoon the mixture round the sides of a lightly greased 20 cm (8 in) flan dish or tart tin to form a ring.

6 Bake for 20 minutes. Reduce the heat to gas mark 5, 190°C (375°F) and bake for a further 10 minutes.
Continued on page 84

Top left: **Gougère with courgettes**; bottom right: **Festive pie** (*see p. 84*); top right and bottom left: **Stir-fried Chinese leaves with green beans** (*see p. 81*)

Gougère with courgettes continued

7 Meanwhile, prepare the filling. Sauté the onion in the butter for 3-4 minutes. Add the garlic, green pepper and courgettes and continue cooking for another 3-4 minutes.

8 Sprinkle over the flour, stir it in well and cook for a further 3 minutes over gentle heat.

9 Stir in the milk. Bring to the boil and simmer, stirring occasionally, for 2-3 minutes. Add the nutmeg and oregano and season well.

10 When the gougère is cooked, spoon the filling into the middle, sprinkle with the grated cheese and put under a hot grill for 3-4 minutes or until the cheese melts and browns lightly. Serve hot.

★

Photograph
page 83

Ingredients
Flaky pastry
200 g (7 oz) wheatmeal flour
30 g (1 oz) rye flour
½ tsp salt
150 g (5 oz) solid vegetable fat
squeeze of lemon juice
up to 150 ml (¼ pint) ice-cold water
Filling
450 g (1 lb) spinach
grated nutmeg
salt and pepper
450 g (1 lb) carrots, chopped
rind and juice of ½ orange
25 g (1 oz) butter
20 g (¾ oz) wholewheat flour
50 g (2 oz) ground walnuts

Serves 4

Festive pie

Put the fat in the freezer for at least 1 hour before beginning this recipe.

1 Mix together the two flours and the salt. Grate in the fat. Add the lemon juice and just enough water to bind the mixture to a dough and chill for at least 4 hours. (You can make this pastry 2-3 days beforehand and keep it in the refrigerator.)

2 Wash the spinach and cook it in its own juices for 6-8 minutes, using a heavy-based saucepan. Purée it with nutmeg and season to taste.

3 Cook the carrots in a little boiling water until completely soft. Drain, reserving the stock, and purée them with the orange rind and juice. Season to taste.

4 Melt the butter in a small pan. Add the flour and stir over gentle heat for a minute or two. Pour on 150 ml (¼ pint) of the carrot stock, bring to the boil and simmer for 2 minutes. Off the heat, stir in the ground walnuts.

5 Preheat the oven to gas mark 7, 220°C (425°F).

6 Roll out and fold the pastry as shown. Use two-thirds of it to line the base and sides of a 23 cm (9 in) flat tin or pie dish. Fill with the carrot purée, then the walnut sauce in a layer, and finally the spinach purée.

7 Roll out the remaining pastry and cut it into strips. Use these to make a lattice top. Bake for 25-30 minutes or until the pastry is well cooked.

Flamiche

1 Make the pastry as in the preceding recipe for Festive Pie. Put the fat in the freezer for at least 1 hour before use.

2 Heat the oil or butter and gently sweat the leeks and garlic for 10-15 minutes in a covered pan.

3 Sprinkle over the soya flour and mix well. Pour on the stock and bring to the boil, stirring. Reduce the heat and simmer for 5 minutes. Season well and leave to cool.

4 Roll out and fold the pastry as shown below. Preheat the oven to gas mark 7, 220°C (425°F).

5 Roll out two-thirds of the pastry and line a 20-23 cm (8-9 in) pie dish with it. Fill with the cooled leek mixture.

6 Roll out the rest of the pastry, cut it into strips and arrange them in a lattice topping. Brush with a little beaten egg and salt and bake for 20-25 minutes.

Ingredients

Flaky pastry
200 g (7 oz) wheatmeal flour
30 g (1 oz) rye flour
½ tsp salt
150 g (5 oz) solid vegetable fat
squeeze of lemon juice
up to 150 ml (¼ pint) ice-cold water

Filling
60 ml (4 tbsp) sunflower oil *or*
    50 g (2 oz) butter
900 g (2 lb) leeks, chopped
3 cloves garlic, crushed
50 g (2 oz) soya flour
300 ml (½ pint) vegetable stock
    (see p. 151)
salt and pepper

Glaze
1 egg beaten with a little salt

Serves 4

Photograph
pages
136-137

ROLLING AND FOLDING FLAKY PASTRY

1 *Take the pastry out of the refrigerator and roll it out into a rectangle.*

2 *Mark this rectangle into thirds and fold the bottom third (the one nearest you) over the centre third.*

3 *Fold over the top third and press the edges to seal them. Give the pastry a quarter turn (through 90 degrees).*

4 *Repeat the rolling and folding 3 more times, giving the pastry a quarter turn each time. Be patient if you find it a little tricky the first time.*

Christmas

A Christmas meal to please all but the most die-hard traditionalist, with a magnificent mushroom brioche as the centrepiece. It is preceded by a smooth cream of cauliflower flavoured with sautéed almonds, and accompanied by Brussels sprouts with chestnuts, glazed carrots and paprika rice. A thick cashew sauce adds savour and richness, balanced by a simple salad based on other green leaves in season.

The Christmas pudding, cake and mincemeat in the mince pies are all made without sugar but taste traditional. A persimmon sorbet offers a refreshing contrast. For a low fat alternative to brandy butter, blend 300 g (11 oz) silken tofu with 1-2 tablespoons maple syrup.

Protein is provided by the rice, nuts and brioche, complemented by a variety of vegetables, both cooked and raw. The rich pudding and pies are followed by fresh fruit and nuts. The result: a festive meal proving that a sense of occasion is compatible with a healthy, balanced diet.

See page 200 for a countdown of the work and planning required, and for details on preparing the sprouts with chestnuts and the glazed carrots.

1 Mince pies (*p. 173*) **2** Christmas cake (*p. 167*) **3** Brandy butter **4** Christmas pudding (*p. 158*) **5** Persimmon and claret water ice (*p. 163*) **6** Brussels sprouts with chestnuts; glazed carrots (*see p. 210*) **7** Paprika rice (*p. 100*) **8** Cashew sauce (*p. 153*) **9** Mushroom brioche (*p. 88*) **10** Green salad (*see above*) **11** Cream of cauliflower and almond soup (*p. 48*)

★

Photograph
pages
86-87

Ingredients

Brioche dough
10 g (½ oz) yeast
1 tsp brown sugar
45 ml (3 tbsp) tepid milk
225-250 g (8-9 oz) wheatmeal
　flour
1 tsp salt
2 eggs
75 g (3 oz) butter

Filling
45 ml (3 tbsp) olive oil
40 g (1½ oz) butter
900 g (2 lb) mushrooms, chopped
2 cloves garlic, crushed
2 sticks celery, chopped
1 crisp eating apple, diced
2 tbsp finely chopped parsley
1 tsp finely chopped marjoram
75-100 g (3-4 oz) fresh breadcrumbs
10 ml (2 tsp) miso
salt and pepper

Serves 8

Mushroom brioche

An impressive party dish, with the golden crust of the brioche surrounding a dark mushroom filling. The filling and the main preparation of the dough can be done ahead of time.

1 Mix the yeast, sugar and milk together thoroughly until smooth and creamy.

2 Mix 225 g (8 oz) flour with the salt in a warm bowl. Make a well in the flour and pour in the yeast mixture. Break in the eggs and stir together to make a paste.

3 In a separate bowl, beat the butter until soft, then beat it into the paste. The dough will be soft and shiny. If it is too slack, add a little extra flour. Turn it into a clean bowl, cover with a cloth and leave to rise for 1-1½ hours in a warm place such as an airing cupboard.

4 Knock back. Knead for 2-3 minutes, put in a floured bowl, cover and leave in a cold place overnight.

5 For the filling, heat the oil and butter and gently sauté the mushrooms, garlic, celery and apple for 3-4 minutes. Cover the pan and sweat over low heat for 10-15 minutes. Mix in the parsley, marjoram and breadcrumbs, beat in the miso and season to taste.

6 Preheat the oven to gas mark 6, 200°C (400°F).

7 Roll out the brioche dough and stuff it as shown, using either a greased baking sheet or a greased 900 g (2 lb) loaf tin. If you have made the filling in advance, reheat it gently before using or it will come away from the crust.

PREPARING THE BRIOCHE

1 *Roll the dough out into a large oblong. If you are using a baking sheet, lay the dough on it and heap up the mushroom filling down the centre.*

2 *Fold up first one side and then the other so that they meet in the centre.*

3 *Moisten all the edges and press them together into a neat seal. You could brush the dough with a little cream at this stage if you want to glaze it.*

4 *If you are using a loaf tin, lift the rolled-out dough with the rolling pin and ease it over the tin.*

5 *Fit the dough carefully into the tin and use a knife to trim off the excess.*

6 *Pile in the filling. Fold the sides up to meet in the centre. Trim, moisten the edges and pinch together to seal.*

8 Bake for 20-25 minutes (if on a baking sheet) or 30-35 minutes (if in a loaf tin).

Raised pie

Another party piece for which the filling can be made in advance. This one uses hot water crust.

1 Heat the oil in a large frying pan, add the diced aubergines and stir-fry briskly for 2-3 minutes until lightly browned.

2 Mix in the mushrooms, cover and sweat over gentle heat for 10-15 minutes or until the vegetables are very soft. Stir occasionally. Mix in the parsley, season to taste and set aside to cool.

3 Meanwhile, in another pan, melt the butter and gently stew the fennel for 10 minutes.

4 Warm the brandy, pour it over the fennel and set it alight. When the flames have died down, put in the tomatoes, cover the pan and cook for another 10 minutes.

5 Add the bulgar wheat and cook for 10 minutes more, adding a little water if necessary. The mixture should be quite thick. Finally stir in the almonds, season and set aside to cool.

6 To make the hot water crust, first mix together the flour and the salt.

7 Continue as shown overleaf. If the dough is a little dry, you may need to add extra boiling water.

Continued

Ingredients
Filling
45 ml (3 tbsp) olive oil
550 g (1¼ lb) aubergines, diced
550 g (1¼ lb) mushrooms, diced
2 tbsp finely chopped parsley
salt and pepper
25 g (1 oz) butter
550 g (1¼ lb) fennel, chopped
45 ml (3 tbsp) brandy
550 g (1¼ lb) tomatoes, skinned
  and chopped
50 g (2 oz) bulgar wheat
50 g (2 oz) blanched almonds,
  coarsely chopped (see p. 209)
Crust
450 g (1 lb) wholewheat flour
1 tsp salt
175 g (6 oz) solid vegetable fat
150 ml (¼ pint) water
beaten egg for glazing

Serves 6-8

Photograph
*pages
54-55*

Raised pie continued

8 Preheat the oven to gas mark 7, 220°C (425°F).

9 Use two-thirds of the dough as shown to line the base and sides of a 20-23 cm (8-9 in) straight-sided cake or pie tin.

10 Put in half the mushrooms and aubergines, then all the fennel and tomato mixture, and finally the rest of the mushrooms and aubergines. Press in well.

11 Lay on the top as shown. Brush it with a little beaten egg to glaze and pierce a hole in the centre so that the steam can escape.

12 Bake for 20 minutes, then reduce the heat to gas mark 5, 190°C (375°F) and bake for a further 50-60 minutes or until the pastry is well cooked. Serve hot.

MAKING THE CRUST

1 Melt the fat and water together, bring to a fierce boil and pour this over the flour and salt. Mix together with a wooden spoon.

2 As soon as the mixture is cool enough to handle, knead it quickly into a ball. Divide into two-thirds and one-third.

3 Work the larger piece of dough over the base and up the sides of the mould, stretching and patting it into position.

4 With your forefinger, make a channel around the base where it joins the side. This is to avoid having too solid a chunk of pastry.

5 Roll out the rest of the dough to fit the top and use the rolling pin to lay it on. Moisten the edges with water.

6 Pinch the edges to seal and make an attractive pattern. Trim off excess dough. You can use the trimmings to make decorations.

BEANS, PEAS & LENTILS

Beans, peas and lentils are far more than just a necessary source of protein. By themselves they are savoury and satisfying; combined with vegetables and cereals they create a balance of complementary flavours, textures and nutrients.

Preparation is simple. You may need to pick them over first for small pieces of grit, especially lentils, then rinse to get rid of surface dust. Whole beans and peas need preliminary soaking—see page 208 for details and cooking times.

In all these recipes, except the Mexican croustade, the bean mixture can be made in advance—in fact should be, if you have time, as the flavours improve and develop. Plainly cooked beans can be frozen, which often saves time.

Haricots Catalan

1 Drain the beans. Cover with fresh water, bring to the boil and boil fast for 10 minutes. Reduce the heat and simmer, covered, for 40-50 minutes or until tender. Drain and set aside.

2 Meanwhile, parboil the French beans in boiling water for 3-5 minutes until just beginning to be tender. Drain and set aside.

3 In a large, heavy-based frying pan, gently sauté the garlic and onions in the oil over moderate heat for about 5 minutes or until the onion is soft and translucent.

4 Stir in the chopped tomatoes and parsley and season well with pepper. Bring to the boil and cook, uncovered, until most of the liquid has evaporated.

5 Stir in all the beans and simmer for 5-6 minutes longer or until heated through. Check the seasoning and serve hot.

Ingredients

175 g (6 oz) haricot *or* pinto beans, soaked overnight
225 g (8 oz) French beans, cut into 5 cm (2 in) lengths
3-4 cloves garlic, finely chopped
100 g (4 oz) onions, finely chopped
30 ml (2 tbsp) oil, preferably olive
550 g (1¼ lb) tomatoes, skinned and finely chopped
2 tbsp finely chopped parsley
salt and pepper

Serves 4

★

Photograph
page 93

Soaking
overnight

★

Ingredients
Short crust
100 g (4 oz) wholewheat flour
½ tsp baking powder
pinch salt
25 g (1 oz) butter
25 g (1 oz) solid vegetable fat
1 tsp brown sugar
30-45 ml (2-3 tbsp) water
10 ml (2 tsp) oil
Filling
15 ml (1 tbsp) sunflower oil
175 g (6 oz) onions, chopped
1 tsp ground coriander
1 tsp ground cumin
175 g (6 oz) red split lentils
350 ml (12 fl oz) boiling water
350 g (12 oz) spinach
15 ml (1 tbsp) lemon juice
salt and pepper
Garnish
2 tbsp sesame seeds

Serves 4

Lentil and spinach quiche

Lentils are particularly suitable as fillings for quiches or pies as they cook to a purée quickly. This recipe is an excellent way of using up any leftover cooked lentils.

1 Mix the flour, baking powder and salt together in a bowl. Rub the fats in with your fingertips until you have a mixture resembling fine breadcrumbs.

2 Dissolve the sugar in 30 ml (2 tbsp) water. Mix in the oil and add this to the flour mixture. Add a little more water if necessary to bind the mixture. The dough should be on the wettish side. Leave to rest for 30 minutes.

3 Preheat the oven to gas mark 6, 200°C (400°F).

4 Roll out the dough to line an 18-20 cm (7-8 in) flan ring. Press it in well, prick the base all over and bake for 5 minutes to set it. This is known as baking "blind".

5 Meanwhile, heat the oil in a large, heavy-based pan and gently fry the onions and spices for 3-4 minutes.

6 Add the lentils to the pan together with the boiling water. Bring back to the boil and simmer, covered, for 10-15 minutes until the lentils turn to a stiff purée.

7 While the lentils are cooking, wash the spinach, drain it well and cook it in its own juices in a covered pan for 6-8 minutes until just done. Drain and chop. Mix it into the lentils with the lemon juice and seasoning.

8 Spread this filling over the prepared flan base. Cover loosely with foil and bake for 25-30 minutes until the pastry is cooked and the filling hot. Sprinkle with sesame seeds and serve hot or warm.

Variations
For an alternative, simpler filling, use 225 g (8 oz) each of lentils and onions. Fry the onions in the oil, as above, using 1 teaspoon turmeric instead of the coriander and cumin. Mix this into the lentils and add about 2 teaspoons wholegrain mustard, 1 tablespoon peanut butter, and salt and pepper to taste.

This filling also lends itself to tartlets, ideal for a cocktail party or buffet (see photograph on pages 44-45). The quantities given are enough for 12 medium or 20 miniature tartlets. As a further variation, skin and roughly chop about 225 g (8 oz) tomatoes. Put one or two pieces in each tartlet before covering with the lentil purée and baking.

From top: **Haricots Catalan** (*see p. 91*); **Chick pea and fennel casserole** (*see p. 94*);
Lentil and spinach quiche

★

Photograph
page 93

Soaking
overnight

Ingredients
175 g (6 oz) chick peas, soaked
    overnight
30 ml (2 tbsp) olive oil
1 clove garlic, crushed
225 g (8 oz) celery, diced
225 g (8 oz) fennel, sliced
225 g (8 oz) green beans, chopped
50 g (2 oz) bulgar wheat
300 ml (½ pint) cider, sweet or dry
300 ml (½ pint) vegetable stock
    (see p. 151)
2 tbsp finely chopped mint
salt and pepper

Serves 4

Chick pea and fennel casserole

Serve with lightly steamed green vegetables and cornbread or barley for a complete meal.

1 Drain the chick peas. Cover with fresh water, bring to the boil and boil fast for 10 minutes. Reduce the heat and simmer, covered, for 45-50 minutes, or until just soft. They need not be fully cooked at this stage as they will get another 20 minutes cooking. Drain and set aside.

2 Heat the oil and lightly fry the garlic for 2-3 minutes. Put in the celery, fennel and green beans and sweat them over low heat, covered, for 5-6 minutes.

3 Add the chick peas and stir-fry for 2-3 minutes. Add the bulgar wheat, cider and stock, bring to the boil, cover and simmer for 20 minutes.

4 Stir in the fresh mint and season well. Cook for another 10 minutes and serve hot.

★

Soaking
overnight

Ingredients
75 g (3 oz) red kidney beans, soaked
    overnight
Crust
50 g (2 oz) fresh breadcrumbs
50 g (2 oz) wholewheat flour
50 g (2 oz) wheatgerm
50 g (2 oz) rolled oat flakes
100 g (4 oz) butter
Filling
275 g (10 oz) sweet potato, peeled
    and diced
salt and pepper
1 small onion, diced
15 ml (1 tbsp) sunflower oil
½ tsp ground cardamom
½ tsp ground cinnamon
1 ripe avocado, diced
juice and grated rind of 1 orange

Serves 4

Mexican croustade

There is a strong Mexican influence in this combination of sweet potato, red kidney beans (chili beans), orange and avocado.

1 Drain the beans. Cover with fresh water, bring to the boil and boil fast for 10 minutes. Reduce the heat and simmer, covered, for 35-40 minutes or until tender. Drain and set aside.

2 Preheat the oven to gas mark 5, 190°C (375°F).

3 To make the crust, mix together the breadcrumbs, flour, wheatgerm and oats. Melt the butter and pour it over the dry ingredients. Mix thoroughly and press into an 18-20 cm (7-8 in) greased flan ring. Bake for 15-20 minutes.

4 Meanwhile, cook the sweet potato in boiling water, covered, for 15-20 minutes. Drain and mash with plenty of salt and pepper.

5 Gently fry the onion in the oil for 3-4 minutes until soft. Add the spices and continue frying over moderate heat, stirring, for a minute or two. Put in the cooked beans and the avocado and fry for a further 2-3 minutes. Add the orange juice and rind and cook for 5 minutes more.

6 Spread the sweet potato over the flan base and cover with the bean and avocado mixture. Cover loosely with foil and bake for 10-15 minutes. Serve hot or warm.

Clockwise from left: **Black-eyed bean croquettes** (*see p. 96*); **Corn and lima bean casserole** (*see p. 96*); **Mexican croustade**

★

Photograph
page 95

Soaking
overnight

Ingredients
100 g (4 oz) lima beans, soaked
    overnight
225 g (8 oz) fresh corn kernels
    (about 2 cobs)
1 small onion, finely chopped
4 sticks celery, cut into 1 cm (½ in)
    lengths
45 ml (3 tbsp) sunflower oil
1 tbsp wholewheat flour
150 ml (¼ pint) yogurt
2 tbsp chopped parsley
salt and pepper
Topping
1½ tbsp sesame seeds
1½ tbsp fresh breadcrumbs
a little oil (preferably sesame)

Serves 4

Corn and lima bean casserole

1 Drain the beans. Cover with fresh water, bring to the boil and boil fast for 10 minutes. Reduce the heat and simmer, covered, for 50-60 minutes. Drain, reserving the stock.

2 Meanwhile, cook the corn in boiling water until tender— about 4 minutes if very fresh, another minute or two if less so.

3 In a large, heavy-based pan, gently fry the onion and celery in the oil for 4-5 minutes until soft. Put in the cooked lima beans and corn and fry for another 2-3 minutes. Sprinkle on the flour, stir well and cook for another 2-3 minutes.

4 Preheat the oven to gas mark 4, 180°C (350°F).

5 Mix together 150 ml (¼ pint) of the bean stock and the yogurt. Stir this into the vegetables and cook over gentle heat for 10-15 minutes, stirring occasionally. Mix in the parsley, season and turn into an ovenproof dish.

6 To make the topping, mix the sesame seeds and breadcrumbs with just enough oil to moisten but not bind them. Sprinkle over the casserole and bake for 10-15 minutes or until crisp.

★

Photograph
page 95

Soaking
overnight

Ingredients
225 g (8 oz) black-eyed beans,
    soaked overnight
100 g (4 oz) fresh breadcrumbs
50 g (2 oz) ground Brazil nuts
100 g (4 oz) Cheddar, grated
1 clove garlic, crushed
1 tsp marjoram
1 tsp dried sage
salt and pepper
Coating
1 egg white, beaten
flour or breadcrumbs
salt and pepper

oil for shallow frying

Makes 8 croquettes

Black-eyed bean croquettes

For a different texture, use cooked short grain rice, millet or buckwheat instead of the breadcrumbs.

1 Drain the beans. Cover with fresh water, bring to the boil and boil fast for 10 minutes. Reduce the heat and simmer, covered, for 35-40 minutes or until tender.

2 Drain the beans again and mash them. Mix with all the other ingredients and season to taste. The mixture should be quite moist. Chill for an hour or two or until firm.

3 Shape into 8 croquettes about 1 cm (½ in) thick. Dip first into beaten egg white and then into seasoned flour or breadcrumbs. Shallow fry for 4-5 minutes on each side.

★

Photograph
*pages
180-181*

Soaking
overnight

Ingredients
175 g (6 oz) aduki beans, soaked
    overnight
30 ml (2 tbsp) olive oil
350 g (12 oz) mushrooms, chopped
1 clove garlic, crushed
Continued

Mushroom and aduki croquettes

These are also good with herbs, such as parsley or coriander, instead of spices. They can be served in a wholemeal bun.

1 Drain the beans. Cover with fresh water, bring to the boil and boil fast for 10 minutes. Reduce the heat and simmer, covered, for 35-40 minutes or until tender. Drain and set aside.

2 Heat the oil in a large pan and gently fry the mushrooms, garlic, chili peppers and cumin for 5-6 minutes or until the mushrooms are very soft.

3 Sprinkle over the flour. Continue cooking over low heat, stirring the flour well in, for 2-3 minutes. Off the heat, mix in the beans and season well. The consistency should be soft but not sloppy. Chill for several hours or overnight.

4 Shape into 8 croquettes about 1 cm (½ in) thick. Dip first into beaten egg and then into oatmeal. Fry in hot oil for 4-5 minutes on each side. Serve hot.

1-2 dried red chili peppers, deseeded and diced
1 tsp ground cumin
30 ml (2 tbsp) wholewheat flour
salt and pepper
Coating
1 small egg, beaten
75 g (3 oz) fine oatmeal

oil for shallow frying

Makes 8 croquettes

Aduki beans in wine

1 Drain the beans. Put them in a pan with fresh water to cover. Add the onion stuck with the cloves, the garlic, carrot, peppercorns, celery and half the olive oil. Bring to the boil and boil fast for 10 minutes. Reduce the heat and simmer, covered, for 35-40 minutes or until tender.

2 Drain the beans again, reserving the stock. Discard the onion, garlic and peppercorns. Mash or purée the carrot and celery into the stock.

3 Heat the remaining oil in a large, heavy-based pan and gently sweat the pickling onions, potatoes and courgettes for 3-4 minutes. Add the beans and cook for 5 minutes. Pour in 300 ml (½ pint) of the bean stock. Stir in the tomato purée, wine and cognac and bring to the boil. Simmer, covered, for 35 minutes or until thick. Season well and serve hot.

Ingredients
225 g (8 oz) aduki beans, soaked overnight
1 onion, peeled
2 cloves
3 cloves garlic, peeled
1 carrot, chopped into 3 pieces
8 peppercorns
2 sticks celery, cut into 2.5 cm (1 in) lengths
30 ml (2 tbsp) olive oil
225 g (8 oz) pickling onions, peeled
225 g (8 oz) potatoes, diced
225 g (8 oz) courgettes, sliced
45 ml (3 tbsp) tomato purée
90 ml (3 tbsp) red wine
45 ml (3 tbsp) cognac
salt and pepper

Serves 4

★

Photograph
page 98

Soaking
overnight

Mung dhal with spinach

1 Wash the mung beans and soak for 2 hours. Drain.

2 Wash the spinach, drain well and cook, covered, for 5 minutes until barely cooked. Drain and chop roughly.

3 Heat the ghee or oil in a frying pan and gently fry the onion and ginger for 2-3 minutes. Add the garlic, cumin and turmeric and fry, stirring, for another minute or two.

4 Add the drained dhal and continue frying over moderate heat for 2-3 minutes. Pour on 300 ml (½ pint) water, bring to the boil, cover and simmer for 20 minutes or until the dhal is tender. Purée if desired.

Continued on page 99

Ingredients
225 g (8 oz) split mung beans
450 g (1 lb) spinach
22.5 ml (1½ tbsp) ghee (see p. 220) *or* oil
100 g (4 oz) onion, finely chopped
2.5 cm (1 in) root ginger, thinly sliced
2 cloves garlic, crushed
2 tsp ground cumin
1 tsp turmeric
50 g (2 oz) creamed coconut, grated
50 ml (2 fl oz) boiling water
salt

Serves 4

★

Photograph
page 98

5 Dissolve the creamed coconut in 50 ml (2 fl oz) boiling water, stirring vigorously until it is well blended. Add this to the dhal together with the chopped spinach. Season with salt and serve hot or warm.

Mung Dhal with Spinach continued

Spiced black beans

This recipe looks good served on contrastingly coloured bulgar wheat, but also goes well with brown rice or couscous.

1 Drain the beans. Cover with fresh water, bring to the boil and boil fast for 10 minutes. Reduce the heat and simmer, covered, for 15-20 minutes. Drain, reserving the stock.

2 Meanwhile, using a heavy-based pan, gently fry the onion and garlic in the oil for 3-4 minutes. Put in the spices and fry for another minute or two, stirring.

3 Add the drained beans, the green peppers, carrots, peanuts and sliced orange. Cook, covered, over gentle heat for 10 minutes, stirring occasionally.

4 Mix in the sherry, lemon juice and shoyu. Add up to 30 ml (2 tbsp) bean stock if the mixture is dry, although the end result should not be watery. Cook, covered, for a further 10-15 minutes. Adjust the seasoning and serve hot, garnished with the extra orange slices.

Ingredients
100 g (4 oz) black beans, soaked overnight
1 onion, finely chopped
2 cloves garlic, crushed
15-30 ml (1-2 tbsp) olive oil
1 tsp grated root ginger
½ tsp ground cumin
½ tsp ground coriander
1 small fresh green chili, finely chopped
2 green peppers, diced
225 g (8 oz) carrots, diced
50 g (2 oz) roasted peanuts
1 orange, peeled and thinly sliced
15 ml (1 tbsp) sherry
juice of ½ lemon
5 ml (1 tsp) shoyu
salt and pepper
Garnish
1 orange, sliced

Serves 4

★
Soaking
overnight

Soya bean casserole

Soya beans take a long time to cook whole but are good in casseroles, especially here with the contrast of water chestnuts.

1 Drain the soya beans. Cover with plenty of fresh water, bring to the boil and boil fast for 1 hour. This long boiling time makes them more digestible. Reduce the heat and simmer, covered, for another hour or until they are soft. Drain, reserving the stock, and set aside.

2 Heat the oil in a large, heavy-based pan and briskly sauté the chili powder, ginger and garlic for 2-3 minutes. Add the vegetables, including the water chestnuts, and continue cooking for 10 minutes over gentle heat with the lid on.

3 In a bowl, mix together the cornflour, sherry and shoyu and blend in the stock. Add to the pan together with the cooked soya beans. Stir well, bring to the boil and simmer, covered, for 10 minutes. Season to taste and serve hot.

Ingredients
100 g (4 oz) soya beans, soaked overnight
15 ml (1 tbsp) sunflower oil
½ tsp chili powder
1 tsp grated root ginger
1 clove garlic, crushed
75 g (3 oz) spring onions, diced
350 g (12 oz) mushrooms, sliced
175 g (6 oz) celery, cut into julienne strips (see p. 222)
100 g (4 oz) carrots, cut into julienne strips (see p. 222)
75 g (3 oz) water chestnuts, thinly sliced
20 g (¾ oz) cornflour
15 ml (1 tbsp) sherry
15 ml (1 tbsp) shoyu
300 ml (½ pint) soya bean stock
salt and pepper

Serves 4

★
Soaking
overnight

From top: **Spiced black beans; Aduki beans in wine** (*see p. 97*); **Mung dhal with spinach** (*see p. 97*); **Soya bean casserole**

GRAINS

As with pulses, the vegetarian store cupboard comes into its own with grains. Apart from rice there are many others, such as wheat, barley, millet, buckwheat and bulgar wheat, to give different textures and unexpected flavours. Cook grains as casseroles, with fresh vegetables or dried beans and lentils, or serve them as accompaniments to other dishes, perhaps with a nut or vegetable sauce. For croquettes, millet and bulgar wheat are the best as they mould easily. Otherwise most grains can be used interchangeably, although the delicate taste of wild rice is probably best appreciated when it is plainly boiled.

Grain dishes are generally simple and quick to make, often using only one pan. Many can be cooked in advance and/or frozen. Thaw overnight in the refrigerator and reheat gently, either in the oven covered with greased paper and foil, or by steaming. There are more ideas for cold grain dishes in the Salad section.

★
Photograph
pages 86-87

Ingredients
15 ml (1 tbsp) oil
1 small onion, finely chopped
2 sticks celery, diced
225 g (8 oz) long-grain brown rice
1 tbsp paprika
500 ml (18 fl oz) boiling water
1 bay leaf
10 ml (2 tsp) shoyu
salt and pepper

Serves 4

Paprika rice

An easy variation on a basic method of cooking long-grain rice. For golden rice, substitute 1-2 teaspoons turmeric (or a pinch of saffron threads) for the paprika. For a simpler version, omit the celery and paprika.

1 Heat the oil in a large, heavy-based pan and gently sauté the onion and celery for 3-4 minutes until beginning to soften.

2 Add the rice and paprika and continue cooking for another 3-4 minutes, stirring and turning the rice to coat it thoroughly with the oil.

3 Pour over the boiling water, add the bay leaf and bring back to the boil.

4 Cover and simmer for 20-25 minutes or until the rice is tender. Remove the bay leaf. Stir in the shoyu and season to taste. Leave to rest for 5-10 minutes before serving. This can be kept warm for up to 20 minutes in a low oven— useful if you want to serve it with, say, stir-fried vegetables, which will need all your attention.

Sweet pilaf with fennel sauce

Pale golden Australian or Californian sultanas look better in this than the dark Afghan ones.

1 In a large, heavy-based pan, fry the onion gently in the oil for 3-4 minutes. Add the spices and cook for 2-3 more minutes to bring out the flavour.

2 Put in the almonds, sultanas, figs or dates, and the rice. Cook for 3-4 minutes, stirring well. Pour over the lemon juice, then the boiling water, and simmer, covered, for about 30-35 minutes or until the rice is tender and all the water absorbed. Season to taste. Keep hot.

3 Meanwhile, prepare the sauce. Simmer the fennel in the boiling water for 40 minutes with the lid on. Strain, discard the fennel and mix the stock with the orange juice.

4 Blend the arrowroot with the cold water. Mix it into the stock, bring to the boil and simmer for 3-4 minutes or until the arrowroot is cooked and you have a clear, smooth sauce. Season to taste and serve with the pilaf.

Ingredients
Pilaf
1 small onion, finely chopped
15 ml (1 tbsp) sunflower oil
1 tsp grated root ginger
1 tsp coriander seeds, crushed
½ tsp fennel seeds
25 g (1 oz) almonds, blanched (see p. 209) and chopped
25 g (1 oz) sultanas
100 g (4 oz) dried figs *or* dates, finely chopped
175 g (6 oz) long-grain brown rice
juice of ½ lemon
425 ml (¾ pint) boiling water
salt and pepper
Sauce
225 g (8 oz) fennel, finely chopped
300 ml (½ pint) boiling water
juice of 2 oranges
15 ml (1 tbsp) arrowroot
15 ml (1 tbsp) cold water

Serves 4

★
Photograph page 102

Risotto verde

This is a basic recipe for cooking short-grain rice. Unlike long-grain rice, it needs the liquid to be added a little at a time in order to cook to the right consistency. Mushrooms, fresh or dried, go well in risottos. So do fresh young peas, broccoli and courgettes. Chopped nuts make a good contrast of textures.

1 Cook the spinach in its own juices for about 6 minutes over moderate heat, covered, using a heavy-based pan. Drain and chop finely.

2 Heat the oil with half the butter and gently fry the onion for 4 minutes. Put in the rice and cook gently, stirring, for 5 minutes. It should be coated with the oil and butter but must not brown.
Continued

Ingredients
450 g (1 lb) spinach, washed
15 ml (1 tbsp) olive oil
50 g (2 oz) butter
1 onion, finely chopped
350 g (12 oz) short-grain brown rice
1 litre (1¾ pints) boiling vegetable stock (see p. 151)
1 clove garlic, crushed
1 tsp dried oregano
75 g (3 oz) Parmesan, grated
juice of ½ lemon
salt and pepper

Serves 4

★
Photograph page 102

3 Add about a quarter of the stock and continue to cook over low heat, stirring occasionally, until all the stock has been absorbed. This will take from 5 to 10 minutes.

4 Add as much again of the stock, together with the spinach, garlic and oregano, and cook in the same way until this stock too has been absorbed.

5 Add the remaining stock gradually, stirring from time to time, until the rice is tender. You may not need quite all the stock. Just before serving, stir in the grated Parmesan, lemon juice and the rest of the butter and season to taste.

Risotto verde continued

Vegetable curry with cashews

The curried vegetables can be prepared well in advance, but the rice is best if freshly cooked, and the cashews should be added at the last minute. Plain yogurt goes well with this.

1 Heat the oil or ghee in a large, heavy-based pan and fry the garlic and spices for 3-4 minutes over medium heat to bring out the flavour.

2 Blanch the aubergines for 4-5 minutes in boiling water. Drain and dice them.

3 Add all the vegetables, including the green chili, to the pan. Fry gently for 5-7 minutes, stirring to mix thoroughly with the spices.

4 Dissolve the grated coconut in the boiling water and mix with the vegetables. Add the tomatoes and cook, covered, for 20 minutes. Keep warm.

5 To cook the rice, bring 500 ml (18 fl oz) water to the boil. Put in the rice, stir once and bring back to the boil. Put the lid on and simmer for 20-25 minutes or until the rice is cooked. Do not salt the water but add salt to taste when the rice is cooked.

6 Toast the cashews under the grill for 2-3 minutes, turning once. Stir them into the vegetables just before serving.

Ingredients
15 ml (1 tbsp) peanut oil *or* ghee
  (see p. 220)
2 cloves garlic, chopped
¼ tsp cayenne
2 tsp ground coriander
1 tsp ground cumin
1 tsp turmeric
1.5 cm (¾ in) root ginger, sliced
2 medium aubergines
1 small cauliflower, divided into
  florets
2 medium potatoes, diced
100 g (4 oz) green beans, chopped
1 fresh green chili, finely chopped
50 g (2 oz) creamed coconut, grated
100 ml (4 fl oz) boiling water
450 g (1 lb) tomatoes, skinned
  and chopped
225 g (8 oz) long-grain brown rice
salt
100 g (4 oz) cashew nuts

Serves 4-6

★

Clockwise from top left: **Sweet pilaf with fennel sauce** (*see p. 101*); **Vegetable curry and yogurt; Risotto verde** (*see p. 101*)

103

★

Photograph
*pages
180-181*

Ingredients
100 g (4 oz) yellow split peas
15 ml (1 tbsp) sunflower oil
1 onion, finely chopped
½ tsp coriander seeds, crushed
½ tsp cumin seeds, crushed
1 cm (½ in) root ginger, chopped
1 tsp turmeric
¼ tsp cayenne
100 g (4 oz) long-grain brown rice
1 fresh green chili, finely chopped
425 ml (¾ pint) boiling water
juice of ½ lemon
2 tomatoes, skinned and chopped
salt

Serves 4

Khichhari

This is the forerunner of our modern kedgeree. It is an ideal dish to make in advance and reheat. Lentils or mung beans, whole or split, can be used instead of the split peas.

1 Steep the split peas in boiling water for 1 hour and drain.

2 In a large, heavy-based pan, heat the oil and fry the onions and spices for 3-4 minutes over medium heat.

3 Add the drained split peas, rice and green chili. Mix well. Pour over the boiling water and the lemon juice. Add the tomatoes, stir once, cover and simmer very gently for 35-40 minutes or until the rice and peas are tender. Season with salt and serve hot or warm.

★

Photograph
page 106

Soaking
overnight

Ingredients
225 g (8 oz) wheat berries, soaked
    overnight and drained
350 g (12 oz) asparagus, cleaned
50 g (2 oz) butter
1 large leek, diced
½ small cauliflower, divided into
    tiny florets
40 g (1½ oz) wholewheat flour
150 ml (5 fl oz) milk
2 tbsp chopped chervil *or* parsley
juice of ½ lemon, or to taste
100 g (4 oz) sorrel *or* lovage,
    chopped
salt and pepper

Serves 4-6

Fricassée Argenteuil

This vegetable dish takes its name from Argenteuil, near Paris, famous for its asparagus. If you are using lovage you will need more lemon juice than if you use sorrel.

1 Put the wheat berries in a pan with plenty of water, bring to the boil and simmer, covered, for 50-60 minutes, adding more water if they dry out. Drain.

2 Tie the asparagus into a bunch. Bring a pan of water to the boil and cook the asparagus for 7-8 minutes until just tender. Drain, reserving the stock. Cut off the tough woody ends of the asparagus and chop the rest into 2.5 cm (1 in) lengths.

3 Melt the butter in a heavy-based pan and gently sweat the leek and cauliflower for 10 minutes, covered. Sprinkle over the flour and cook for another 2-3 minutes, stirring from time to time.

4 Mix 300 ml (½ pint) of the asparagus stock with the milk. Add this to the pan and bring to the boil, stirring constantly to prevent lumps forming.

5 Put in the cooked wheat berries, chervil and lemon juice. Return to the boil and simmer for 2-3 minutes. Stir in the asparagus and sorrel or lovage. Season well, simmer for another 2-3 minutes for the flavours to develop and mingle and serve straightaway.

Couscous

A vegetarian adaptation of the traditional North African dish. If you have not got a proper couscous steamer, an ordinary sieve or strainer that fits over a deep, heavy-based saucepan works perfectly well.

1 Heat the oil and fry the spices for 3-4 minutes over moderate heat to bring out their flavour. Add the onion and cook for another 2-3 minutes until it just begins to soften. Mix in the garlic, vegetables and raisins.

2 Put the couscous in a fine mesh sieve or steamer lined with muslin. Pour boiling water over it so that the grains are all moistened. This will speed up the cooking time considerably.

3 Set the steamer over the vegetables. Put the lid on and cook over gentle heat for 20 minutes, stirring the vegetables occasionally. The steam from the vegetables will cook the couscous in this time.

4 Season both the couscous and the vegetables with salt, adding pepper only if you think they need it. Put the couscous on a serving dish and arrange the vegetables over it.

Ingredients
30 ml (2 tbsp) sunflower oil
1 tsp cayenne
2 tsp yellow mustard seeds
1 tsp paprika
1 onion, finely chopped
3 cloves garlic, crushed
2 green peppers, deseeded and diced
350 g (12 oz) courgettes, sliced
2 medium potatoes, diced
175 g (6 oz) okra, diced
350 g (12 oz) tomatoes, skinned
   and chopped
50 g (2 oz) raisins
225 g (8 oz) couscous
boiling water
salt and pepper

Serves 4-6

★
Photograph
page 106

Barley and tomatoes in sour cream

This is delicious hot but is equally good served cold, without the cheese topping, as an unusual salad.

1 Heat the oil in a large pan over moderate heat and fry the barley for 3-4 minutes. Pour on enough boiling water to cover it by 5 cm (2 in). Cover and simmer for 50-60 minutes or until tender. Drain and set aside.

2 Preheat the oven to gas mark 5, 190°C (375°F).

3 Roughly chop half the tomatoes and mix them into the barley with the olives, mushrooms, dill weed, sour cream and half the cheese. Season well and turn into a lightly greased ovenproof dish.

4 Slice the remaining tomatoes and arrange them in a layer on top. Sprinkle with the remaining cheese. Bake for 10-15 minutes or until the cheese has melted and begins to brown.

Ingredients
5 ml (1 tsp) oil
225 g (8 oz) pot barley
boiling water
550 g (1¼ lb) tomatoes, skinned
50 g (2 oz) black olives, stoned and
   finely chopped
225 g (8 oz) mushrooms, diced
2 tsp dried dill weed
150 ml (5 fl oz) sour cream
100 g (4 oz) Cheddar, grated
salt and pepper

Serves 4-6

★
Photograph
page 106

Polenta with spicy sauce

A traditional North Italian dish, perfect polenta should be light and soft on the inside with a crisp outer shell. A sauce that could be used instead of the spicy one given here is the green split pea sauce on page 152. Polenta goes well with steamed green vegetables (French beans or broccoli) or with sautéed aubergines, courgettes and peppers.

1 Bring the water to the boil. Sprinkle on the cornmeal gradually, stirring well to prevent any lumps forming. Add the salt and butter and continue cooking over low heat, covered, for 20 minutes. Stir the polenta frequently as it cooks to ensure that it does not catch or become lumpy. When cooked it should be thick and of a creamy consistency.

2 Pour into a wide, lightly greased dish to cool and set. A dish about 33 x 23 cm (13 x 9 in) is ideal. The polenta should be about 1 cm (½ in) thick.

3 For the sauce, gently fry the onion and garlic in the oil for 3-4 minutes or until just limp. Add the chili and red peppers and cook for another 3-4 minutes. Stir in the tomatoes and tomato purée, cover and simmer for 15-20 minutes or until you have a rich, thick sauce. Season well.

4 When the polenta is quite cold, cut it into small squares. Dip each one first into beaten egg and then into cornmeal. Deep fry, a few at a time, until brown. Serve hot, covered with the sauce.

Ingredients
1.1 litre (2 pints) water
225 g (8 oz) yellow cornmeal
1 tsp salt
50 g (2 oz) butter
Sauce
1 large onion, finely chopped
2 cloves garlic, crushed
30 ml (2 tbsp) olive oil
¼-½ tsp chili powder *or* 1 dried chili, finely chopped
2 red peppers, deseeded and diced
450 g (1 lb) tomatoes, skinned and chopped
15 ml (1 tbsp) tomato purée
salt and pepper
Coating
1 egg, beaten
extra cornmeal

oil for deep-frying

Serves 4

★

Savoury millet

If you have never cooked millet before, this simple method makes an excellent introduction. It is particularly popular with children.

1 Heat the oil in a large, heavy-based pan and lightly fry the onion, pepper and garlic for 3-4 minutes. Add the millet and cook for a further 2-3 minutes until it just begins to brown.

2 Heat the milk and water together until hot but not boiling. Pour over the millet and bring to the boil. Stir once, cover and simmer for 20 minutes or until the millet is cooked.

3 Quickly stir in the grated cheese and chopped parsley, reserving a little of each for the garnish. Season well and serve immediately, sprinkled with the remaining cheese and parsley.

Ingredients
30 ml (2 tbsp) sunflower oil
1 onion, finely chopped
1 red pepper, deseeded and diced
2 cloves garlic, crushed
225 g (8 oz) millet grains
700 ml (1¼ pints) milk and water mixed—roughly half and half
100 g (4 oz) Cheddar, grated
4 tbsp finely chopped parsley
salt and pepper

Serves 4-6

★
Photograph
page 109

Clockwise from top: **Fricassée Argenteuil** (*see p. 104*); **Barley and tomatoes in sour cream** (*see p. 105*); **Polenta with spicy sauce**; **Couscous** (*see p. 105*)

107

★

Photograph
*pages
188-189*

Ingredients
2 medium aubergines, thickly sliced
olive oil for frying
30 ml (2 tbsp) tahini
30 ml (2 tbsp) water
juice of ½ lemon
1 clove garlic, crushed
5 ml (1 tsp) shoyu
Millet pilaf
1 small onion, finely chopped
15 ml (1 tbsp) olive oil
1 large clove garlic, crushed
1 tsp ground coriander
175 g (6 oz) millet grains
100 g (4 oz) dried apricots, washed
4 cloves
225 ml (8 fl oz) white wine *or* cider
450 ml (16 fl oz) boiling water
salt and pepper

Serves 4

Byzantine millet pilaf

The combination of apricots and grains, topped with aubergines baked in a sesame sauce, is influenced by Middle Eastern cookery.

1 Preheat the oven to gas mark 4, 180°C (350°F).

2 Lightly sauté the aubergine slices in the olive oil until just browned and softened. Arrange them in layers in a shallow ovenproof dish.

3 Mix the tahini with the water in a bowl. Add the lemon juice, garlic and shoyu and blend thoroughly. Pour this over the aubergine slices and bake, uncovered, for 20 minutes. Keep warm.

4 Meanwhile, gently fry the onion in 15 ml (1 tbsp) olive oil for 3-4 minutes until soft. Add the garlic, coriander and millet and fry for another 2-3 minutes.

5 Cut the apricots into thin slivers. Add them to the frying pan together with the cloves, white wine or cider and boiling water. Bring back to the boil and simmer for 20 minutes or until the millet is cooked. Season well and serve hot with the aubergines.

★

Ingredients
5 ml (1 tsp) oil
75 g (3 oz) millet grains
425 ml (¾ pint) boiling water
½ packet silken tofu—approx.
    150 g (5 oz)
30 ml (2 tbsp) shoyu
50 g (2 oz) almonds, finely chopped
50 g (2 oz) wheatgerm
salt and pepper
1 tbsp finely chopped parsley
    (optional)
Coating
100 g (4 oz) millet flakes

oil for shallow frying

Makes 8 patties

Millet and tofu patties

Almonds and wheatgerm give texture and flavour to these delicate croquettes. They are best if prepared the previous day and refrigerated overnight, as this makes them easier to handle. You could use regular tofu if you would like a firmer texture.

1 Heat the oil in a large, heavy-based pan and gently fry the millet until it turns light brown. Pour on the boiling water, cover and simmer for 20 minutes or until the millet is soft. Leave until quite cool. Drain if necessary.

2 Blend the millet, tofu and shoyu to a thick paste in a liquidizer. Turn into a bowl and beat in the almonds and wheatgerm. Season well and add the parsley. Chill thoroughly, preferably overnight in the refrigerator.

3 Divide into 8 pieces and shape these into flat cakes. The texture is quite soft so they need careful handling.

4 Dip each one into millet flakes and shallow fry for 2-3 minutes on either side until golden brown. Serve immediately, accompanied by a sauce or dip such as the horseradish and mustard on page 152 or the lime relish on page 155.

From top: **Kasha ring** (*see p. 110*); **Millet and tofu patties; Savoury millet**
(*see p. 107*); In saucepans: **tomato sauce** (*see p. 72*); **mustard sauce for kasha ring**

★

Photograph
page 109

Ingredients
15 ml (1 tbsp) sunflower oil
225 g (8 oz) leeks, diced
225 g (8 oz) celeriac, diced
225 g (8 oz) Jerusalem artichokes,
    well scrubbed and diced
225 g (8 oz) mushrooms, diced
1 clove garlic, crushed
5 ml (1 tsp) oil
150 g (5 oz) buckwheat groats
570 ml (1 pint) boiling water
1 tsp caraway seeds
1 tsp paprika
45 ml (3 tbsp) red wine
salt and pepper
Sauce
1 packet silken tofu—approx.
    300 g (11 oz)
1 clove garlic, crushed
2 tsp English *or* Dijon mustard
½ tsp turmeric
1 tbsp capers

Serves 4-6

Kasha ring

Kasha *in Russian means any cooked cereal, but buckwheat is the most usual. Here, it is mixed with vegetables and served with a spicy mustard sauce.*

1 Heat the sunflower oil in a heavy-based pan and cook the vegetables and garlic over gentle heat, covered, for 10-15 minutes.

2 Meanwhile, in another pan, heat 5 ml (1 tsp) oil and fry the buckwheat over medium heat for about 3-4 minutes or until it begins to brown. Pour over the boiling water. Bring back to the boil, cover and simmer for 20 minutes or until the buckwheat is just tender. Drain.

3 Preheat the oven to gas mark 4, 180°C (350°F).

4 Mix together the cooked buckwheat and vegetables. Stir in the caraway, paprika and red wine. Season well and press the mixture into a lightly greased ring mould of about 1.5 litres (2½-3 pints) capacity. Cover loosely with foil and bake for 40 minutes.

5 Meanwhile, prepare the sauce by blending the tofu, garlic, mustard and turmeric until completely smooth. Add the capers and blend for another 15 seconds.

6 Heat the sauce very gently, preferably in a double boiler. It must not boil or it will curdle, and should be warm rather than hot. Turn out the kasha ring on a warmed serving dish and serve with the sauce.

PASTA, PIZZA & PANCAKES

These are all basic ways of cooking flour dough or batter, except for potato pancakes, which use finely grated potato. Wheat flour is the most common, although buckwheat has a long tradition in recipes for pancakes from Brittany to Russia, as well as in a certain type of pasta in northern Italy. Cornmeal is of course the staple flour used for Mexican *tortillas*.

Some kind of sauce or filling is almost always used. It may be as simple as the oil and garlic sauce for spaghetti, or even just melted butter, or it may be as robust as the refried bean filling for the *tortillas*. A sauce that will top a pizza will also accompany pasta; fillings for cannelloni or lasagne go well in pancakes, too, and vice versa. You will find recipes here for more unusual sauces as well as for the indispensable and ever versatile tomato sauce.

PASTA

Bought pasta, fresh or dried, is a great standby. It can be made from refined or wholewheat flour, with or without eggs, plain or coloured green with spinach. But if you prefer it home made, there are machines to help you turn it out in various shapes and sizes. Even without a machine, it is not difficult to make ravioli, lasagne, cannelloni and tagliatelle at home.

Home-made ravioli are a particularly appealing way to start a meal. They can be made quite small, only 2.5 cm (1 in) square, as shown in the photographs, or larger. They are also shown made in semicircles, but they can be triangular or twisted into more complicated shapes. Once made and filled, they should be left to dry out for about 30 minutes before they are cooked.

Continued

Pasta continued

Wholewheat pasta has a denser texture than refined pasta. I use a recipe enriched with eggs in preference to a plain water/flour mixture, as I feel this gives the best flavour.

The sauces in this chapter can in theory be used for any kind of pasta you like. However, as a general guide, thick sauces of the tomato variety go best with spaghetti or tubular pasta such as macaroni, while the smoother, more buttery sauces go better with flat ribbon noodles like tagliatelle.

★

Ingredients
350 g (12 oz) wholewheat flour
large pinch salt
4 eggs
15 ml (1 tbsp) olive oil

a little beaten egg

**Makes 500 g (1 lb 2 oz)
(Serves 4 as a main course
or 6 as a starter)**

Wholewheat pasta

Stir the flour and salt together in a large bowl and make a well in the centre. Break in the eggs and add the olive oil. Make the dough as shown below. All pasta should be rolled out thinly, but especially wholewheat pasta as it is so substantial. To make green pasta, substitute about 100 g (4 oz) chopped cooked spinach for one of the eggs.

MAKING PASTA DOUGH

1 *Mix the eggs and oil together with a fork, gradually drawing in all the flour from the edges.*

2 *Knead the dough well for a good 5 minutes until it loses all its stickiness and becomes shiny.*

3 *Cover the dough and leave it to rest for half an hour, then roll it out as thinly as you possibly can.*

Cooking pasta
Pasta must always be freshly cooked. Bring a large pan of water to the boil and put in plenty of salt. If the pan is big enough, there is no need to add a little oil as some cooks do to prevent the pasta from sticking together. It should be cooked "al dente"—until just tender but offering a very slight resistance to the bite. The only way to be sure of this is to test a piece by biting. Wholewheat tagliatelle will take from 8-10 minutes to cook, the same as wholewheat spaghetti. They are much more filling than pasta made with refined flour. As soon as the pasta is cooked, drain and serve immediately.

Cooking directions and times for stuffed pasta (lasagne, ravioli, cannelloni) are given in the appropriate recipes. These can all be cooked in advance, frozen and reheated. To reheat, heat the oven to gas mark 4, 180°C (350°F). Cover the dish tightly with foil or a lid and bake for one hour.

MAKING SQUARE RAVIOLI

1 *Dot teaspoonsful of filling on half the dough at regular intervals. It may help to mark out a grid first in squares of 2.5-5 cm (1-2 in).*

2 *Brush the edges and in between the rows of filling with a little beaten egg, and carefully cover with the other half of the dough.*

3 *Press firmly along the edges and between the rows to seal, and use a pastry wheel to cut out the individual ravioli.*

Fennel and tomato filling

1 Blanch the fennel in boiling water for 5 minutes and drain.

2 Heat the olive oil and stew the fennel with the garlic for 10 minutes until quite soft.

3 Add the tomatoes and basil and stew for a further 10 minutes until the mixture is soft enough to mash. Season well and let it cool before using.

4 To cook the ravioli, bring a large pan of salted water to the boil. Drop in the ravioli and cook, uncovered, for 12-15 minutes. Drain and serve immediately, sprinkled generously with grated Parmesan.

Ingredients
225 g (8 oz) fennel, finely chopped
30 ml (2 tbsp) olive oil
1 clove garlic, crushed
225 g (8 oz) tomatoes, skinned and chopped
2 tsp chopped basil
salt and pepper
For serving
grated Parmesan

Serves 4-6

★
Photograph
page 114

Oil, garlic and chili sauce

This is one of the quickest of all pasta sauces. It is made while the pasta is cooking.

1 Using a large, heavy-based pan, heat the oil and sauté the garlic and chili over moderate heat for 2-3 minutes. The garlic should turn golden but must on no account burn.

2 As soon as the pasta is cooked, drain it, turn it into the pan and mix quickly to coat it with the oil. Mix in the parsley and season with salt (and pepper if you think it needs it). Serve immediately.

Ingredients
30 ml (2 tbsp) olive oil
2-3 cloves garlic, crushed
1 dried chili, very finely diced
2-3 tbsp finely chopped parsley
salt and pepper

Serves 4-6

Photograph
*pages
190-191*

Pesto

1 Grind the pine kernels in a blender. Add the basil and garlic and blend again briefly. Add the grated cheese gradually, blending thoroughly.

2 Pour in the olive oil a little at a time, still blending. Season well. Serve with freshly cooked pasta.

Ingredients
75 g (3 oz) pine kernels
6-9 tbsp chopped fresh basil
6 cloves garlic, crushed
100 g (4 oz) Parmesan, grated
150 ml (¼ pint) olive oil
salt and pepper

Serves 4-6

Walnut and mushroom sauce

1 Heat 15 ml (1 tbsp) of the oil and gently fry the onion, garlic and spices for 3-4 minutes until the onion begins to soften.

2 Add the mushrooms, cover and cook over gentle heat for 10 minutes, stirring occasionally. Add the tomatoes and tomato purée, season and cook for another 10 minutes.

3 In a separate pan, heat the remaining oil and fry the chopped walnuts gently for 4-5 minutes until lightly browned. Stir half the walnuts into the sauce.

4 To serve, mix into freshly cooked pasta, sprinkle with the remaining walnuts and the parsley and serve immediately.

Ingredients
20 ml (4 tsp) olive oil
1 large onion, diced
1 clove garlic, crushed
1 tsp cinnamon
1 tsp ground allspice
1 tsp finely grated root ginger
225 g (8 oz) mushrooms, diced
450 g (1 lb) tomatoes, skinned and chopped
15 ml (1 tbsp) tomato purée
salt and pepper
100 g (4 oz) shelled walnuts, roughly chopped
1 tbsp finely chopped parsley

Serves 4-6

★

Butter and cream sauce with peas

1 Bring a pan of water to the boil. Put in the peas, cover and cook steadily until the peas are tender. Drain.

2 Cream the butter by beating it vigorously in a large mixing bowl until light and fluffy. Gradually beat in the cream then the grated cheese. Mix the peas into the sauce. Set over very low heat to keep warm.

3 Mix into freshly cooked pasta, season and serve at once.

Ingredients
175 g (6 oz) peas
100 g (4 oz) butter
60 ml (4 tbsp) single cream
50 g (2 oz) Parmesan, grated
salt and pepper
For serving
extra grated Parmesan

Serves 4-6

Photograph
page 116

Celery and almond sauce

1 Heat the olive oil and fry the onions and celery with the garlic over gentle heat for 2-3 minutes. Cover and continue cooking for 10-15 minutes until the vegetables are really tender. Add the stock, cover and cook for another 5-10 minutes until the sauce is creamy. Season to taste.

2 In a separate pan, heat 5 ml (1 tsp) oil and fry the almonds for 4-5 minutes until lightly browned. Serve the sauce over freshly cooked pasta, sprinkled with the almonds.

Ingredients
60 ml (4 tbsp) olive oil
225 g (8 oz) onions, diced
225 g (8 oz) celery, finely chopped
2 cloves garlic, crushed
150 ml (¼ pint) light vegetable stock (see p. 151)
salt and pepper
5 ml (1 tsp) oil
100 g (4 oz) slivered almonds (see p. 209)

Serves 4-6

Photograph
page 116

Clockwise from top: **Ravioli with fennel and tomato filling** (*see p. 113*); **Pasta with walnut and mushroom sauce; Spaghetti with pesto**

MAKING TAGLIATELLE

1 *Gently fold the sheet of dough over on itself like a Swiss roll.*

2 *Cut this carefully into thin strips of about 1 cm (½ in). Try not to press too hard.*

3 *Unfold each strip and spread it out to dry for half an hour before it is cooked.*

MAKING LASAGNE AND CANNELLONI

1 *Cut the dough into oblongs about 12.5 x 10 cm (5 x 4 in).*

2 *For cannelloni, put 1-2 tbsp of the filling on each oblong and brush the edge with beaten egg.*

3 *Roll up the oblongs from the long side and press to seal.*

Lasagne with leeks and lentils

If you make your own lasagne, it is easy to make them into strips that will comfortably fit your baking dish. Do not make them too big or they will be clumsy to boil and drain. If you are using bought dried lasagne, 225 g (8 oz) will be enough.

1 Put the lentils in a pan with plenty of water to cover. Bring to the boil and simmer, covered, for 25 minutes. Drain, reserving the stock.

2 Heat the oil and gently fry the leeks, carrot, mushrooms and garlic for 5-6 minutes or until fairly soft.

3 Add the cooked lentils, tomatoes, herbs and shoyu, cover and cook for 15-20 minutes, adding a little lentil stock if the mixture is too dry. Season to taste.

4 Preheat the oven to gas mark 4, 180°C (350°F).
Continued

Ingredients

100 g (4 oz) brown lentils, washed
15 ml (1 tbsp) olive oil
450 g (1 lb) leeks, finely diced
1 medium carrot, diced
225 g (8 oz) mushrooms, diced
2 cloves garlic, crushed
450 g (1 lb) tomatoes, skinned and chopped
1 tsp dried oregano
1 tsp dried marjoram
15 ml (1 tbsp) shoyu
salt and pepper
350-450 g (12 oz-1 lb) fresh lasagne
300 ml (½ pint) béchamel sauce (see p. 152)
50 g (2 oz) Parmesan, grated

Serves 4

★

Clockwise from top: **Tagliatelle with butter and cream** (*see p. 115*); **Tagliatelle with celery and almond sauce** (*see p. 115*); **Lasagne with leeks and lentils**

117

Lasagne with leek and lentil sauce continued

5 Meanwhile, cook the lasagne by boiling them in a large pan of salted water for 8-10 minutes or until just tender. As soon as they are cooked, drain them, run cold water over them and spread them out on a damp cloth. This will help prevent them sticking.

6 Put a layer of lasagne in a lightly greased baking dish. Cover with a layer of lentil mixture and one of béchamel sauce. Continue in this order until you have used all your ingredients, ending with a layer of sauce. Sprinkle over the grated Parmesan and bake for 30 minutes.

★

Ingredients
350 g (12 oz) spinach
1 large onion, diced
1 clove garlic, crushed
15 ml (1 tbsp) oil
1 green pepper, deseeded and diced
100 g (4 oz) ground almonds
300 ml (½ pint) water
1 tsp dried thyme
grated nutmeg
salt and pepper
450-550 g (1-1¼ lb) cannelloni
tomato sauce (see p. 72)
50 g (2 oz) Parmesan, grated
For serving
extra grated Parmesan

Serves 4-6

Spinach and almond cannelloni

1 Blanch the spinach in boiling water for 1 minute. Drain thoroughly and chop finely.

2 Gently fry the onion and garlic in the oil for 3-4 minutes until soft. Add the green pepper and cook for 3-4 minutes more.

3 Preheat the oven to gas mark 6, 200°C (400°F).

4 Stir in the chopped spinach and cook over moderate heat for another 2 minutes. Add the almonds, water and thyme and bring to the boil, stirring. Season with the nutmeg, salt and pepper.

5 Fill the cannelloni with this stuffing as on page 117. Arrange them in a lightly greased dish and cover with tomato sauce. Sprinkle with the grated Parmesan and bake for 20-25 minutes. Serve with extra Parmesan.

Ingredients
450-550 g (1-1¼ lb) short-cut macaroni
100 g (4 oz) French beans, sliced
300 ml (½ pint) yogurt
225 g (8 oz) ricotta or cottage cheese
1 bunch spring onions, chopped
1 red pepper, deseeded and diced
½ tsp caraway seeds
10 ml (2 tsp) shoyu
salt and pepper
50 g (2 oz) Parmesan, grated

For serving
extra grated Parmesan

Serves 4-6

Macaroni with French beans

1 Preheat the oven to gas mark 4, 180°C (350°F) and bring a large pan of water to the boil.

2 Salt the water and cook the macaroni at a rolling boil until just resistant to the bite—about 8-10 minutes. Drain.

3 Blanch the French beans for 1-2 minutes in boiling salted water and drain.

4 Mix together the yogurt and ricotta or cottage cheese. Add the macaroni, the French beans, spring onions and red pepper. Mix well, add the caraway and shoyu and season to taste.

5 Turn into a lightly oiled ovenproof dish and sprinkle with the grated Parmesan. Bake for 25-30 minutes. Serve hot.

Clockwise from top: **Spinach and almond cannelloni; Macaroni with French beans; Macaroni with chick peas** (*see p. 120*); **Pizza** (*see p. 120*)

Photograph
page 119

Soaking
overnight

Ingredients
225 g (8 oz) chick peas, soaked
    overnight
450 g (1 lb) short-cut macaroni
2 cloves garlic, crushed
15 ml (1 tbsp) olive oil
1 tbsp finely chopped basil
For serving
3 tbsp freshly grated Parmesan

Serves 4-6

Macaroni with chick peas

The combination of chick peas with pasta has been known since the time of Horace. Sometimes called "thunder and lightning", this is very simple to make, and the peas and pasta complement each other nutritionally.

1 Drain the chick peas. Put them in a large pan with plenty of fresh water, bring to the boil and boil hard for 10 minutes. Reduce the heat, skim off any scum and simmer, covered, until soft—about 50-60 minutes, depending on the age of the peas.

2 Meanwhile, cook the macaroni in a large pan of boiling salted water until just resistant to the bite—about 8-10 minutes. Drain.

3 Using a large, heavy-based pan, sauté the garlic gently in the oil for 3-4 minutes without letting it brown.

4 Drain the chick peas and add them, with the macaroni, to the pan with the garlic. Mix in the basil and stir and turn over low heat for a minute or two to ensure that all the flavours are absorbed and the mixture heated through. Season to taste and serve hot, sprinkled with the grated Parmesan.

PIZZA

Pizzas need little introduction. They can be a substantial part of a meal or delicious party nibbles. Vary the classic tomato topping by using different vegetables and herbs, and decorate with anything from cheese and artichoke hearts to olives, chopped herbs, capers and green peppercorns.

★

Photograph
page 119

Ingredients
Pizza base
10 g (½ oz) fresh yeast
60 ml (4 tbsp) tepid milk
225 g (8 oz) wholewheat flour
pinch of salt
1 large egg, lightly beaten
30-45 ml (2-3 tbsp) olive oil

Makes one 25 cm (10 in) pizza

Tomato and onion topping
1 large onion, diced
2 cloves garlic, crushed
30 ml (2 tbsp) olive oil
Continued

Pizza with tomato and onion

I use a rich dough, slightly more cake-like than the standard bread dough, which I think makes an excellent pizza base. If you prefer, use a plain wholewheat dough (see page 174).

1 Preheat the oven to gas mark 2, 160°C (300°F).

2 Mix the yeast with the tepid milk until creamy.

3 Warm the flour and salt in a large bowl for 5 minutes in the oven. This is not absolutely essential but enables the yeast to work more quickly.

4 Mix the flour, yeast mixture, egg and olive oil together and work into a ball, kneading well. This takes about 5 minutes. The dough should be fairly soft. If it is too sticky, add a little extra flour.

5 Put the dough into a clean bowl to rise. Cover with a damp cloth and leave for 1-1½ hours, until roughly doubled in size and resilient to the touch. Continue as below.

4 sticks celery, diced
550 g (1¼ lb) tomatoes, skinned
  and chopped
30 ml (2 tbsp) tomato purée
2 tsp dried oregano
2 tsp chopped fresh basil
salt and pepper
75 g (3 oz) mozzarella, sliced
black olives

ROLLING OUT PIZZA DOUGH

1 *Punch the dough down with your fist to knock the gas out of it. Knead again for a few minutes until quite smooth.*

2 *Roll the dough out into a 25 cm (10 in) circle, or shape into a rectangle 20 x 25 cm (8 x 10 in).*

3 *Set the dough on a lightly oiled baking tray or sheet. Prick it all over and cover with the topping.*

6 While the dough is rising, make the topping. Gently fry the onion and garlic in the oil for 3-4 minutes until soft.

7 Put in the celery and cook for 5 minutes. Add the tomatoes, tomato purée and herbs, cover and cook for 20-25 minutes. Season to taste.

8 Spread this over the pizza base as shown above. Leave for 10-15 minutes to rest and preheat the oven to gas mark 6, 200°C (400°F).

9 Arrange the mozzarella slices and black olives over the pizza and bake for 25-30 minutes.

Mushroom topping for pizza

1 Gently fry the onions and garlic for 3-4 minutes in the oil until soft.

2 Put in the mushrooms, tomato purée and marjoram and cook, covered, for 20-25 minutes. You should have a thick sauce. If it is too liquid, take the lid off and boil hard for a few minutes until it has reduced to the proper consistency. Season to taste.

Ingredients
350 g (12 oz) onions, sliced
1 clove garlic, crushed
30 ml (2 tbsp) olive oil
450 g (1 lb) button mushrooms,
  sliced
30-45 ml (2-3 tbsp) tomato purée
1 tsp dried marjoram
salt and pepper

★
Photograph
*pages
168-169*

PANCAKES

There is nothing difficult about cooking pancakes. The main essential is a good frying pan. Strictly speaking, if there is oil in the batter the pan does not need greasing, but I find it helps to use just a little oil.

Cooked pancakes, apart from blinis, keep very well. Wrapped carefully in greaseproof paper or polythene film, they will keep up to 3 days in the refrigerator or 2 months in the freezer. Single pancakes will thaw within an hour; a stack of pancakes should be left at room temperature for several hours. Filled pancakes can also be frozen. In this case, let the filling cool before use, as otherwise the pancake may become too soggy.

To reheat, put in a lightly oiled ovenproof dish, brush with melted butter or oil, cover with foil or a lid and heat at gas mark 4, 180°C (350°F) for 10-15 minutes if unfilled, 20 minutes if filled.

Buckwheat flour can be used instead of up to half the wholewheat. It produces savoury pancakes with a dark, speckled appearance, which are especially good with strong flavours and sour cream. They are substantial, so make them as thin and lacy as you can.

★

Photograph
page 125

Ingredients
100 g (4 oz) wholewheat flour
pinch of salt
1 egg
300 ml (½ pint) milk
5 ml (1 tsp) oil

oil *or* butter for frying

Makes 8-10 pancakes

Wholewheat pancakes

This recipe can be used for sweet or savoury pancakes. Serve sweet pancakes with maple syrup, or just with a generous squeeze of lemon juice and brown sugar to taste.

1 Mix the flour and salt in a bowl. Beat together the egg, milk and oil. Pour this into the flour, stirring constantly and mixing in the flour until you have a smooth batter. (If you use a liquidizer, first blend the milk, egg, salt and oil for 15-30 seconds, then add the flour and blend for a further 30 seconds to a smooth batter.)

2 Let the batter stand for half an hour or so before making the pancakes. Blend or beat again just beforehand as some of the flour will almost certainly have settled at the bottom.

3 Heat a little oil or butter—about 5 ml (1 tsp)—in a frying pan until it smokes. Pour in 2 tablespoons of batter, quickly tipping the pan so the batter spreads out evenly into a circle.

4 Cook for 2-3 minutes. Toss or flip over with a slice and cook the other side for a further 2-3 minutes.

If you are going to eat the pancakes straightaway, stack them on top of one another on a lightly oiled plate and keep warm in a moderately hot oven or under a low grill. If you are going to keep them to use later, turn each one out on a cool surface as it is cooked. This ensures a good texture. If they are stacked before cooling, their own steam will make them soggy.

Pancake Fillings

All the fillings given here are savoury. They can all be made well in advance, and pancakes stuffed with them freeze well. Other ideas for fillings are some of the pasta sauces already given or small quantities of bean or pea casseroles.

To stuff pancakes, put a tablespoon or two of filling on each one, roll up and arrange in a lightly greased ovenproof dish. Brush with a little melted butter or extra oil, cover with foil or a lid and heat for 15-20 minutes in a moderate oven.

Red cabbage and raisin filling

Crisp eating apples are best for this. This filling is also good with the potato pancakes on page 127.

1 Fry the onion gently in the oil until very soft—about 10-15 minutes.

2 Add the cabbage, apple, raisins and spices and cook, covered, for another 5 minutes over moderate heat.

3 Pour on the red wine and braise over low heat for 15 minutes. Stir occasionally, adding a little water if necessary. Season well.

Ingredients
1 medium onion, finely chopped
15 ml (1 tbsp) sunflower oil
350 g (12 oz) red cabbage, finely shredded
175 g (6 oz) grated apple
50 g (2 oz) raisins
1 tsp paprika
1 tsp cinnamon
45 ml (3 tbsp) red wine
salt and pepper

Enough for 8-10 pancakes

★
Photograph
page 125

Beetroot and chive filling

1 Scrub the beetroot and top and tail it. Bring a pan of water to the boil and cook the beetroot, covered, until tender. This takes 20-30 minutes depending on the size of the beetroot. Drain, peel and dice finely.

2 Gently fry the onion for 3-4 minutes in the oil until soft. Sprinkle over the flour and cook, stirring, for 2-3 minutes.

3 Off the heat, mix in the cooked beetroot and the herbs. Cool slightly, then stir in the yogurt or sour cream and season.

Ingredients
450 g (1 lb) raw beetroot
1 medium onion, finely chopped
15 ml (1 tbsp) olive oil
2 tsp wholewheat flour
1 tbsp snipped chives
3 tbsp finely chopped parsley
200 ml (7 fl oz) yogurt *or* sour cream
salt and pepper

Enough for 8-10 pancakes

Photograph
page 125

★

Ingredients
450 g (1 lb) broccoli florets
1 small onion, finely chopped
15 ml (1 tbsp) sunflower oil
1 clove garlic, crushed
1 tsp ground cumin
25 g (1 oz) pine kernels
150 ml (5 fl oz) béchamel sauce
 (see p. 152)
salt and pepper

Enough for 8-10 pancakes

Broccoli and pine kernel filling

This also makes a good accompaniment to the mushroom and aduki croquettes on page 96.

1 Lightly steam the broccoli for 5-6 minutes.

2 Gently fry the onion in the oil for 2-3 minutes. Add the garlic, cumin and pine kernels and continue cooking over moderate heat for 4-5 minutes so that the aroma of the spices is brought out and the pine kernels are lightly toasted.

3 Add the steamed broccoli and cook for another minute or two. Remove the pan from the heat and blend in the white sauce with a wooden spoon. Season to taste.

★

Photograph
*pages
186-187*

Ingredients
8 pancakes (see p. 122)
Fennel filling
450 g (1 lb) fennel, finely sliced
50 g (2 oz) butter
50 g (2 oz) Parmesan, freshly grated
salt and pepper
Spinach filling
450 g (1 lb) fresh spinach, washed
½ tsp grated nutmeg
black pepper
Tomato filling
1 onion, chopped
1 clove garlic, crushed
30 ml (2 tbsp) olive oil
450 g (1 lb) tomatoes, skinned
 and chopped
3 sticks celery, diced
½ tsp aniseeds
15 ml (1 tbsp) tomato purée
salt and pepper
For serving
extra grated Parmesan

Serves 4

Galette

This makes a spectacular dish for a dinner party.

1 Blanch the fennel for 10 minutes in boiling water. Drain well.

2 Melt the butter in a small pan and stew the fennel for 10 minutes over gentle heat, covered. Purée it with the grated Parmesan and add salt and pepper to taste.

3 Preheat the oven to gas mark 4, 180°C (350°F).

4 Cook the spinach in its own juices for 7-8 minutes in a covered pan. Chop it very finely and season with nutmeg and black pepper.

5 Gently fry the onion and garlic for 3-4 minutes in the olive oil. Stir in the tomatoes, celery, aniseeds and tomato purée and cook uncovered, over moderate heat, for 10-15 minutes or until you have a thick sauce. Season well.

6 Assemble the galette in a lightly greased 18 cm (7 in) spring mould. Put in one pancake, then sandwich in the different fillings (reserving some of the tomato sauce) between the pancakes. End with a pancake.

7 Bake for 10-15 minutes. Turn out and serve with the remaining tomato sauce and extra grated Parmesan.

Clockwise from top: **Wholewheat pancakes** (*see p. 122*) with fillings: **beetroot and chive** (*see p. 123*); **broccoli and pine kernel**; **red cabbage and raisin** (*see p. 123*); **Potato pancakes** (*see p. 127*); **Blinis with sour cream** (*see p. 127*); **Tortillas** (*see p. 126*).

★
Photograph
page 125

Soaking
overnight

Ingredients
Bean Filling
350 g (12 oz) red kidney *or* pinto
  beans, soaked overnight
45 ml (3 tbsp) oil
1 large onion, chopped
3 cloves garlic, crushed
2 tsp ground cumin
¼ tsp ground coriander
1½ tsp salt
1 green pepper, deseeded and finely
  diced
pepper
Tortillas
325 ml (12 fl oz) water
40 g (1½ oz) butter
100 g (4 oz) cornmeal
175 g (6 oz) wholewheat flour
1 tsp salt

Makes 12 tortillas

Tortillas

These are classic Mexican pancakes made here from cornmeal mixed with wholewheat flour. Refried beans are beans which are first boiled, then fried with spices and vegetables to make a hearty and satisfying filling.

1 Drain the beans. Bring them to the boil in plenty of fresh water and boil fiercely for 10 minutes. Cover and simmer for 40-50 minutes until soft. Drain and mash.

2 Heat the oil in a frying pan and gently fry the onion, garlic and spices with about half the salt for 10 minutes over gentle heat.

3 Put in the green pepper, cover and cook for another 5-8 minutes. Mix with the mashed beans and season well with the rest of the salt and the pepper. Keep warm.

4 Make the tortillas as shown below. Divide the filling between them and serve hot.

MAKING TORTILLAS

1 *Bring the water to the boil and add half the butter. Stir in the cornmeal over low heat. Cover, cook for 5 minutes and stir in the remaining butter until smooth.*

2 *Leave this to cool. Mix the wholewheat flour and salt together in a bowl. Stir in the cooled cornmeal.*

3 *Knead this to a soft dough. You may need to add a little more water or flour if it is too dry or too sticky.*

4 *Divide into 12 and shape each piece into a ball. Roll each one out into a 15-18 cm (6-7 in) circle.*

5 *Cook in an ungreased frying pan for 2-3 minutes on each side over moderate heat until flecked with dark spots.*

6 *Spoon 2-3 tablespoons of filling into each tortilla.*

Potato pancakes

These are excellent with a sharp or sweet sauce or vegetable. Try the beetroot and chive filling on page 123 or the red cabbage and raisin filling on the same page.

1 Peel the potatoes and grate them finely. Squeeze out all excess moisture.

2 In a separate bowl, beat the eggs and blend in the miso. Mix in the potatoes and remaining ingredients and season according to taste.

3 Heat the butter and oil in a large frying pan. Put in heaped tablespoons of the mixture—you should be able to do 2 or 3 at a time. Fry for about 3-4 minutes on each side, pressing the pancakes down flat as they fry with a wooden spoon. Drain on kitchen paper and serve hot.

Ingredients
3 large potatoes
2 eggs
5 ml (1 tsp) miso
1 small onion, finely chopped
3-4 tbsp cornmeal
2 tsp paprika
salt and pepper
For frying
25 g (1 oz) butter
30 ml (2 tbsp) oil

Makes 8-10 pancakes

Photograph
page 125

Blinis

Russian yeast pancakes, traditionally served with sour cream, these are also good with yogurt or the olive pâté on page 42.

1 Crumble the yeast and sugar together, mix with the warm water and leave for 5 minutes until creamy and frothy. Beat in the egg yolk.

2 Sift the flours together with the salt. Beat the yeast mixture into the flour until quite smooth and the consistency of thick cream.

3 Leave in a warm place until at least double in bulk. This will take about 1 hour. Beat the mixture down, using a whisk or wooden spoon.

4 Whip the egg white to a soft peak. Fold 1 tablespoon into the batter and then fold in the rest of the egg white. Leave to rest for 20 minutes.

5 Heat a little butter in a large frying pan. Fry tablespoons of the batter over medium heat for 2-3 minutes on each side. You should be able to do 2 or 3 at a time: this batter will not spread out. Keep the first batch warm while you do the next. Serve hot.

Ingredients
5 g (¼ oz) fresh yeast
pinch of sugar
80 ml (3½ fl oz) warm water
1 egg, separated
50 g (2 oz) plain unbleached flour
50 g (2 oz) buckwheat flour
pinch of salt
butter for frying

Makes 6-8 blinis

Photograph
page 125

EGGS & CHEESE

At one time eggs and cheese were regarded as a mainstay of the vegetarian diet, and it is still often the case that if you order a vegetarian meal when eating out you end up with either an omelette or a cheese salad. It is true that they seem an obvious replacement for meat, being such a good source of protein, but now we are more aware of the health aspect of diet and realize that it is no good giving up the hidden fats in meat just to replace them with high-fat dairy products and eggs which, while important, should play a secondary part.

People who change to a meatless diet sometimes experience a craving for fats. The answer to this can be a little grated cheese. It goes a long way when sprinkled over a bean or grain dish and makes the food more satisfying without upsetting the balance of the diet. There are now an increasing number of cheeses on the market made with vegetable rennet, which is good news for those strict vegetarians whose choice has in the past been limited.

Ingredients
1 clove garlic
425 ml (¾ pint) dry white wine
15 ml (1 tbsp) lemon juice
450 g (1 lb) Emmental *or* Gruyère, grated
1-2 tbsp wholewheat flour (optional)
grated nutmeg
salt and pepper
30 ml (2 tbsp) Kirsch
For serving
1 large wholewheat loaf, cut into cubes

Serves 4

Fondue

A classic dish, ideal for easy entertaining. It is both rich and sustaining, so accompanying dishes should be light, such as green salads, with fruit or a sorbet to follow. To eat it, each guest spears a piece of bread with a fork and dips in.

1 Rub the inside of a flame-proof casserole or fondue pan with the garlic. Pour in the wine and lemon juice and bring slowly to boiling point.

2 Add the grated cheese and the flour, if used—this depends on whether you prefer a thicker consistency. Beat well until the cheese melts and the mixture is completely smooth. *Continued*

Top: **Fondue**; bottom: **Blue cheese and onion quiche** (*see p. 130*)

Fondue continued

3 Season with grated nutmeg, salt and pepper. Stir in the Kirsch and serve hot. If the fondue becomes too thick, add a little more hot wine.

Variations
Raw vegetables can be used instead of bread. The basic sauce can be flavoured with mustard, paprika or caraway seeds.

★

Photograph
page 129

Ingredients
short crust pastry made with 175 g
    (6 oz) wholewheat flour
    (see p. 92)
900 g (2 lb) onions, diced
45 ml (3 tbsp) olive oil
150 ml (¼ pint) sour cream
30-45 ml (2-3 tbsp) white wine
3 eggs, beaten
50 g (2 oz) blue cheese, grated
1 tsp caraway seeds
pinch of cayenne

Serves 4-6

Blue cheese and onion quiche

Egg and cheese combinations lend themselves perfectly to tart fillings. Stilton is particularly successful here, but Gorgonzola and Danish Blue also work well.

1 Preheat the oven to gas mark 6, 200°C (400°F).

2 Roll out the pastry to fill a 23 cm (9 in) flan ring. Prick the base well and bake for 5 minutes to set it.

3 Gently fry the onions for 5-10 minutes in the oil until quite translucent. Let them cool completely.

4 Mix together all the other ingredients. Stir in the onions, pile the filling into the flan case and bake for 35 minutes. Serve warm or cold.

Variations
Vegetables can be added to the cheese and egg mixture. Broccoli, leeks, spinach, courgettes, asparagus and tomatoes are all ideal. Lightly steam or sauté 450 g (1 lb) vegetables. Mix them with 300 ml (½ pint) milk and the eggs and cheese as above. Season well, pile into the flan case and cover with another 50 g (2 oz) grated cheese.
Cheddar, Gouda, Emmental and Gruyère are all suitable, on their own or in combination. Cottage cheese, ricotta, sour cream or yogurt can be substituted for some of the milk. Herbs and spices can be added to taste.

Photograph
*pages
180-181*

Ingredients
450 g (1 lb) greens—spinach, Swiss
    chard, spinach beet, spring
    cabbage or pak-choi
4 tbsp finely chopped parsley
6-8 spring onions, finely chopped
8 eggs
30 ml (2 tbsp) yogurt
30 ml (2 tbsp) water
salt and pepper
Continued

Frittata verde

A substantial version of an omelette, served flat and not rolled up. It makes a good snack, or it can be eaten with a baked potato and salad for a simple supper.

1 Lightly boil or steam the greens (for cooking times see page 217). Chop finely and add to the parsley and onions.

2 Beat together the eggs, yogurt and water. Stir the mixture into the vegetables.

3 Heat just enough oil to cover the bottom of a large omelette pan. Pour in the mixture, beating lightly with a fork until it begins to cook.

4 Cook gently for 5-10 minutes. The exact time depends on the size of your pan. The omelette should be well browned on the bottom and thoroughly heated through. This takes longer in a smaller pan where the mixture is thicker.

5 Sprinkle with the grated Parmesan, if liked, and brown the top for 2 minutes under a hot grill. Transfer to a serving dish with a palette knife. Serve warm or cold.

a little oil (or oil and butter)
    for frying
2 tbsp grated Parmesan (optional)

Serves 4

Baked eggs with lentils

A dish inspired by Spain which is ideal for supper or brunch.

1 Bring the lentils to the boil in a large pan of water and simmer them, covered, for 35-40 minutes until soft. Drain.

2 Heat the oil in a large, heavy-based pan and fry the onion, garlic and peppers gently for about 5 minutes, until soft.

3 Mix in the cooked lentils and the tomatoes, parsley, bay leaf and water. Season well. Cook over moderate heat, stirring, for 10-15 minutes or until most of the liquid has evaporated and the mixture is fairly thick.

4 Preheat the oven to gas mark 6, 200°C (400°F).

5 Spoon the mixture into a lightly greased ovenproof dish, removing the bay leaf. Make four slight hollows with the back of a spoon. Break in the eggs. Sprinkle with the sherry, cover and bake for 20 minutes or until the egg whites are firm. Serve at once, garnished with the parsley.

Ingredients
100 g (4 oz) green or brown lentils
30 ml (2 tbsp) oil, preferably olive
1 medium onion, finely chopped
2 cloves garlic, crushed
1 green pepper, deseeded and diced
1 red pepper, deseeded and diced
450 g (1 lb) tomatoes, skinned
    and chopped
2 tbsp finely chopped parsley
1 bay leaf
60 ml (4 tbsp) water
salt and pepper
4 eggs
30 ml (2 tbsp) pale dry sherry
Garnish
sprigs of fresh parsley

Serves 4

Photograph
page 133

Aubergine and cheese bake

1 Dust the aubergine slices with flour and fry them, a few at a time, in hot oil until just brown and soft. This will take about 2 minutes on each side. When adding more oil, make sure it is well heated before putting in the aubergines. Drain them on kitchen paper.

2 In the same pan, gently fry the onions for 3-4 minutes until translucent. Put in the tomatoes and cook for a further 10 minutes until the mixture has reduced to a thick pulp. Cool.
Continued

Ingredients
450 g (1 lb) aubergines, sliced
flour for dusting
oil for frying
350 g (12 oz) onions
350 g (12 oz) tomatoes, skinned
    and chopped
2 eggs
100 g (4 oz) ricotta
30 ml (2 tbsp) yogurt
1 tsp dried oregano
salt and pepper
25 g (1 oz) Parmesan, grated

Serves 4

★
Photograph
page 133

Aubergine and cheese bake continued

3 Preheat the oven to gas mark 4, 180°C (350°F).

4 Beat the eggs with the ricotta and yogurt. Add the tomato and onion mixture and season with oregano, salt and pepper.

5 Lightly grease a 23 cm (9 in) ovenproof dish. Put in a layer of aubergine slices, cover with some sauce and sprinkle with a little grated cheese. Continue in this order, ending with a generous sprinkling of cheese. Bake for 25-30 minutes.

Ingredients
300 ml (½ pint) milk
1 onion
1 bay leaf
350 g (12 oz) courgettes, sliced
40 g (1½ oz) butter
25 g (1 oz) wholewheat flour
3-4 eggs, separated
50-75 g (2-3 oz) Cheddar, grated
salt and pepper

Serves 4

Courgette soufflé

1 Heat the milk with the onion and bay leaf to just below boiling point. Remove from the heat and leave for 20 minutes.

2 Lightly steam the courgettes for 4-5 minutes.

3 Preheat the oven to gas mark 6, 200°C (400°F).

4 Heat the butter, stir in the flour and cook, stirring, over low heat for 2 minutes. Strain the milk into the pan and bring to boiling point, stirring. Simmer for 2-3 minutes.

5 Off the heat, beat in the egg yolks, one at a time. Mix the courgettes into the sauce. Add the cheese and season lightly.

6 Beat the egg whites until stiff but not dry. Stir 1 tablespoon into the sauce, then gently fold in the remaining egg whites.

7 Spoon into a lightly greased 1-1½ litre (2-2½ pint) soufflé dish and bake for 25 minutes. The centre should be firm. If it is still too soft, give it another 5 minutes. Serve immediately.

Variation
Avocado soufflé
Instead of the courgettes, use 1-2 avocados, diced, sprinkled with lime juice and mixed with 6 green olives, stoned and chopped, and 450 g (1 lb) tomatoes, skinned and chopped.

Photograph
pages
190-191

Ingredients
225 g (8 oz) broccoli florets
40 g (1½ oz) butter
25 g (1 oz) wholewheat flour
150 ml (¼ pint) milk
3 eggs, separated
salt and pepper
Filling
tomato sauce (see p. 72)
Garnish
2-3 tbsp freshly grated Parmesan
tomato slices (optional)

Broccoli roulade

1 Steam the broccoli lightly for 5-6 minutes. Chop it finely.

2 Melt the butter, stir in the flour and cook over low heat for 2 minutes. Add the milk and bring to boiling point, stirring well to avoid lumps. Simmer for 2-3 minutes.

3 Preheat the oven to gas mark 5, 190°C (375°F) and line a 33 × 23 cm (13 × 9 in) Swiss roll tin with greaseproof paper.
Continued

From top: **Courgette soufflé; Baked eggs with lentils** (*see p. 131*); **Aubergine and cheese bake** (*see p. 131*)

Broccoli roulade continued

4 Off the heat, beat the egg yolks into the sauce, one at a time. Season well and mix in the broccoli.

5 Whisk the egg whites until stiff but not dry and gently fold them into the broccoli mixture.

6 Spread this over the prepared Swiss roll tin and bake for 17-20 minutes.

7 Turn out on a clean tea towel covered with a fresh sheet of greaseproof paper. Peel off the old sheet. Spread the filling over the roulade and roll it up, using the tea towel. Don't worry if it cracks slightly. Sprinkle with the grated cheese and put back in the oven for 5 minutes before serving.

Variation

Substitute 100 g (4 oz) green or brown lentils for the broccoli. Simmer them in plenty of water for 35-40 minutes and drain. For a filling, use the salsify sauce on p. 153.

★

Photograph
pages
136-137

Ingredients
75 g (3 oz) Cheddar, grated
25 g (1 oz) Stilton, grated
225 g (8 oz) fresh breadcrumbs
1 tbsp finely chopped parsley
1 tsp finely chopped rosemary *or*
    thyme
2 eggs
1-2 tsp French mustard
salt and pepper

oil for deep-frying

Makes 12-16 croquettes

Cheese and herb croquettes

These are deep-fried for a crispy outer coating.

1 Mix the grated cheeses with 175 g (6 oz) breadcrumbs and the herbs. Add 1 egg and 1 egg yolk and the mustard. Mix well and season to taste.

2 Divide into 12 or 16 pieces and shape into small cylinders. Dip each one into the egg white and then roll it in the remaining breadcrumbs. Deep-fry for 5-7 minutes in hot oil. Drain on kitchen paper before serving.

Photograph
pages
44-45

Ingredients
150 ml (¼ pint) water
50 g (2 oz) butter
50 g (2 oz) wheatmeal *or*
    wholemeal flour
50 g (2 oz) Cheddar, grated
2 eggs
pinch of mustard powder
pepper

**Makes 12 medium or 18
    miniature puffs**

Cheese puffs

1 Preheat the oven to gas mark 7, 220°C (425°F) and bring the water and butter to the boil in a heavy-based pan.

2 Sieve the flour into a bowl. Tip the bran remaining in the sieve into the bowl. Off the heat, shoot all the flour into the boiling water and butter and beat very well for about 5 minutes or until the mixture is glossy. Mix in 1 egg at a time, beating thoroughly until well amalgamated, and stir in the cheese, mustard and pepper.

3 Pipe the mixture out into small balls on a lightly greased baking sheet and bake for 15-20 minutes. Allow to cool before filling. Do not fill the puffs more than an hour or two before eating or they will be soggy.

Cheese puff fillings
Avocado

1 Peel and stone the avocado.

2 Mash it with the lemon juice and mayonnaise.

3 Dice the hard-boiled egg and mix it in. Season to taste.

Artichoke hearts

1 Mash the artichoke hearts with the yogurt and dill weed.

2 Season to taste.

Photograph
pages
44-45

Ingredients
1 avocado
15 ml (1 tbsp) lemon juice
30 ml (2 tbsp) mayonnaise
  (see p. 149)
1 hard-boiled egg
salt and pepper

Ingredients
6 artichoke hearts
150 ml (¼ pint) yogurt
1 tsp dried dill weed
salt and pepper

Cheese shortbread

1 Preheat the oven to gas mark 6, 200°C (400°F).

2 Mix the flour with the semolina. Rub the butter in until the mixture is the consistency of fine breadcrumbs. Add the cheese and seasonings.

3 Press into a 20-23 cm (8-9 in) square tin and mark into the desired shapes. Bake for 15-20 minutes and allow to cool.

Ingredients
100 g (4 oz) wholewheat flour
50 g (2 oz) semolina
100 g (4 oz) butter
100 g (4 oz) Cheddar, grated
pinch of cayenne
pinch of mustard powder
salt

Makes nine 7.5 cm (3 in) square biscuits

★
Photograph
pages
44-45

Cheese water biscuits

1 Preheat the oven to gas mark 7, 220°C (425°F).

2 Mix together the flour, baking powder and salt. Rub in the fat until the mixture is the consistency of fine breadcrumbs.

3 Add just enough milk to make a soft dough. Roll out to a thickness of not more than 0.5 cm (¼ in).

4 Brush with a little extra milk and sprinkle on the grated cheese. Cut into whatever shapes you please. Bake on a baking sheet for 20 minutes and allow to cool before eating.

Ingredients
225 g (8 oz) wholewheat flour
1½ tsp baking powder
½ tsp salt
50 g (2 oz) solid vegetable fat
50 ml (2 fl oz) milk
25 g (1 oz) Cheddar, finely grated

Makes about 18-20 small biscuits

★
Photograph
pages
186-187

Cheese dip

For a party piece, use a whole Edam cheese. Slice the top third off. Scoop out the centre, leaving a 2.5 cm (1 in) shell. Make a dip with the scooped-out cheese, then spoon it back.

Grate the hard cheese very finely. Beat in the cream cheese and cream and finally the other ingredients—some or all of them according to taste. You may not need to add salt as the cheese will be quite salty already. Serve at room temperature.

Ingredients
175 g (6 oz) hard cheese—Edam, Cheddar, Swiss or a mixture
50 g (2 oz) cream cheese
30 ml (2 tbsp) single cream
1 tbsp wholegrain mustard
50 g (2 oz) chopped gherkins, spring onions or olives
cayenne

Photograph
pages
44-45

Picnics

Any food that tastes good cold and can be eaten with the fingers or from a container is ideal for picnics, snacks or packed lunches: quiches and tarts (the wholefood flamiche shown here is particularly nourishing); rissoles and croquettes based on nuts, eggs or cheese; and all kinds of salads, from a simple leaf one to the protein-rich salad shown here, which combines red kidney beans, chick peas, lima beans and French beans.

Pitta bread is perfect for sandwiches (if you prefer home-made bread, try the soda bread on page 178 or the rosemary and walnut scones on page 184). Besides the fillings given here, which combine salad vegetables and cheese, you could use tomato with mozzarella, coleslaws or other salads, particularly the more substantial ones, or the tortilla filling on page 126. Tiny cherry tomatoes, if you can find them, make a good accompaniment.

To finish with, fresh fruit is ideal, from apples to cherries, strawberries or little kumquats which can be eaten whole.

1 Pitta stuffed with cottage cheese and beansprouts in mayonnaise with chopped herbs 2 Red cabbage, carrot and alfalfa salad (*p. 147*) 3 Cheese and herb croquettes (*p. 134*) 4 Salad of raw spinach and young dandelion leaves in vinaigrette with chopped hard-boiled egg 5 Wholewheat rolls (*p. 175*) 6 Pitta stuffed with cubed feta cheese, cucumber, celery and olives 7 Flamiche (*p. 85*) 8 Cashew patties (*p. 40*) 9 Many bean salad (*p. 142*)

SALADS & DRESSINGS

Salads of fresh, raw vegetables are a rich source of vitamins and minerals and as such play an important part in any healthy diet. Ideally, they should form part of at least one meal a day and can even be the basis of the meal itself.

A growing number of greengrocers and specialist market gardeners are supplying a wider and wider range of vegetables and saladings, and it's worth searching these out, or growing your own fresh produce if you can. For extra nutrients add fresh or dried fruit, nuts or sprouts. For a substantial main dish try a salad with cooked dried beans or peas, pasta or grains. The range of dressings can be varied beyond mayonnaise and vinaigrette. Whatever kind you use, have it ready and toss the salad in it straightaway to preserve nutrients. Leaf salads should be prepared and dressed at the last possible moment.

Soaking
overnight

Ingredients
100 g (4 oz) wheat berries, soaked
   overnight and drained
100 g (4 oz) pot barley
2 bananas, sliced
4 dried figs, finely sliced
50 g (2 oz) pecans, coarsely chopped
1 fresh green chili, diced
peanut butter dressing (see p. 150)

Serves 4

Mixed grain on lettuce

Other grains—rice, buckwheat, rye—can be used in this salad, in any proportion you like. You could fry the barley first (see page 206) for a few minutes if you prefer.

1 Bring a large pan of water to the boil. Put in the wheat berries and the barley. Bring back to the boil and simmer, covered, for 50-60 minutes or until tender. Drain.

2 When cold, mix the grains with the fruit, nuts and chili.

3 Stir the dressing into the salad, and serve, preferably on a bed of crisp greens.

Clockwise from top left: **Couscous salad** (*see p. 140*); **Mixed grain salad with peanut butter dressing**; **Marinaded buckwheat salad** (*see p. 140*); **Barley salad** (*see p. 140*); **with vinaigrette** (*see p. 149*)

Photograph
page 139

Ingredients
175 g (6 oz) buckwheat groats
5 ml (1 tsp) oil
570 ml (1 pint) water
1 orange, peeled and thinly sliced
50 g (2 oz) daikon, grated
5 g (¼ oz) arame *or* hijiki, soaked
 in warm water for 10 minutes
50 g (2 oz) pumpkin seeds
100 g (4 oz) firm tofu, finely
 chopped

Marinade
60 ml (4 tbsp) sunflower oil
15 ml (1 tbsp) sherry
15 ml (1 tbsp) shoyu
2 cloves garlic, crushed
juice of ½ lemon
2 tsp finely grated root ginger
60 ml (4 tbsp) orange juice

Serves 4

Marinaded buckwheat

1 Fry the buckwheat in the oil for 2-3 minutes.

2 Bring the water to the boil. Pour it over the buckwheat, stir once, cover the pan and simmer for 20 minutes. All the water should be absorbed. If not, drain the buckwheat.

3 Mix together all the marinade ingredients and pour them over the warm buckwheat. Leave to cool.

4 When the buckwheat is cool, add the other ingredients. Chill the salad in the refrigerator for about half an hour before serving.

Photograph
page 139

Ingredients
100-150 g (4-5 oz) pot barley
50 g (2 oz) hazelnuts
1 small cauliflower, divided into
 small florets
½ cucumber, diced
1 tbsp blue poppy seeds
90 ml (6 tbsp) vinaigrette (see
 p. 149)
salt and pepper

Serves 4

Barley

The hazelnuts can be used fresh, but they taste even better if you toast them gently first. The barley could be fried, too, as in the first recipe.

1 Boil the barley in plenty of water for 50-60 minutes. Drain.

2 Toast the hazelnuts for 2-3 minutes under the grill or in a moderate oven and chop them coarsely.

3 Mix the barley and hazelnuts with the cauliflower, cucumber and poppy seeds. Stir in the vinaigrette and season to taste.

Photograph
page 139

Soaking
overnight

Ingredients
100 g (4 oz) chick peas, soaked
 overnight
225 g (8 oz) couscous
5 ml (1 tsp) miso
570 ml (1 pint) boiling water
30 ml (2 tbsp) olive *or* walnut oil
15 ml (1 tbsp) sesame oil
15 ml (1 tbsp) lemon juice
2 cloves garlic, crushed
4 tbsp chopped coriander leaves
12-15 spring onions, chopped
salt and pepper

Serves 4

Couscous

Couscous and chick peas combine to make a substantial main salad. Without the chick peas this makes a lighter side salad which goes well with any bean or vegetable dish.

1 Drain and rinse the chick peas. Put them in a large pan with plenty of fresh water, bring to the boil and boil hard for 10 minutes. Reduce the heat, skim off any scum and simmer, covered, until soft—about 50-60 minutes. Drain and set aside.
Continued

2 Put the couscous in a large, heavy-based pan. Mix together the miso and the boiling water and pour this over the couscous. Stir well, bring back to the boil and simmer, covered, for 5 minutes, stirring occasionally. Remove from the heat and leave to cool. All the water should have been absorbed. If not, drain off the excess.

3 When the couscous is cool, fluff it up with a fork. Mix in the chick peas, oils, lemon juice, garlic, chopped coriander and spring onions. Reserve a little chopped coriander for a garnish if you like. Season with salt and plenty of pepper.

Spiced rice

1 Gently fry the onion in the oil for 3-4 minutes until soft.

2 Put in the spices and rice and fry for another 2-3 minutes.

3 Pour over the boiling water, bring back to the boil and simmer until all the water is absorbed and the rice is tender— about 25-30 minutes.

4 Meanwhile, steam the green beans for 3-4 minutes until barely tender.

5 Mix all the dressing ingredients together and pour over the warm rice. Season well and leave to cool

6 When the rice is cool, mix with the remaining ingredients.

Ingredients
1 onion, finely chopped
15 ml (1 tbsp) sunflower oil
1 tsp turmeric
¼ tsp cayenne
150 g (5 oz) long-grain brown rice
400 ml (14 fl oz) boiling water
100 g (4 oz) green beans, chopped
100 g (4 oz) pineapple, diced
3 tbsp creamed coconut, grated
10-12 radishes, quartered
Dressing
30 ml (2 tbsp) sunflower oil
15 ml (1 tbsp) white wine vinegar
45 ml (3 tbsp) pineapple juice
½ tsp grated root ginger
salt and pepper

Serves 4

*Photograph
page 143*

Lentil and mint in yogurt

This salad quite definitely improves with keeping and is even better eaten the day after it is made.

1 Cook the lentils in plenty of boiling water until tender. This takes 35-40 minutes. Drain and leave to cool.

2 Heat a very little oil—just a few drops—and fry the fenugreek and cardamom seeds for 3-4 minutes or until they turn dark. Crush them well.

3 Mix together the crushed spices, yogurt, curd cheese and garlic. Stir this into the cooled lentils. Add the chopped onions and herbs and season well.

Ingredients
150 g (5 oz) green lentils
a little oil
1 tsp fenugreek seeds
6 cardamom seeds
150 ml (¼ pint) yogurt
100 g (4 oz) curd cheese
1 clove garlic, crushed
12 spring onions, chopped
1 tbsp finely chopped mint
1 tbsp finely chopped parsley
salt and pepper

Serves 4

*Photograph
page 143*

Paprika pasta

Ingredients
100 g (4 oz) pasta—shells *or* short-
  cut macaroni
50 g (2 oz) black olives, stoned and
  sliced
4 tomatoes, skinned and chopped
1 small fennel bulb, diced
Dressing
150 ml (¼ pint) yogurt
2 tomatoes. skinned and roughly
  chopped
juice of ½ lemon
1 tsp paprika
dash of shoyu
2 tsp chopped basil

Serves 4

Lettuce or chicory goes well with this salad, but red chicory (radicchio rosso) looks particularly good and echoes the Italian touches of pasta and basil.

1 Bring a large pan of water to the boil, salt it and cook the pasta until just tender to the bite—this may take from 7 to 15 minutes depending on the kind of pasta. Drain and cool.

2 Blend all the ingredients for the dressing together until smooth and stir into the cooled pasta.

3 Mix with the olives, tomatoes and fennel.

Many bean

Photograph
*pages
136-137*

Soaking
overnight

Ingredients
50 g (2 oz) red kidney beans, soaked
  overnight
50 g (2 oz) chick peas, soaked
  overnight
50 g (2 oz) lima *or* cannellini beans,
  soaked overnight
100 g (4 oz) French beans, cut into
  1 cm (½ in) lengths
Marinade
50 ml (2 fl oz) white wine vinegar
75 ml (3 fl oz) mixed olive and
  sunflower oil
15 ml (1 tbsp) lemon juice
1 tsp grated lemon rind
2 cloves garlic, crushed
15 ml (1 tbsp) white wine
1 dried red chili, very finely chopped
1 bunch spring onions, chopped

Serves 4

The kidney beans should be soaked and cooked separately unless you want the whole salad to be pink.

1 Drain the beans and peas. Cover with fresh water, bring to the boil and boil fiercely for 10 minutes. Reduce the heat and simmer until tender. The kidney beans will take 35-40 minutes, the chick peas and lima beans up to an hour, depending on how fresh they are. Drain.

2 Steam the French beans for 3-4 minutes. They should be still quite crunchy, only just beginning to be tender.

3 Mix together all the marinade ingredients.

4 Mix all the beans and peas together and pour the marinade over them. Leave for several hours in a cool place before serving. Drain off any excess dressing.

Spinach, apple and potato

Photograph
*pages
54-55*

Ingredients
450 g (1 lb) spinach, washed
225 g (8 oz) potatoes
225 g (8 oz) crisp eating apples,
  diced
50 g (2 oz) blue cheese
150 ml (¼ pint) yogurt
salt and pepper

Serves 4

Cauliflower, lightly cooked and divided into florets, can be substituted for the potato. It can be left raw and the spinach, too, in which case vinaigrette would be better than the yogurt.

1 Cook the spinach in a covered pan without adding any extra water for about 6 minutes until just tender. Chop roughly.

2 Boil the potatoes until just tender. Drain, peel and cut into cubes. Leave to cool and mix with the spinach and apple.

3 Mash or blend the blue cheese with the yogurt. Gently turn this dressing into the salad and season to taste.

From top: **Paprika pasta salad; Spiced rice salad** (*see p. 141*); **Lentil and mint salad in yogurt** (*see p. 141*)

Leaf salads

Ingredients
Lettuce
Endive, Batavian and curly
Chicory
Radicchio rosso
Young spinach leaves
Lamb's lettuce (corn salad)
Watercress
Sorrel
Nasturtium leaves
Lovage
Celery leaves
Young dandelion leaves
Rocket

Aim for a variety of contrasting tastes and textures. As well as the various kinds of lettuce, add chicory for a slightly bitter crispness and its relative, radicchio rosso, for colour. Endive, curly or Batavian, is very popular in France, as are lamb's lettuce (corn salad) and young dandelion leaves. So is sorrel, which, with its strong, acid taste, needs to be used in moderation, like celery leaves. Lovage tastes of celery too, but is milder. Young spinach leaves are firm and crunchy. Both watercress and nasturtium leaves have a peppery tang. If you can find rocket, you will realize why the Italians love it.

I like to keep a wooden bowl for salads and rub garlic into the wood as a first step. The bowl never needs washing, only wiping with kitchen paper. The flavours of the dressing thus seep gradually into the wood.

To add extra interest to a leaf salad, use sprouted seeds, thinly sliced onions or shallots, nuts or thin slices of fruit—the pale white-green of a crisp apple, the softer green of avocado or melon, or darker green kiwi fruit.

Avocado and kiwi

Photograph pages 186-187

Ingredients
2 large avocados, diced
4 kiwi fruit, peeled and sliced
1 tbsp finely chopped parsley
1 tbsp snipped chives
90 ml (6 tbsp) vinaigrette
    (see p. 149)
½ small cucumber, cut into julienne
    strips (see p. 222)
2 sticks celery, cut into julienne
    strips (see p. 222)
1 lettuce
1 bunch watercress, cleaned—
    approx. 50 g (2 oz)

Serves 4

1 Toss the avocados and kiwi fruit with the herbs and half the vinaigrette.

2 Toss the julienne of cucumber and celery in the remaining vinaigrette.

3 To serve, arrange the lettuce leaves and watercress in a dish. Pile on the avocado and kiwi fruit and arrange the cucumber and celery julienne on top.

Chicory, orange and watercress

Photograph pages 54-55

Ingredients
3 heads chicory
2 bunches watercress, cleaned—
    approx. 100 g (4 oz)
2 oranges, peeled and sliced
50 g (2 oz) cream cheese
150 ml (¼ pint) yogurt
2 tbsp snipped chives
salt and pepper

Serves 4

1 Separate the chicory into blades. Arrange it on a serving dish or in a bowl with the watercress and orange slices. Chill for half an hour.

2 Beat together the cheese and yogurt. Stir in the chives and season to taste. Just before serving, pour the dressing over the salad.

Celeriac and courgette

1 Cut the celeriac into julienne strips, see page 222 (they need not be as small as a normal julienne) and toss it in the lemon juice to stop it discolouring.

2 Cut the other vegetables into strips of the same size. Mix all the ingredients with the dressing.

Ingredients
1 small celeriac
juice of ½ lemon
225 g (8 oz) courgettes
1 small swede
1 small daikon
tahini and orange dressing (see p. 151)

Serves 4

Photograph *page 146*

Olive and orange

1 Blend the vinaigrette with the honey and cayenne.

2 Mix the oranges, olives and spring onions with the dressing and chill for an hour or two.

3 Just before serving, arrange the watercress or young spinach leaves in a bowl and pile the salad on top.

Ingredients
90 ml (6 tbsp) vinaigrette (see p. 149)
5 ml (1 tsp) honey
pinch of cayenne
4 large oranges, peeled and divided into segments
25-50 g (1-2 oz) green olives, stoned and finely sliced
1 bunch spring onions, chopped
For serving
watercress *or* young spinach leaves

Serves 4

Photograph *page 146*

Cucumber and strawberry

1 Mix together the yogurt, garlic and herbs.

2 Arrange the cucumber and strawberries in a bowl and gently mix in the dressing. Chill for 1 hour before serving.

Ingredients
250 ml (8 fl oz) yogurt
1-2 cloves garlic, crushed
2 tbsp finely chopped mint
1 tbsp finely chopped parsley
1 large cucumber *or* 2 small ones, diced or sliced
350 g (12 oz) strawberries, coarsely chopped

Serves 4

Photograph *page 146*

Beetroot, celery and apple

1 Mix the beetroot, celery and apple well. The beetroot can be finely chopped instead of grated if you prefer.

2 Moisten with the olive oil and lemon juice and season.

Ingredients
225 g (8 oz) raw beetroot, peeled and grated
4 sticks celery, chopped
225 g (8 oz) crisp dessert apples, peeled and chopped
30 ml (2 tbsp) olive oil
juice of ½ lemon
salt and pepper

Serves 4

Photograph *page 146*

COLESLAWS

Shredded cabbage—red, green or white—makes an excellent
base for substantial salads. A food processor is ideal for
preparing them. If you shred the cabbage by hand, cut the
pieces as finely as possible. Allow 225 g (8 oz) cabbage
for 4 people and use the same weight of other ingredients:
fresh or dried fruit, nuts and seeds, grated root vegetables,
crisp celery or fennel, sprouts and herbs. Serve with a
vinaigrette, mayonnaise dressing (see pages 148-149).

Coleslaw with apricots

1 Toast the cashew nuts for 2-3 minutes under a hot grill
until lightly browned.

2 Cut the apricots into very fine slivers. Mix with all the
other ingredients. The poppy seeds can be sprinkled over the
top if you prefer, and any of the alternative dressings could
be substituted.

Ingredients
50-75 g (2-3 oz) cashew nuts
50-75 g (2-3 oz) dried apricots
225 g (8 oz) red *or* white cabbage,
   shredded
4 sticks celery, chopped
2 tsp blue poppy seeds (optional)
90 ml (6 tbsp) mayonnaise
   (see p. 149)

Serves 4

Coleslaw with fennel

Mix all the ingredients together. The dill weed could be
used to garnish.

Ingredients
225 g (8 oz) white cabbage, shredded
100 g (4 oz) fennel bulb, chopped
75 g (3 oz) mung bean sprouts
25 g (1 oz) pumpkin seeds
1 tbsp dried dill weed
90 ml (6 tbsp) mayonnaise
   (see p. 149)

Serves 4

Red cabbage, alfalfa and carrot

1 Mix together the oil, lemon juice and apple juice
concentrate and season to taste. Mix half with the red cabbage
and half with the grated carrot, keeping them separate.

2 Arrange the salad in rings with the red cabbage on the
outside, then the grated carrot, and the alfalfa sprouts
in the centre.

Ingredients
45 ml (3 tbsp) sunflower oil
45 ml (3 tbsp) lemon juice
15 ml (1 tbsp) apple juice
   concentrate
salt and pepper
275 g (10 oz) red cabbage, finely
   shredded
225 g (8 oz) carrots, finely grated
50 g (2 oz) alfalfa sprouts

Serves 4

Photograph
*pages
136-137*

From top: **Beetroot, celery and apple** (*see p. 145*); **Celeriac and courgette in
tahini and orange dressing** (*see p. 145*); **Cucumber and strawberry** (*see p. 145*);
Olive and orange (*see p. 145*); **Coleslaw with apricots; Coleslaw with fennel**

Photograph
*pages
186-187*

Ingredients
350 g (12 oz) button mushrooms,
    sliced
15 ml (1 tbsp) oil
1 clove garlic, crushed
50 g (2 oz) shelled walnuts
½ packet silken tofu—approx.
    150 g (5 oz)
15 ml (1 tbsp) lemon juice
salt and pepper
3-4 spring onions, sliced lengthways

Serves 4

Mushroom salad in tofu

1 Toss the mushrooms in the oil with the garlic.

2 Toast the walnuts for 2-3 minutes under a hot grill. Chop them roughly.

3 Mix together the tofu and lemon juice. Season well and stir into the mushroom slices.

4 Either mix in the spring onions and toasted walnuts or arrange them on top as a garnish.

Photograph
*pages
188-189*

Ingredients
60 ml (4 tbsp) sunflower oil
15 ml (1 tbsp) red wine vinegar
10 ml (2 tsp) shoyu
salt and pepper
100 g (4 oz) mung bean sprouts
100 g (4 oz) button mushrooms,
    diced
1 red or yellow pepper, diced
4 sticks celery, diced

Serves 4

Beansprouts Oriental

1 Combine the oil, vinegar and shoyu and season to taste.

2 Mix together the other ingredients. Toss with the dressing and chill before serving.

DRESSINGS

As well as the usual vinaigrette and mayonnaise dressings, yogurt or tofu, flavoured with cheese, tahini, shoyu or miso, can be used. It is worth making your own mayonnaise, not only for the taste but because you can be sure of avoiding the additives contained in commercial brands.

The term vinaigrette covers a multitude of combinations. As a guide, start with 3 parts of oil to 1 of vinegar or lemon juice. Walnut oil and sesame oil give characteristic nutty tastes; sunflower and safflower oil are good for lighter dressings. Herbs and spices can be added, for example, tarragon, parsley, chives, horseradish, cayenne, chili and garlic. Bear in mind the type of salad you are dressing: bland food such as beans needs a good sharp vinaigrette, while crisper saladings benefit from a richer mixture. My own preference is for a sharp yet light dressing, as in this recipe.

Basic vinaigrette

Mix all the ingredients together and shake well. I use a jar with a screw top.

Variations

Add a peeled and mashed avocado and blend until smooth. The result is more like a mayonnaise than a vinaigrette. Good with a simple green or tomato salad or with a coleslaw.

Add 15-30 ml (1-2 tbsp) soya flour and 5 ml (1 tsp) honey and blend until smooth. This looks similar to egg mayonnaise and is a useful recipe for those who prefer not to eat dairy products. Other non-dairy mayonnaise substitutes are the avocado vinaigrette above and the almond dip on page 43.

Ingredients
60-90 ml (4-6 tbsp) oil (olive *or* sunflower *or* a mixture to taste)
15 ml (1 tbsp) wine or cider vinegar
15 ml (1 tbsp) lemon juice
1 large clove garlic, crushed
large pinch of mustard powder
salt and pepper

Makes 90-120 ml (6-8 tbsp)

Mayonnaise

1 Beat the egg yolks. These should be at room temperature, as otherwise the mayonnaise may curdle.

2 Add up to half the oil drop by drop, beating the mixture constantly. I find it easiest to drop in using a fork.

3 When half the oil has been added, beat in 15 ml (1 tbsp) vinegar. Then beat in the remaining oil, about a tablespoon at a time, until the mixture is very thick.

4 Thin down with some or all of the remaining vinegar and season to taste.

Mustard, garlic, tarragon and other flavourings can be added to taste. For a lower fat dressing, mix equal quantities of mayonnaise and yogurt.

Ingredients
2 egg yolks
300 ml (½ pint) oil (sunflower, olive *or* a mixture, according to preference)
30 ml (2 tbsp) white wine vinegar
salt and pepper

Makes about 350 ml (12 fl oz)

Cottage cheese

Blend all the ingredients together until smooth and season to taste.

Ingredients
225 g (8 oz) cottage cheese
30 ml (2 tbsp) mayonnaise
juice of ½ lemon
15 ml (1 tbsp) honey (optional)
2 tbsp chopped herbs—chives, parsley *or* watercress
salt and pepper

Makes about 300 ml (½ pint)

Photograph
page 139

Ingredients
175 g (6 oz) peanut butter
150 ml (¼ pint) water
10 ml (2 tsp) miso
pinch of cayenne
up to 5 ml (1 tsp) honey *or* lemon
   juice (optional)

Makes about 300 ml (½ pint)

Peanut butter

Blend the peanut butter, water, miso and cayenne together until smooth. Blend in the honey or lemon juice to taste for a sweeter or a sharper dressing. This goes well with cold grains or pasta.

Ingredients
30 ml (2 tbsp) tahini
30 ml (2 tbsp) water
15 ml (1 tbsp) sunflower oil
juice of ½ orange
1 tsp finely grated root ginger

Makes about 100 ml (4 fl oz)

Tahini and orange

1 Mix the tahini and water together. You need to do this or the tahini may curdle.

2 Add all the other ingredients and mix thoroughly. Good with grains, raw vegetables and green salads.

Variation
Omit the oil and ginger and add 150 ml (¼ pint) yogurt. This makes about 175 ml (6 fl oz). Lemon juice could be used instead of orange.

STOCKS, SAUCES & RELISHES

Vegetable stock can be every bit as rich in flavour and wholesome as a meat-based one. Recipes are given for a light and a dark version, either of which can replace milk or water to add flavour to sauces and soups.

Of the sauces here, the most adaptable is béchamel, made with wholewheat flour, which provides the basis for a range of variations. The rich brown sauce is a good example of how to create a tasty gravy substitute without using meat products. Nut-based sauces play a large part in vegetarian cuisine and supply extra protein.

Sauces need not be thickened with flour. Vegetable purées make delicious bases, as in the celery and dill or tomato sauce. A version of tomato sauce using orange is given here, but for a basic one use the recipe given on page 72.

Stock

Other root vegetables can be added to this—turnip, celeriac and parsnip are all good. Green vegetables such as cabbage or broccoli are strongly flavoured and should be added sparingly if at all, but the water they have cooked in could be used. The strained vegetables can be puréed and added to a thick soup.

Light stock

1 Heat the oil and sweat all the vegetables and herbs very gently for 5 minutes. Take care not to let the vegetables colour.

2 Add the water, bring to the boil and simmer for 1½-2 hours, covered. Strain and cool. This will keep for 3-4 days in the refrigerator, or it can be frozen.
Continued

Ingredients
15 ml (1 tbsp) olive oil
4 potatoes, roughly chopped
2 carrots, roughly chopped
1 large onion, roughly chopped
1 stick celery, roughly chopped
1 bay leaf
sprig of thyme
1.5 litres (2½ pints) water
For dark stock
miso *or* shoyu to taste

Makes about 1.5 litres (2½ pints)

★

Stock continued

Dark stock
Instead of gently sweating the vegetables, fry them until well browned, especially the onions. Add the miso or shoyu, bring to the boil and simmer as before. Instead of water, use left-over liquid from cooking aduki, black-eyed or red kidney beans, or from soaking dried mushrooms.

★
(including variations)

Ingredients
300 ml (½ pint) milk
½ onion
6 peppercorns
1 bay leaf
40 g (1½ oz) butter
25 g (1 oz) wholewheat flour
salt and pepper

Makes 300 ml (½ pint)

White (béchamel) sauce

Strictly speaking "white sauce" is a misnomer, as wholewheat flour makes a speckled beige sauce. You can also use cornmeal: this gives a lighter, golden version, more like a custard, which is suitable as a basis for a sweet sauce. I find a ratio of more fat than flour gives a softer mixture, it is easier to stir in the milk, and the finished result is lighter. For a less rich sauce, use skimmed milk, soya milk, or half milk and half stock. For a cream sauce, add 2-3 tablespoons cream.

1 Bring the milk gently to the boil with the onion, peppercorns and bay leaf. Off the heat, leave to stand for 10 minutes, covered. Strain.

2 Melt the butter and when it foams sprinkle over the flour. Cook this mixture over gentle heat for 2-3 minutes, stirring. Add the milk, about a quarter at a time, stirring well to avoid lumps and making sure all the uncooked roux (the flour and butter mixture) is incorporated.

3 Bring to boiling point and simmer, stirring occasionally for 3-5 minutes. Season to taste.

Variations
Green split pea sauce with cayenne
Cook 50 g (2 oz) green split peas until quite soft—about 45 minutes. Drain and purée. Stir into the white sauce and season to taste with cayenne. This is a good way of adding extra protein to a plain grain or vegetable dish.

Horseradish and mustard
As the white sauce is coming to the boil, stir in 1 tablespoon grated horseradish and ¼ teaspoon mustard powder. Serve with croquettes, pancakes or simple steamed vegetables.

Cheese or Herb
While the sauce is hot, add 50-100 g (2-4 oz) grated Cheddar or 1-2 tablespoons chopped herbs such as dill, tarragon or parsley. Cook, stirring, for another minute or two until the cheese has melted or the herbs have flavoured the sauce.

Salsify sauce

Use this as a filling for the lentil roulade on page 134 or as sauce for the stuffed cabbage on page 66.

1 Boil the salsify for 20-25 minutes. Peel and dice.

2 Gently fry the onions and garlic in the butter for about 3-4 minutes until soft, add the salsify and cook for another 2-3 minutes until lightly browned.

3 Stir in the flour, yogurt and lemon juice. Mash until you have a fairly smooth but not perfectly blended consistency.

Ingredients
1 kg (2 lb) salsify, scrubbed
2 medium onions, diced
2 cloves garlic, crushed
40 g (1½ oz) butter
10 ml (2 tsp) wholewheat flour
90 ml (6 tbsp) yogurt
lemon juice to taste

Makes about 300 ml (½ pint)

★

Rich brown sauce

A good brown sauce using no liquid other than water is quick and simple to make. The fried vegetables are essential to the flavour and the miso and shoyu add colour as well as seasoning. Wholewheat flour adds its own delicious taste, but must be thoroughly cooked if the result is not to be gluey.

1 Melt the butter and sweat the vegetables for 10 minutes in a covered pan.

2 Sprinkle over the flour and cook, stirring, for 3-4 minutes. Put in the water and bay leaf. Bring to the boil, still stirring, and simmer for 4-5 minutes.

3 Dissolve the miso in a tablespoon of the sauce and mix this back into the pan. Add the shoyu and simmer for a further few minutes. Taste for seasoning and add more miso or shoyu if desired. Remove the bay leaf before serving.

Ingredients
40 g (1½ oz) butter
25 g (1 oz) mushrooms, minced
2 sticks celery, minced
1 small carrot, minced
1 small onion, minced
25 g (1 oz) wholewheat flour
570 ml (1 pint) water
1 bay leaf
10 ml (2 tsp) miso
5 ml (1 tsp) shoyu

Makes about 700 ml (1¼ pints)

★
Photograph
page 154

Cashew sauce

This goes well with the mushroom brioche on page 88.

1 Toast the cashew nuts for 3-4 minutes under the grill until golden brown.

2 Grind to a fine powder in a blender. Pour in 570 ml (1 pint) water and blend until the mixture resembles a very thin milk.

3 Heat the oil in a small saucepan, add the flour and cook over low heat for 3 minutes. Gradually pour on the cashew milk and bring to the boil, stirring constantly.

4 Add shoyu and seasoning. Cook gently for a further 10 minutes. Stir occasionally and add more water if necessary.

Ingredients
100 g (4 oz) cashew nuts
570-900 ml (1-1½ pints) water
30 ml (2 tbsp) oil
20 g (¾ oz) flour
10 ml (2 tsp) shoyu
salt and pepper

Makes 570-900 ml (1-1½ pints)

★
Photograph
*pages
86-87*

★

Chestnut and wine sauce

This is an ideal accompaniment for pastry dishes.

Ingredients
50 g (2 oz) dried chestnuts, soaked
    for 1 hour
25 g (1 oz) butter
50 g (2 oz) mushrooms, finely
    chopped
75 ml (3 fl oz) red wine
15 ml (1 tbsp) brandy
1 bay leaf
sprig of thyme
salt and pepper

Makes about 300 ml (½ pint)

1 Boil the chestnuts in their soaking water until soft. This takes about 40 minutes. Purée the chestnuts with 60 ml (4 tbsp) of their cooking liquid.

2 Heat the butter and gently sauté the mushrooms in it for 5 minutes. Add the chestnut purée, red wine, brandy, bay leaf and thyme and simmer for 5 minutes. Season to taste and serve hot, discarding the bay leaf and thyme.

★

Photograph
*pages
54-55*

Tomato and orange sauce

A fresh-tasting variation on basic tomato sauce, which will keep for 3-4 days in the refrigerator.

Ingredients
1 large onion, finely chopped
1 clove garlic, crushed
30 ml (2 tbsp) olive oil
450 g (1 lb) tomatoes, skinned
    and chopped
2 tsp dried oregano
juice and grated rind of 1 orange
salt and pepper

Makes 300 ml (½ pint)

1 Lightly fry the onion and garlic in the oil for 3-4 minutes. Add the tomatoes and oregano and cook, covered, for 20 minutes, stirring occasionally.

2 Stir in the orange rind and juice and cook, covered, for a further 5 minutes. Season to taste and serve hot.

Clockwise from top right: **Date and orange relish; Avocado and fennel sauce; Chestnut and wine sauce; Celery and dill sauce; Rich brown sauce** *(p. 153)*

Celery and dill sauce

Buttermilk goes well with the distinctive flavour of dill, but you can omit it if you would prefer a thicker, not too sharp sauce.

1 Heat the butter and sweat the celery in a covered pan for 10 minutes.

2 Add the dill weed and stock and simmer for 5 minutes. Allow to cool a little.

3 Liquidize. Add the buttermilk and season to taste. Reheat gently before serving.

Ingredients
25 g (1 oz) butter
4 sticks celery, finely chopped
4-6 tsp fresh dill weed
150 ml (¼ pint) vegetable stock
  (see p. 151)
150 ml (¼ pint) buttermilk
salt and pepper

Makes about 300 ml (½ pint)

Avocado and fennel sauce

If no extra liquid is added this makes a good dip. Yogurt or tofu can be blended in for a creamier consistency.

1 Heat the oil and sauté the fennel briskly for 3-4 minutes. Pour on boiling water to cover and simmer for 10 minutes. Drain, reserving the liquid.

2 Blend the fennel and avocado with a little of the cooking liquid until smooth. Add more liquid until you have the required consistency. Season. Reheat gently before serving.

Ingredients ★
5 ml (1 tsp) oil
225 g (8 oz) fennel, very finely
  chopped
1 ripe avocado, chopped
salt and pepper

Makes about 250 ml (8 fl oz)

Lime relish

Wash the lime well but do not peel it. This relish will keep for a day or two but is best eaten as soon as possible. It goes well with couscous, curry, samosas and burgers like the mushroom and aduki croquettes on page 96.

Mix the vegetables, lime and ginger together and toss them in the vinegar. Season to taste.

Ingredients ★
100 g (4 oz) carrot, grated
½ cucumber, peeled and grated
6 spring onions, finely chopped
½ lime, very finely chopped
1 tsp grated root ginger
15 ml (1 tbsp) white wine vinegar
salt and pepper

Makes about 175 g (6 oz)

Photograph
*pages
180-181*

Date and orange relish

A simple recipe that can be eaten straight away. It is excellent as a chutney in cheese sandwiches or as an accompaniment to croquettes on page 96.

Put all the ingredients into a heavy-based saucepan with a lid. Cook gently, covered, for 30-45 minutes. stirring occasionally to break the mixture down, and adding a little extra liquid if necessary. Allow to cool before serving.

Ingredients ★
2 oranges, peeled and chopped
225 g (8 oz) dried dates, chopped
45 ml (3 tbsp) vinegar
2 tbsp muscovado sugar
juice and rind of ½ lemon
1 tsp mustard seeds
1 tbsp powdered cinnamon
pinch of cayenne
60 ml (2 tbsp) water *or* orange
  juice

Makes about 425 ml (¾ pint)

PUDDINGS

From a wholefood point of view, if not strictly a vegetarian one, desserts make a very positive contribution to a meal. If the main course has been light and lacking in protein, serve cheesecake made with tofu, a soufflé, mousse or roulade using eggs, or a milk pudding. If you prefer to avoid cream, try a cashew "cream" (made with cottage cheese), yogurt, or custard made with cornmeal as an accompaniment, and use yogurt also to make delicious ice cream.

Fresh fruit salad is one of the best possible endings to a meal. Base it on a colour theme—green and white looks cool and refreshing, red soft fruit with peaches or nectarines is lovely for a party—or on a simple contrast of fruits, such as pomegranate and banana. Dried fruits really come into their own in sweets, whether individually, as mixed fruit compotes or puréed, give a nutritious as well as delectable final touch to a meal.

★ *(sauce)*

Ingredients
4 medium pears (Comice *or*
    Williams), ripe but still firm
50 ml (2 fl oz) honey
300 ml (½ pint) orange juice
570 ml (1 pint) water
1 vanilla pod
Sauce
50 g (2 oz) butter
25 g (1 oz) carob powder
1 egg
2.5 ml (½ tsp) vanilla essence
30 ml (2 tbsp) maple syrup

Serves 4

Pears with carob sauce

Carob powder makes an excellent substitute for chocolate in this version of poires Belle Hélène.

1 Peel the pears, leaving on the stalks. Dissolve the honey in the orange juice and water over low heat, add the vanilla pod and poach the pears, covered, for 15-20 minutes or until tender. Allow to cool completely in the syrup. Remove the vanilla pod.

2 For the sauce, melt the butter, stir in the carob powder and whisk in the egg, vanilla essence and maple syrup. Stir over gentle heat for 10 minutes until the sauce thickens slightly and is completely smooth. You may need to add a little of the pear syrup to thin to a coating consistency. Coat each pear liberally with the warm sauce.

Millet pudding with apricots

Those who like rice pudding, but do not care for it made with brown rice, will find this a delicious alternative. The soya milk gives it a rich, creamy quality. It is good on its own or with puréed or stewed fruit.

1 Preheat the oven to gas mark 3, 170°C (325°F).

2 Gently fry the millet in the oil for 4-5 minutes until golden brown. Pour over the soya milk, bring to the boil and simmer for 5 minutes.

3 Transfer to an ovenproof dish, sprinkle over the cinnamon (and any or all of the optional extras listed with the ingredients) and bake for 45-60 minutes.

4 Stew the apricots in their soaking water for 10 minutes or until warm. Serve in a separate bowl.

Ingredients
100 g (4 oz) millet grains
5 ml (1 tsp) oil
570 ml (1 pint) soya milk
1 tsp powdered cinnamon
Optional extras
10 ml (2 tsp) honey
50 g (2 oz) roasted hazelnuts
50 g (2 oz) raisins
50 g (2 oz) preserved ginger, chopped

225 g (8 oz) Hunza apricots, soaked in hot water for 1 hour

Serves 4

★

Behind: **Millet pudding with apricots**; foreground: **Pears with carob sauce**

★ *(sauce)*

Photograph
pages
188-189

Rhubarb with cashew cream

Made with low fat cottage cheese, the nut "cream" makes a perfect accompaniment to cooked fruit—and a healthy alternative to cream.

Ingredients
1 large firm pear
1 tbsp demerara sugar
175 ml (6 fl oz) red wine
550 g (1¼ lb) rhubarb, chopped
   into 2.5 cm (1 in) lengths
1 pink grapefruit, peeled and
   chopped
15-30 ml (1-2 tbsp) honey
Cashew cream
100 g (4 oz) cashew nuts
100 g (4 oz) cottage cheese
15-30 ml (1-2 tbsp) honey
up to 150 ml (¼ pint) water

Serves 4

1 Peel the pear and cut it into chunks. Dissolve the sugar in the wine in a small pan and stew the pear, covered, over very low heat for 15 minutes. Strain, reserving the juice.

2 In a separate pan, stew the rhubarb and grapefruit with the honey over low heat for 10 minutes or until the rhubarb is tender but not disintegrating. Strain, reserving the juice.

3 Put the pear juice and rhubarb juice in a pan together and boil down hard until reduced by at least half and beginning to be thick. Combine the pear, rhubarb and grapefruit in a serving bowl and pour the juice over. Leave to cool.

4 To make the cashew cream, blend all the ingredients together until very smooth. Serve with the rhubarb.

★

Photograph
pages
86-87

Rich fruit pudding

Rich but sugar free, this makes an ideal Christmas pudding.

Ingredients
225 g (8 oz) Lexia raisins
45 ml (3 tbsp) fruit juice, warmed
50 g (2 oz) rolled oat flakes
50 g (2 oz) self-raising wholewheat
   flour
75 g (3 oz) solid vegetable fat, grated
¼ tsp ground nutmeg
½ tsp grated root ginger
½ tsp ground allspice
25 g (1 oz) stem ginger, finely
   chopped
juice and rind of ½ orange
juice and rind of ½ lemon
3 eggs
45 ml (3 tbsp) sherry *or* brandy

Serves 4-6

1 Soak the raisins for 15-30 minutes in the fruit juice.

2 Mix together the oats and flour. Rub in the fat, add the spices and stem ginger and mix well. Add the raisins and the orange and lemon rind and juice.

3 In a separate bowl, beat the eggs thoroughly. Add them to the mixture with the sherry or brandy and stir very well for at least 5 minutes.

4 Butter a 900 ml (1½ pint) bowl and pour in the pudding mixture. Cover with greaseproof paper and a double layer of foil and steam for 1½-2 hours.

Photograph
pages
168-169

Fruit jelly

I use orange juice or red grape juice for this. Suitable fruit are oranges, pineapple, grapes, apricots, peaches, kiwi fruit or guavas (see page 218 for advice on preparation). Apples and bananas must be tossed in lemon juice to prevent discoloration.

Ingredients
300 ml (½ pint) fruit juice
5 ml (1 tsp) agar powder
100 g (4 oz) fresh fruit, chopped

Makes 4 small jellies

1 Bring the fruit juice to the boil with the agar. Whisk thoroughly and boil until the agar has dissolved. Leave to cool slightly.

2 Stir in the prepared fruit, pour into moulds and leave
to set. Dip the moulds into cold water first if you are going to
turn out the jellies.

Fruit compote

*This is good both at breakfast and at the end of a meal. It needs
to be started the day before but is very easy to make.*

1 Soak the dried fruit overnight with the spices in the water
and fruit juice concentrate.

2 Next day, bring to the boil and simmer for 25 minutes.
Remove the spices, add the seeds of the pomegranate
and cook for a further 5 minutes, adding more water if
necessary. Serve the compote warm or cold, sprinkled with
the chopped pistachios.

Variation
For a more substantial version, which is also good hot, spoon
the compote into an ovenproof dish. Cover with 100-175 g
(4-6 oz) muesli (see page 206), stirring some of it into the
fruit, and bake at gas mark 4, 180°C (350°F) for 30-35 minutes.

Ingredients
225 g (8 oz) dried apricots
50 g (2 oz) prunes
50 g (2 oz) dried pears
50 g (2 oz) dried figs
50 g (2 oz) Lexia raisins
6 cloves *or* allspice berries
1 cinnamon quill
570 ml (1 pint) water
15 ml (1 tbsp) fruit juice concentrate
1 fresh pomegranate
Garnish
50 g (2 oz) shelled pistachios,
  chopped

Serves 4

Photograph
pages
180-181

Soaking
overnight

Trifle

*Frozen raspberries are suitable for this. You can use sugar-free
jam and omit the whipped cream if you like.*

1 Preheat the oven to gas mark 5, 190°C (375°F) and line a
15 cm (6 in) cake tin with greaseproof paper.

2 Beat the eggs and sugar thoroughly until they "form the
ribbon", that is until they turn pale yellow and become
thick and frothy. Do not overbeat.

3 Fold in the flour carefully and thoroughly. Spoon the
mixture into the prepared cake tin and bake for 25 minutes.
Turn out and cool.

4 When cold, split the cake in half and spread with the jam.
Sandwich together again and cut into small pieces.

5 Put these in a serving dish, cover with the raspberries
and sprinkle with the sherry or liqueur. Spread the custard on
top and leave to set. Serve chilled, decorated with whipped
cream and toasted almonds if liked.

Ingredients
2 eggs
50 g (2 oz) light raw sugar
50 g (2 oz) wheatmeal flour
2-3 tbsp jam
225 g (8 oz) raspberries
sherry *or* liqueur to taste
300 ml (½ pint) egg custard *or*
  cornmeal custard (see overleaf)
Garnish (optional)
whipped cream
toasted flaked almonds

Serves 4

Photograph
pages
168-169

Custard

A traditional custard must be heated very gently and not allowed to come near boiling point; a double boiler is ideal for cooking it. Cornmeal custard is a simple alternative which omits the eggs and sugar.

★

Ingredients
2 eggs
25 g (1 oz) light raw sugar
300 ml (½ pint) milk

Makes 300 ml (½ pint)

★

Photograph
pages
168-169

Ingredients
25 g (1 oz) cornmeal
15 ml (1 tbsp) maple syrup
300 ml (½ pint) milk
1 vanilla pod

Makes 300 ml (½ pint)

Traditional custard
Beat the eggs and sugar together. Add the milk and heat gently until thick enough to coat the back of a spoon.

Cornmeal custard
1 Mix the cornmeal and maple syrup with a little of the milk to make a smooth paste.

2 Heat the remaining milk with the vanilla pod until nearly boiling. Pour this over the cornmeal paste and mix until smooth.

3 Return to the pan and reheat gently until thick, stirring constantly. Remove the vanilla pod before serving.

For a thinner, pouring custard, use only 10 g (½ oz) cornmeal.

Photograph
pages
54-55

Ingredients
225 g (8 oz) cranberries
225 ml (8 fl oz) orange juice
2 cloves
¼ tsp powdered cinnamon
6 tbsp demerara sugar
30 ml (2 tbsp) water
10 ml (2 tsp) agar powder
6 eggs, separated
2.5 ml (½ tsp) vanilla essence
150 ml (¼ pint) double cream
15 ml (1 tbsp) brandy *or* rum

Serves 4

Spiced cranberry soufflé

You can use fresh or frozen cranberries for this, or any soft fruit—strawberries or raspberries that do not look quite good enough to serve as they are would be ideal.

1 Put the cranberries in a small pan with the orange juice and spices. Cover and simmer until they have turned to a thick sauce. Remove from the heat and allow to cool.

2 Boil 4 tablespoons of the sugar with the water and agar for 4-5 minutes or until you have a thick caramel sauce.

3 Whisk the egg whites until stiff. Still whisking, pour over the caramel. Add the vanilla, whisk again and chill for 1 hour in the refrigerator.

4 Fold the cranberry sauce into the egg whites. Pile into a 1 litre (2 pint) soufflé dish and chill.

5 Beat the egg yolks with the rest of the sugar until pale yellow and frothy. Add the cream and the brandy or rum and beat again thoroughly. Serve this sauce with the soufflé.

Prune and brandy mousse

1 Stew the prunes in just enough water to cover until soft. This takes about 35-40 minutes.

2 Drain the prunes and purée them with the brandy, egg yolks and yogurt until smooth.

3 Whisk the egg whites until stiff and fold in. Spoon into individual glasses and chill before serving.

Ingredients
225 g (8 oz) prunes, soaked for 3-4 hours or overnight and stoned
15 ml (1 tbsp) brandy
2 eggs, separated
150 ml (¼ pint) yogurt

Serves 4

Photograph
page 162

Lemon and whisky roulade

1 Preheat the oven to gas mark 5, 190°C (375°F) and line a 33 × 23 cm (13 × 9 in) Swiss roll tin with oiled greaseproof paper. (See also Broccoli roulade, page 132.)

2 Beat together the eggs, honey and lemon rind in a bowl over a pan of hot water until thick and mousse-like. Still beating, add the lemon juice very gradually. This will take 10-15 minutes.

3 Off the heat, fold in the flour carefully and thoroughly. Pour into the prepared tin and level out. Bake for 15-20 minutes until just firm.

4 Tip the roulade out on a clean sheet of greaseproof paper, roll it up with the paper and allow to cool.

5 Whip the cream and fold in the whisky and sugar.

6 Unroll the cold roulade, spread the cream over it and roll up again. Decorate with extra cream and/or lemon slices or lemon zest.

Ingredients
3 eggs
40 g (1½ oz) honey
grated rind and juice of 1 small lemon
75 g (3 oz) wheatmeal flour
150 ml (¼ pint) whipping cream
15 ml (1 tbsp) whisky
2 tsp light raw sugar
Garnish
extra whipping cream
lemon slices
lemon zest

Serves 4

★

Photograph
page 162

Tofu cheesecake

This is a light flan with the look of traditional cheesecake. The filling is delicate so handle it carefully.

1 Preheat the oven to gas mark 4, 180°C (350°F).

2 Melt the butter, honey and sugar together in a pan, bring to the boil and stir in the oats.

3 Press the mixture into a 20.5 cm (8 in) flan ring, preferably one with a loose base, and bake for 15-20 minutes.

4 Blend all the ingredients for the filling until smooth. Pour over the base and chill for 24 hours before serving.

Ingredients
Base
100 g (4 oz) butter
15 ml (1 tbsp) honey
1-2 tbsp demerara sugar
225 g (8 oz) rolled oat flakes
Filling
1 packet silken tofu—about 300 g (11 oz)
100 g (4 oz) cottage cheese
2 bananas, peeled
10 ml (2 tsp) honey
juice and rind of ½ lemon

Serves 4

Photograph
page 162

Green and white fruit salad

A refreshing sweet for a summer day. The pear should be of a firm type such as Comice. Other possibilities are green or white figs, sliced in half lengthways, greengages or bananas.

1 Scoop the melon flesh out into balls. Peel, stone and halve the lychees. Pip the grapes but leave them whole. Mix all the fruit together about 2 hours before eating.

2 Blend all the ingredients for the dressing together. Mix with the fruit and chill.

Ingredients
½ honeydew melon
225 g (8 oz) lychees
225 g (8 oz) green grapes
2 kiwi fruit, sliced
1 small firm pear, diced
Dressing
30 ml (2 tbsp) lemon juice
15 ml (1 tbsp) honey
15 ml (1 tbsp) Pernod
150 ml (¼ pint) white grape juice

Serves 4

Peach and claret water ice

A good alternative when peaches are out of season is kaki, also known as persimmon or Sharon fruit. This ice can be served on its own or with extra fresh fruit—one peach or persimmon per person—peeled and cut into thin slivers.

1 Simmer the peaches in the water with the sugar and the lemon rind and juice for 15 minutes.

2 Strain, pressing some of the peach flesh through the sieve if you like. Add the claret and freeze until mushy—about 1 hour.

3 Whisk the egg white and fold it in. Freeze again.

Ingredients
6-8 medium peaches, peeled and
  very finely chopped
570 ml (1 pint) water
100 g (4 oz) demerara sugar
rind and juice of 1 lemon
100 ml (4 fl oz) claret
½ egg white

Serves 4

★
Photograph
*pages
86-87*

Blackcurrant yogurt ice cream

Redcurrants, blackberries, bilberries or gooseberries could also be used, as could stoned black cherries.

1 Mix together the yogurt, vanilla essence and honey and freeze until mushy—about 1 hour.

2 Put the blackcurrants in a pan with the orange juice and sugar. Cover and simmer over low heat for 5 minutes (gooseberries would take about 10 minutes).

3 Remove from the heat and let the fruit steep for 30 minutes. Strain and allow to cool completely.

4 Stir the fruit into the yogurt. Freeze for an hour. Whisk the egg whites until stiff, fold them in and freeze for 1-2 hours or until firm.

Ingredients
570 ml (1 pint) yogurt
5 ml (1 tsp) vanilla essence
30 ml (2 tbsp) honey
100-175 g (4-6 oz) blackcurrants,
  topped and tailed
30 ml (2 tbsp) orange juice
25 g (1 oz) light raw sugar
2 egg whites

Serves 6

★
Photograph
*pages
186-187*

Clockwise from top left: **Prune and brandy mousse** *(see p. 161)*; **Green and white fruit salad**; **Lemon and whisky roulade** *(see p. 161)*; **Tofu cheesecake** *(see p. 161)*

163

CAKES, BISCUITS & PASTRY

Wholefood cakes may not be as light as a traditional sponge, but they have a compensating richness of texture and flavour. The cakes in this chapter use wholewheat or soya flour and oat flakes; only one (parkin) uses any sugar. The others are sweetened with dried fruit, carob powder, fruit juice, grated carrot, honey or molasses, all of which make excellent sweeteners without the health problems associated with sugars. Three of them (the carob, banana and rich fruit cakes) are made without eggs, showing how easy it is to use substitutes and cut down the cholesterol intake. The banana cake also uses oil as a fat rather than butter, helpful for those on a diet low in saturated fats.

Of the biscuits, none uses sugar. The pastries are enriched with sugar and egg yolk but there is no sugar in the toppings or fillings. All these recipes are suitable for freezing, and keep well for several days in airtight containers.

★

Ingredients
175 g (6 oz) dried figs
300 ml (½ pint) apple juice
75 g (3 oz) butter
2 eggs
175 g (6 oz) self-raising wholewheat
　　flour
2 tsp ground allspice
½ tsp fennel seeds
225 g (8 oz) grated carrot

Carrot and fig cake

1 Stew the figs for 30 minutes in the apple juice, drain and purée.

2 Preheat the oven to gas mark 3, 160°C (325°F) and line an 18 cm (6 in) tin with greaseproof paper.

3 Beat the butter until creamy.

4 Beat the eggs, mix with the flour and spices, and beat into the butter.

5 Stir in the carrot and the fig purée. Spoon into the prepared tin and bake for 1 hour. Allow to cool for 10 minutes and turn out.

Clockwise from top right: **Parkin** (*see p. 166*); **Carrot and fig cake**; **William's carob cake** (*see p. 166*)

★

Photograph
page 165

Ingredients
150 g (5 oz) carob powder
75 g (3 oz) desiccated coconut
75 g (3 oz) soya flour
50 g (2 oz) rolled oat flakes
50 g (2 oz) wholewheat flour
225 g (8 oz) raisins
1 tbsp powdered cinnamon
100 g (4 oz) butter, cut into small
    pieces
45 ml (3 tbsp) oil
300 ml (½ pint) apple *or* grape juice
Filling
30 ml (2 tbsp) carob powder
30 ml (2 tbsp) tahini
15 ml (1 tbsp) honey

William's carob cake

1 Preheat the oven to gas mark 3, 170°C (325°F) and line a 20.5 cm (8 in) cake tin with greaseproof paper.

2 Mix together the dry ingredients and mix in the butter and oil until smooth.

3 Stir in the fruit juice and spoon the mixture into the prepared cake tin. Cover with foil. Bake for 50-60 minutes or until a skewer inserted into the centre comes out clean. This cake does not rise. Cool for 10 minutes and turn out.

4 Mix the carob powder and tahini with a little water to a paste. Add the honey and more water until the filling has a spreading consistency. You could enrich it with a little cream if you like.

5 Split the cake and spread the filling thinly over the centre and on the top. Sandwich together again.

Variation (filling)
Mix together 30 ml (2 tbsp) tahini, 30 ml (2 tbsp) apple juice concentrate and 5-10 ml (1-2 tsp) carob powder. Leave to stand for 30-60 minutes. This has a glossy look and makes a very good icing. It can also be used in sandwiches.

★

Photograph
page 165

Ingredients
100 g (4 oz) wholewheat flour
225 g (8 oz) rolled oat flakes
100 g (4 oz) coarse oatmeal
pinch of salt
½ tsp bicarbonate of soda
¼ tsp baking powder
3 tsp ground ginger
100 g (4 oz) butter
150 ml (¼ pint) molasses
25 g (1 oz) muscovado sugar
15 ml (1 tbsp) honey
75 ml (3 fl oz) milk
2 eggs, beaten
75 ml (3 fl oz) apple juice

Makes 9 squares

Parkin

A traditional oatmeal and ginger cake from the North of England, where it is often eaten with cheese and apples.

1 Preheat the oven to gas mark 3, 170°C (325°F) and line a 20.5 cm (8 in) square baking tin with greaseproof paper.

2 Mix the first 7 ingredients together in a bowl.

3 Put the butter, molasses, muscovado sugar and honey in a pan and bring to boiling point, stirring occasionally. Pour this over the dry ingredients and mix thoroughly.

4 Put the milk, eggs and apple juice in the same pan. Heat to roughly blood heat, stirring to amalgamate all the remaining treacly mixture. Do not worry if it curdles.

5 Add this to the contents of the bowl, mix well and spoon into the prepared baking tin. Sprinkle a little extra milk on the surface if you prefer it glazed. Bake for 30-35 minutes or until a skewer inserted into the centre comes out clean.

Banana cake

You could substitute other fruit for half the banana: pear, apple, apricot or pineapple are particularly good. They must be very finely chopped to give the best flavour.

1 Preheat the oven to gas mark 5, 190°C (375°F).

2 Mix all the ingredients together. The consistency should be soft and moist. Spoon into a greased 450 g (1 lb) loaf tin and bake for 50-60 minutes, or until a skewer inserted into the centre comes out clean. Cool for 10 minutes before turning out.

Ingredients
450 g (1 lb) ripe bananas, mashed
50 g (2 oz) chopped nuts
100 ml (4 fl oz) sunflower oil
100 g (4 oz) raisins
75 g (3 oz) rolled oat flakes
150 g (5 oz) wholewheat flour
2.5 ml (½ tsp) almond essence
pinch of salt

★
Photograph
pages
168-169

Rich fruit cake

Made without sugar or eggs, this is nevertheless an ideal cake for special occasions—birthdays, Christmas or weddings.

1 Preheat the oven to gas mark 3, 170°C (325°F) and line a 23 cm (9 in) square cake tin with greaseproof paper.

2 Cream the honey and oil together.

3 Mix the soya flour with the water and gradually add to the oil and honey mixture, beating well. Beat in the rum and the grated rind and juice of the orange and lemon. Add the almonds, figs and dates.

4 Mix the flour with the salt and spice and mix together the currants, sultanas and raisins.

5 Stir half the flour and half the currant mixture into the soya cream, then stir in the remainder. Spoon into the prepared tin and bake for 3¼-3½ hours, or until a skewer inserted into the centre comes out clean. Cool for 10 minutes and turn out.

Ingredients
100 ml (4 fl oz) clear honey
175 ml (6 fl oz) oil
75 g (3 oz) soya flour
300 ml (½ pint) water
15 ml (1 tbsp) rum
grated rind and juice of 1 orange
grated rind and juice of 1 lemon
50 g (2 oz) flaked almonds
100 g (4 oz) dried figs, chopped
100 g (4 oz) dried dates, chopped
225 g (8 oz) wholewheat flour
pinch of salt
2 tsp mixed spice
225 g (8 oz) currants
225 g (8 oz) sultanas
225 g (8 oz) raisins

Photograph
pages 86-87

Sunflower crunch

1 Preheat the oven to gas mark 6, 200°C (400°F) and lightly grease a 33 × 23 cm (13 × 9 in) Swiss roll tin.

2 Mix together all the dry ingredients.

3 Melt the butter and honey and boil together for 3-4 minutes. Pour this over the dry ingredients and mix well. Press firmly into the prepared Swiss roll tin and bake for 15-20 minutes. Allow to cool before cutting.

Ingredients
350 g (12 oz) rolled oat flakes
4 tbsp granola (see p. 182)
3 tbsp sunflower seeds
3 tbsp sesame seeds
3 tbsp chopped nuts
4 tbsp wholewheat flour
1 tsp baking powder
175 g (6 oz) butter
45 ml (3 tbsp) honey

Makes 12-15 squares or fingers

★
Photograph
pages
168-169

Children's parties

Food for children's parties can be healthy yet still appeal to a sweet tooth—there is no need for it to be rich in sugar.

Even the traditional jellies and trifle can have a wholefood slant. Make the jellies with fresh fruit and set them with agar; use a wheatmeal cake as the basis for the trifle—it doesn't have to be decorated with whipped cream. For the birthday cake, try a banana cake decorated with yogurt-coated raisins, as shown here, or the carob cake on page 166.

Spread sandwiches with peanut butter and mashed banana, or with dates, puréed and mixed with cream cheese and sesame seeds.

Fill buns or rolls with herb-flavoured croquettes. Miniature pizzas are always popular; so are carob bourbon biscuits, cut into shapes, and sunflower seed biscuits made with crunchy oatmeal. Savoury popcorn is easy to make: heat a little oil in a heavy pan, add a handful of corn at a time, put the lid on and keep the pan covered until all the corn has popped. Toss it in a little shoyu to taste.

1 Apple juice **2** Wheatmeal trifle with cornmeal custard (*pp. 159 and 160*) **3** Mushroom and aduki "burgers" (*p. 96*) **4** Banana cake (*p. 167*) with carob icing (*p. 166*) **5** Carob bourbon biscuits (*p. 170*) **6 & 11** Sandwiches made with wholewheat bread (*p. 174 and above*) **7** Lemonade **8** Popcorn (*see above*) **9** Yogurt milk shake **10** Sunflower crunch (*p. 167*) **12** Pizzas (*p. 120*) **13** Fruit jellies (*p. 158*)

★

Photograph
pages
188-189

Ingredients
175 g (6 oz) cake *or* biscuit crumbs
25-50 g (1-2 oz) raisins, chopped
40 g (1½ oz) hazelnuts, finely
    chopped
50 g (2 oz) ground almonds
50 g (2 oz) blackcurrant jam,
    preferably sugar-free
15 ml (1 tbsp) brandy
Coating
275 g (10 oz) carob chocolate

Makes 25-30 truffles

Carob truffles

If you melt only a little carob chocolate—2 or 3 squares at a time—it's easier to give each truffle a thin coating. Use two forks to turn the truffles over.

1 Mix all the ingredients except the carob chocolate thoroughly. Divide into walnut-sized balls.

2 Melt the carob chocolate over low heat. Dip each truffle in and turn it until coated. Leave to set.

★

Photograph
pages
168-169

Ingredients
150 g (5 oz) butter
30 ml (2 tbsp) honey
2 egg yolks
175 g (6 oz) wholewheat flour
30 ml (2 tbsp) cornmeal
15 ml (1 tbsp) carob powder
½ tsp vanilla essence
Filling
25 g (1 oz) butter
15 ml (1 tbsp) tahini
15 ml (1 tbsp) peanut butter
15 ml (1 tbsp) thick honey

Makes about 20 pairs of biscuits

Carob bourbon biscuits

This can be cut into the traditional bourbon "fingers" about 7.5 × 2.5 cm (3 × 1 in) or, for a party, they look pretty if differently shaped pastry cutters are used.

1 Preheat the oven to gas mark 4, 180°C (350°F) and lightly grease a baking sheet.

2 Beat together the butter, honey and egg yolks until creamy.

3 Mix in the flour, cornmeal, carob powder and vanilla essence.

4 Roll out to a thickness of 0.5 cm (¼ in) on a floured board, prick with a fork and cut into the desired shapes. Bake for 10-15 minutes. Turn out on a rack and allow to cool.

5 For the filling, beat all the ingredients together and sandwich a little between each pair of biscuits.

★

Ingredients
225 g (8 oz) dried dates, chopped
100 g (4 oz) butter
2 ripe bananas, mashed
2 eggs
75 g (3 oz) wholewheat flour
50 g (2 oz) carob powder
100 g (4 oz) chopped walnuts
5 ml (1 tsp) vanilla essence

Makes 16 squares

Brownies

1 Preheat the oven to gas mark 4, 180°C (350°F) and lightly grease a 20.5 cm (8 in) square baking tin.

2 Cook the dates in just enough water to cover them for 20 minutes or until soft and reduced to a stiff purée. Cool. Then beat them with the butter until light and fluffy.

3 Beat in the bananas and then the eggs, one at a time.

4 Stir in the flour, carob powder, walnuts and vanilla essence and mix gently but thoroughly.

5 Turn into the prepared baking tin and bake for 40 minutes. Allow to cool in the tin before cutting.

Clockwise from top left: **Brownies; Orange daties** *(see p. 172)*; **Apricot slice** *(see p. 172)*

★

Photograph
page 171

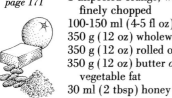

Ingredients
450 g (1 lb) dried dates, chopped
1 unpeeled orange, washed and
  finely chopped
100-150 ml (4-5 fl oz) water
350 g (12 oz) wholewheat flour
350 g (12 oz) rolled oat flakes
350 g (12 oz) butter *or* solid
  vegetable fat
30 ml (2 tbsp) honey

Makes about 18 slices

Orange daties

Date purée gives these slices a moist quality and rich flavour, highlighted by a fresh orange tang. They will keep 4-5 days in an airtight container, and also freeze well.

1 Preheat the oven to gas mark 6, 200°C (400°F) and lightly grease a 33 × 23 cm (13 × 9 in) Swiss roll tin.

2 Put the dates and orange in a pan with the water. Cook gently, covered, for 20 minutes or until soft. Cool slightly and liquidize until smooth.

3 Mix together the flour, oat flakes, butter and honey. Spread half of this over the prepared Swiss roll tin and press down evenly.

4 Cover with the date mixture and then with the remaining dough. It is easier to do this if you roll it out first on greaseproof paper. Bake for 25-30 minutes and allow to cool before cutting into slices.

★

Photograph
page 171

Ingredients
225 g (8 oz) dried apricots
short crust pastry (p. 92) made
  with 175 g (6 oz) flour
Topping
100 g (4 oz) flaked almonds
100 g (4 oz) ground almonds
5 ml (1 tsp) vanilla essence
2 eggs
30 ml (2 tbsp) apple juice
  concentrate

Makes 12 slices

Apricot slice

Instead of ordinary short crust, you could use the rich short crust given in the next recipe (for mince pies).

1 Stew the apricots in just enough water to cover for 35-40 minutes until soft.

2 Preheat the oven to gas mark 6, 200°C (400°F) and lightly grease a 23 cm (9 in) baking sheet.

3 Roll the pastry out to fit the baking sheet, prick it all over and bake for 4 minutes to set it.

4 Decrease the oven heat to gas mark 5, 190°C (375°F).

5 Purée the apricots and spread them over the pastry base.

6 Mix the topping ingredients together, spread them over the apricots and bake for 20 minutes. Cool and cut into slices.

Mince pies

The quantity of mincemeat given is much more than is needed for the mince pies, as it is not worth making in small amounts. It keeps in the freezer for 2-3 months, bottled for 2-3 weeks. If you are bottling it, leave overnight in a cool place first.

1 Stew the apples with the spice and fruit juice for about 10 minutes until soft, adding a little water only if necessary.

2 Remove from the heat and mix in the other ingredients.

3 For the pastry mix the flour and salt together, make a well in the centre and add the remaining ingredients.

4 Gradually incorporate the flour into the ingredients, rubbing lightly with the fingertips, until you have a soft dough. Wrap in greaseproof paper and chill for 1 hour.

5 Preheat the oven to gas mark 6, 200°C (400°F).

6 Roll the pastry out to a thickness of 0.5 cm (¼ in) and cut out 18 to 20 8 cm (3 in) rounds for bases and the same number of 6.5 cm (2½ in) rounds for lids. Line 6.5 cm (2½ in) patty tins with the bases and half fill with mincemeat. Cover with the lids and bake for 15-20 minutes. Turn out on a rack to cool.

Ingredients
Mincemeat
750 g (1½ lb) cooking apples, peeled and chopped
1 tbsp mixed spice
15 ml (1 tbsp) fruit juice
175 ml (6 fl oz) honey
225 g (8 oz) raisins
225 g (8 oz) currants
100 g (4 oz) mixed peel, finely chopped
100 g (4 oz) slivered almonds
15-30 ml (1-2 tbsp) brandy
30 ml (2 tbsp) molasses
Makes 1.1 kg (2½ lb) mincemeat

Pastry
450 g (1 lb) wholewheat flour
pinch of salt
175 g (6 oz) brown sugar
225 g (8 oz) butter, chopped
4 egg yolks
2-3 drops vanilla essence

Makes 18-20 mince pies

Photograph
pages
86-87

Oatcakes

These can be made any size you like. Small rounds 5 cm (2 in) in diameter are good for cocktail parties; 7.5 cm (3 in) is a useful size for cheese biscuits. You could also make them square or oblong.

1 Preheat the oven to gas mark 6, 200°C (400°F) and lightly grease a baking sheet.

2 Mix together the dry ingredients. Rub the fats into the mixture and add enough milk to bind into a rough dough.

3 Roll out to a thickness of about 1 cm (just under ½ in). Cut into the required shapes and bake for 12-15 minutes or until crisp. Cool on a rack.

Ingredients
225 g (8 oz) fine oatmeal
225 g (8 oz) wholewheat flour
1 tsp salt
100 g (4 oz) solid vegetable fat, grated
100 g (4 oz) butter, cut into small pieces
a little milk to mix—approx. 3-4 tsp

Makes about 25 small biscuits

★

Photograph
pages
186-187

BREAD

Making your own bread is by no means a time-consuming chore: the longest part is the rising and proving, but don't forget that while this is happening it is the yeast that is doing the work and not you.

All you need is flour, water (or milk) and yeast, with salt to taste. Soft wholewheat flour makes a dense loaf that keeps well; strong flour gives a lighter texture. The inclusion of a little rye or barley flour adds a distinctive flavour. Cornmeal can be used on its own or mixed with wheat flour.

Fresh yeast is specified here; if you are using dried yeast, you need only half the amount. Other raising agents—soda or baking powder—are used for quick breads, mixed and baked in under an hour. Molasses or honey is added for flavour and texture, but is not needed to activate the yeast. (See also page 204.)

All yeast bread, soda bread and scones freeze well, so it is worth making plenty.

★

Photograph
page 177

Ingredients
700 g (1½ lb) wholewheat flour
1 tsp salt
25 g (1 oz) fresh yeast
5 ml (1 tsp) molasses
25 g (1 oz) soya flour
425 ml (¾ pint) warm water
15 ml (1 tbsp) sunflower oil

Makes approx. 1 kg (2¼ lb)

Wholewheat bread

This is a simple, basic recipe—delicious as it is, or you can vary it by adding grains, herbs or cheese. The soya flour adds taste as well as protein.

1 Mix the flour and salt together in a warm dry bowl.

2 Stir the yeast, molasses and soya flour until creamy. Pour on 150 ml (¼ pint) of the warm water and beat vigorously until the yeast has dissolved. Leave in a warm place for 5 minutes or so until the surface is frothy.

3 Pour the yeast mixture over the flour. Add the remaining water and oil and stir with a spoon until the dough starts to form. Continue as shown opposite.

174

MAKING BREAD

1 *Knead until the individual ingredients combine. The point to watch for is the change in texture. The dough should take on a uniform smoothness and feel velvety.*

2 *Leave in a bowl, covered with a damp cloth, in a warm place free from draughts. After about an hour the dough should roughly double in size. It will be spongy but firm in texture and will come away cleanly from the sides of the bowl.*

3 *Tip the dough out of the bowl and punch your fist into the centre to knock out all the gas. This is called "knocking back" or "knocking down". Knead again for a few minutes.*

4 *For loaves, cut the dough into 450 g (1 lb) lumps. Shape into loaves and set in greased tins to prove (rise a second time).*

5 *To make a plait, divide each lump into three, roll into long cylinders and twist together. For a cob, shape the dough into a smooth ball.*

6 *To make rolls, cut the dough into 75 g (3 oz) pieces. Shape into rounds or crescents, or slash the sides with scissors to make "daisy wheels".*

4 When shaped, leave bread to prove in a warm, draught-free place. Loaves take 20-30 minutes, rolls 10-15, to double in size. Preheat oven to gas mark 7, 220°C (425°F).

5 Bake loaves for 35-40 minutes if in a tin, 30-35 minutes if on a baking sheet (e.g. plait or cob); bake rolls for 15-20 minutes. The bread is done if it sounds hollow when tapped on the base. Turn out on a wire rack to cool.

Variations
Sprouted and cooked grains
These add flavour and texture to a basic dough. Sprouted wheat or rye gives a light, slightly sweet loaf, while cooked grains make the bread moist and chewy. After the first rising, and before shaping the dough knead in 50-75 g (2-3 oz) of cooked or sprouted grains to each 450 g (1 lb) dough. Prove and bake as above.

Savoury breads
Cheese and thyme

A savoury bread can be made in the same way by kneading in 25 g (1 oz) of grated Cheddar with 2 teaspoons dried thyme before the second rising. Glaze the loaf if you like by brushing it with a little beaten egg or milk just before you put it in the oven. Sesame seeds make a good decoration.

Cheese and garlic

As cheese and thyme, but use garlic powder instead of thyme. Blue poppy seeds are an attractive decoration for this.

Cheese and onion

As above, but adding 1 very finely chopped onion instead of the herbs. Sprinkle the top with extra grated cheese.

★

Photograph
pages
188-189

Ingredients
50 g (2 oz) fresh yeast
15 ml (1 tbsp) molasses
700 ml (1¼ pints) warm water
550 g (1¼ lb) wholewheat flour
550 g (1¼ lb) rye flour
1½ tsp salt
60 ml (4 tbsp) oil
1 tbsp carob powder
1 tbsp caraway seeds

Makes four 450 g (1 lb) loaves

Rye bread

This uses the batter method, a good way of dealing with a dough containing low-gluten flour. The yeast, water and wholewheat flour form a batter and the yeast ferments for an hour with the flour, reacting with the gluten in it, before being kneaded with the low-gluten flour (rye in this recipe). The resulting dough is lighter, softer and easier to handle.

1 Mix the yeast and molasses with the warm water in a large bowl. Stir in the wholewheat flour and beat thoroughly to form a smooth batter. Leave for 1 hour to ferment.

2 Beat in the remaining ingredients to form a soft dough. Knead for a few minutes until the dough feels smooth. Add a little extra flour if necessary, but the dough should not be too dry.

3 Divide into four and shape each piece into a long loaf. The bread will be less sticky if you release some of the moisture in the dough by pricking it all over with a fork. Leave to rise for 45-60 minutes. Rye bread is usually baked on a baking sheet rather than in a tin.

4 Preheat the oven to gas mark 7, 220°C (425°F).

5 Bake the bread for 30-35 minutes or until the base sounds hollow when tapped. Turn out on a rack and allow the bread to cool completely.

Clockwise from bottom left: **Wholewheat bread** *(see pp. 174-176)*— rolls shaped in daisy wheels or crescents, sliced plain loaf, whole loaf with cooked rice, cob with sprouted wheat, plait, and cheese and garlic rolls; **Oaten rolls** *(see p. 178)*

Photograph
page 177

Oaten rolls

The oats are softened by a preliminary soaking. They give the rolls a rich, sweet flavour and a pleasantly moist texture.

Ingredients
25 g (1 oz) fresh yeast
15 ml (1 tbsp) honey
425 ml (¾ pint) warm milk
225 g (8 oz) coarse oatmeal
450 g (1 lb) wholewheat flour
1 tsp salt

Makes twelve 75 g (3 oz) rolls

1 Mix together the yeast and honey. Whisk in the warm milk, stir in the oatmeal and leave to stand for 45-60 minutes, by which time the oats will have swelled and softened slightly and the surface of the mixture will be frothy.

2 Stir in the flour and salt to form a soft dough. Knead thoroughly. If the mixture is a little sticky add more flour, but not too much—the texture should be soft but not dry. Leave in a clean bowl to rest for 30 minutes.

3 Knead again lightly for 2 minutes. Divide into 12 pieces and shape into rounds. Make an indentation in the centre of each one with the handle of a wooden spoon.

4 Put to rise on a greased baking sheet for 30 minutes. They will rise slightly, but not as much as a wholewheat loaf. Preheat the oven to gas mark 7, 220°C (425°F).

5 Bake the rolls for 15-20 minutes, or until the bases sound hollow when tapped, and turn them out on a rack to cool.

Photograph
page 183

Soda bread

Buttermilk gives a distinctive taste and texture. The bread freezes well but tastes best of all still warm from the oven.

Ingredients
450 g (1 lb) wholewheat flour
450 g (1 lb) fine wholewheat (pastry or chapatti) flour *or* wheatmeal flour
2 tsp bicarbonate of soda
1 tsp salt
100 g (4 oz) butter, cut into pieces
425 ml (¾ pint) buttermilk

Makes one large 1.1 kg (2½ lb) round *or* two small ones

1 Preheat the oven to gas mark 7, 220°C (425°F).

2 Mix together both the flours, the bicarbonate of soda and the salt. Rub in the butter.

3 Make a well in the middle and gradually add the buttermilk until you have a soft but not sloppy dough. You may need a little extra buttermilk—it will depend on the flour.

4 Knead the dough quickly and lightly, just enough to shape it into a rough ball. Put in on a floured baking sheet and flatten it out to a circle about 3.5 cm (1½ in) thick.

5 With a floured knife, cut two slashes in the form of a cross almost, but not quite, through it, to divide it into quarters or "farls".

6 Bake for 25 minutes, then reduce the heat to gas mark 5, 190°C (375°F) and bake for 25 minutes or until the crust is browned. The exact time depends on how wet the dough is.

Heaven's rolls

Linseeds are popular in Austria, and are used here, like the wheatgerm, to add flavour as well as nutrients.

1 Mix the yeast and honey until creamy. Whisk in 150 ml (¼ pint) water and leave to ferment for 5 minutes in a warm place.

2 Mix together the dry ingredients.

3 Mix the ferment into the dry ingredients with the remaining water, add the oil and knead well for 5-7 minutes, adding a little more flour if the mixture is sticky. Leave in a clean bowl, covered, to rise for 30 minutes.

4 Punch the dough down with your fist, knead briefly and divide into 12. Shape each piece into a roll and put on a greased baking sheet to prove for 10-15 minutes. Preheat the oven to gas mark 7, 220°C (425°F).

5 Bake for 15-20 minutes or until the bases sound hollow when tapped. Turn out on a wire rack to cool.

Ingredients
25 g (1 oz) fresh yeast
30 ml (2 tbsp) honey
300 ml (½ pint) warm water
500 g (1 lb 2 oz) wholewheat flour
50 g (2 oz) sunflower seeds
50 g (2 oz) linseeds
50 g (2 oz) wheat flakes
50 g (2 oz) wheatgerm
1 tsp salt
15 ml (1 tbsp) oil

Makes twelve 75 g (3 oz) rolls

★
Photograph
*pages
180-181*

Cornbread

Yellow cornmeal gives a golden colour as well as an appetizing nutty flavour and crisp texture. You can use a mixture of cornmeal and wheat flour for different tastes and consistencies.

1 Preheat the oven to gas mark 6, 200°C (400°F).

2 Mix the cornmeal thoroughly with the bicarbonate of soda and the salt.

3 Beat the egg thoroughly, add the yogurt, honey and oil and beat again until well mixed.

4 Mix all the ingredients together to make a soft batter. If it seems too runny, add a little more flour. Spoon into a lightly greased sandwich tin or bun tin and bake for 15-20 minutes or until risen, golden brown and firm to the touch. Turn out on a rack to cool.

Variations
Milk and baking powder can be used instead of yogurt and bicarbonate of soda. More eggs will give a lighter, richer, more cake-like mixture. For a sweeter tea-time bread, use extra honey and add dried fruit. For a savoury bread, add grated cheese, chopped peppers or onion with paprika or chili powder.

Ingredients
175 g (6 oz) cornmeal
1½ tsp bicarbonate of soda
½ tsp salt
1 egg
150 ml (¼ pint) yogurt
10 ml (2 tsp) honey
30 ml (2 tbsp) oil

Makes one 15 cm (6 in) round *or* **nine small buns**

★
Photograph
*pages
54-55*

Brunch

A meal to enjoy on a lazy Sunday morning, most of which, including the khichhari, croquette mixture and pancake batter, can be prepared in advance. To start with serve home-made muesli and granola (the latter also used in special muffins); fruit compote and fruit juice; rye bread with honey, apple butter or peanut butter, or rolls made with sunflower seeds, linseeds, wheat flakes and wheat germ. These could be followed by boiled eggs or by an omelette with an Italian name but which might also derive from Persian cookery, generously filled with a mixture of fresh herbs and greens: sorrel, spinach, lovage, mint, parsley or chives.

For those who arrive nearer lunchtime khichhari, ancestor of the traditional British breakfast dish kedgeree, or strongly spiced bean and mushroom croquettes make more filling dishes. Pancakes are delicious with either yogurt or maple syrup. Cream cheese, Gjetost and Jarlsberg make a varied selection of cheeses.

As an alternative to coffee there is a wide range of herb teas; rosehip with hibiscus or mint with lime are particularly refreshing.

1 & 7 Granola (*p. 182*) 2 Rye bread (*p. 176*)
3 Pancakes (*p. 122*) 4 Lime relish (*p. 155*)
5 Mushroom and aduki croquettes (*p. 96*)
6 Muesli (*p. 206*) with yogurt
8 & 14 Fruit compote (*p. 159*) 9 Frittata verde (*p. 130*)
10 Heaven's rolls (*p. 179*) 11 Granola muffins (*p. 182*)
12 Yogurt (*p. 220*) 13 Khichhari (*p. 104*)

★

Photograph
pages
180-181

Ingredients
Granola
½-⅔ part oil
½-⅔ part honey
3 parts rolled oat flakes
1 part wheatgerm
1 part bran
1 part soya flour
1 part wholewheat flour
1 part sesame seeds
1 part sunflower seeds
1 part chopped nuts
powdered cinnamon to taste
Muffins
100 g (4 oz) wholewheat flour
50 g (2 oz) granola
25 g (1 oz) wheatgerm
25 g (1 oz) bran
1½ tsp baking powder
½ tsp salt
2 small eggs
150 ml (¼ pint) milk
30 ml (2 tbsp) maple syrup

Makes 9-12 buns or muffins

Granola muffins

You can use a simpler granola mix if you like, but the one given here is particularly good and can also be used as a cereal, a quick crumble topping, or mixed with yogurt for a nutritious snack. It keeps several weeks in an airtight tin.

Granola
1 Preheat the oven to gas mark 2, 160°C (300°F).

2 Whisk together the oil and honey and mix thoroughly with the dry ingredients.

3 Spread on a lightly greased baking tray or dish and bake for ½-1 hour, turning the top layer under from time to time so that the entire mixture browns evenly.

Muffins
1 Preheat the oven to gas mark 6, 200°C (400°F).

2 Mix together all the dry ingredients.

3 In a separate bowl, beat the eggs thoroughly and add the milk and maple syrup. Beat the mixture again and mix with the dry ingredients.

4 Spoon the mixture into a greased deep bun tin and bake for 18-20 minutes. Serve warm. Delicious for brunch or teatime.

★

Ingredients
1 large egg
175 g (6 oz) cooked carrots, mashed
1 unpeeled eating apple, grated
60 ml (4 tbsp) sunflower oil
100 g (4 oz) wholewheat pastry flour
2 tsp baking powder
pinch of salt
25-50 g (1-2 oz) light raw sugar
½ tsp powdered cinnamon
1 tsp gomashio (optional)

Makes 9 buns or muffins

Carrot and apple muffins

The sweetness of carrots combines well with apples to make these little buns or muffins — an excellent way of using up leftover carrots. Eat them with soups or salads.

1 Preheat the oven to gas mark 6, 200°C (400°F).

2 Beat the egg thoroughly and mix with the carrots, apple and oil.

3 Mix together the flour, baking powder, salt, sugar and cinnamon, with the gomashio if used. Stir into the egg mixture until you have a smooth thick consistency like batter. If it is too sloppy, add a little extra flour.

4 Fill 9 greased bun or muffin tins and bake for 15-20 minutes until firm. Serve warm.

Clockwise from top: **Carrot and apple muffins**; **Soda bread** (*see p. 178*); **Malted fruit loaf** (*see p. 184*); **Rosemary and walnut scones** (*see p. 184*)

★

Photograph
page 183

Ingredients
350 g (12 oz) wholewheat flour
4 tsp baking powder
½ tsp salt
50 g (2 oz) walnuts, finely chopped
1½ tbsp finely chopped rosemary
50 ml (2 fl oz) sunflower oil
1 large egg, beaten
200 ml (7 fl oz) milk

Makes 10-12 scones

Rosemary and walnut scones

A subtle variation on traditional English scones, good with soup or as a lunchtime snack.

1 Preheat the oven to gas mark 7, 220°C (425°F).

2 Mix together the flour, baking powder and salt and add the chopped walnuts and rosemary.

3 Combine the oil, egg and milk. Add to the dry ingredients and mix to a soft dough.

4 Pat out to a thickness of 1.5 cm (¾ in) and cut into 5 cm (2 in) rounds. Bake for 10 minutes and serve warm.

★

Photograph
page 183

Ingredients
450 g (1 lb) wholewheat flour
1 tsp salt
25 g (1 oz) mixed spices
50 g (2 oz) muscovado sugar
25 g (1 oz) fresh yeast
15 ml (1 tbsp) malt extract
25 g (1 oz) soya flour
300 ml (½ pint) warm water
15 ml (1 tbsp) sunflower oil
100 g (4 oz) raisins
1 egg, lightly beaten with a little
    salt
Glaze
15 ml (1 tbsp) malt extract
15 ml (1 tbsp) apple juice
    concentrate

Makes two 450 g (1 lb) loaves

Malted fruit loaf

I buy good-quality mixed spice—ground cloves, nutmeg and cinnamon—and add extra powdered cinnamon, but you could use any combination you like. Ginger, coriander and a little pepper can all be added.

1 Mix together the flour, salt, spices and sugar.

2 Mix the yeast with the malt extract, soya flour and warm water and leave to ferment in a warm place for 5 minutes or until the surface of the liquid is quite frothy.

3 Add the ferment and the oil to the dry ingredients. Mix well with a wooden spoon and then knead well for 5-7 minutes. Lightly knead in the raisins and put into a clean bowl to rise for 30 minutes, covered with a damp cloth.

4 Punch the dough down with your fist, knead again lightly and divide it between two greased loaf tins. Leave to rise for 30 minutes.

5 Heat the oven to gas mark 6, 200°C (400°F). Brush the tops of the loaves with the beaten egg and bake them for 30-35 minutes.

6 While still hot from the oven, brush with the malt extract mixed with the apple juice. You may not need quite all of it.

MENU AND MEAL PLANNER

Whether you're a full-time vegetarian or would merely like a vegetarian meal as an occasional change from a meat-based one, it can be difficult to structure a meal, to decide what to serve with what. This part of the book is designed to help you prepare varied and interesting meals, well balanced in taste, texture and nutrients. There are menus to help you entertain; menus for a weekend, combining simply prepared meals with more elaborate ones; and menus for a whole week for a family, with the emphasis on simpler cooking while providing balanced, nutritious meals. There is a section on buying, storing, preparing and cooking ingredients, including ideas for garnishes and tips on how to choose the most suitable kitchen equipment. Finally there is a section on daily nutritional needs and how best to supply them.

★ *indicates that the dish is suitable for freezing*

Summer dinner party

Contrasting fillings make a multicoloured centrepiece for a light summer evening meal. The vegetable-based menu is given substance by the wholewheat pancakes and more protein is provided by the vegetarian cheeses and the tofu in the salad dressing.

Button mushrooms are garnished with walnuts and spring onions in a tofu and lemon dressing (*see p. 148*).

A layered galette of wholewheat pancakes with three different vegetable fillings—spinach, fennel, and tomato and onion (*see p. 124*). The pancakes can be made in advance and frozen; the fillings will keep for 1-2 days in the refrigerator. Serve sprinkled with grated Parmesan.

Blackcurrant and yogurt ice cream looks rich and creamy, but is low in fat and sugar. Its clean sharp taste is enhanced with orange (*see p. 163*).

Avocado and kiwi salad with a julienne of celery and cucumber, tossed in a herb vinaigrette (*see p. 144*).

Globe artichoke served with an individual bowl of lemon and garlic sauce is a quick and easy first course which can be prepared well in advance (*see p. 37*).

A selection of cheeses—from the top: Coulommiers, blue cheese, goat's cheese—all made without animal rennet and served with oatcakes and cheese biscuits (*see pp. 135, 173*).

Winter dinner party

Rich, thick soup, subtly spiced pilaf with millet and aubergines, individual spinach darioles, salad and a compote of winter fruit make a substantial meal, most of which can be prepared in advance.

Spinach leaves are stuffed with tomatoes and flavoured with basil (or oregano, if liked) and with spring onions (*see p. 67*).

Byzantine millet pilaf with coriander, apricots and aubergines in sesame sauce can be prepared in advance and frozen (*see p. 108*).

Rye bread uses both wholewheat and rye flour. Molasses, carob powder and caraway add colour and spice (*see p. 176*).

Mushroom soup with red wine, flavoured with parsley, bay, marjoram and tarragon, can made made in advance and frozen (*see p. 57*).

188

Mung bean sprouts are combined with sweet peppers, button mushrooms and celery in a shoyu-flavoured dressing to provide a colourful salad (*see p. 148*).

Rhubarb, pink grapefruit and pears in wine can be served hot or cold. The "cream" to go with them is based on cashew nuts and cottage cheese (*see p. 158*).

Carob truffles are a delicious mixture including chopped fruit and nuts with a coating of melted carob chocolate (*see p. 170*).

189

Impromptu dinner party

If special guests turn up unexpectedly and you have only
a couple of hours to prepare a meal, this menu can be created quickly and
easily from what you might have at hand.

Tomato sauce is easy
to make in quantity and
keeps well, whether
frozen or in the
refrigerator
(*see p. 72*).

Spaghetti aglio, olio e peperoncino
is the Italian name for this
quickly-made dish
of pasta with
garlic and
chili, much
liked in its
native land.
Grated
cheese is
optional (*see p. 113*).

Potatoes, lightly steamed and
sprinkled with toasted almonds,
are a good accompaniment to the
roulade, but steamed
carrots or celery
would be good too
(*see p. 217*).

Make an **impromptu salad**
with whatever you have to
hand: use leftover grains or
beans, and nuts or raisins
as well as fresh salad
vegetables as here,
dressed with
vinaigrette
(*see p. 149*).

A **roulade** always looks
impressive, but in fact is
easy to make once you have
mastered the technique—it
only needs one or two
practice runs (*see p. 132*).

Oranges,
sliced and
marinated in
orange and lemon
juice with honey and Grand Marnier to taste,
and decorated with the orange zest.

191

Menu organizer

A frequent criticism of vegetarian food is that it takes so long to prepare. The secret of success is organization—making sure that the beans are put to soak in advance and that time is allowed for preparation. To help with this, a countdown is given for each menu showing exactly what needs to be done and when (apart from dishes that are self-explanatory, such as quickly assembled salad or fruit combinations). Many dishes freeze well, so, as with non-vegetarian food, it's a good idea to make extra quantities to freeze for a later meal.

The following fifteen menus are suitable for dinner parties for all seasons of the year and all occasions from Christmas dinner to informal gatherings. The first three are illustrated in detail on the preceding pages. Of the others, the first Christmas menu is shown on pages 86-87 and the Thanksgiving menu on pages 54-55.

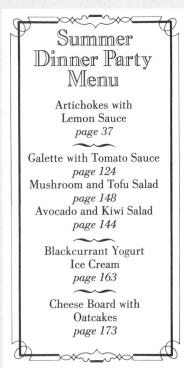

Summer Dinner Party Menu

Artichokes with
Lemon Sauce
page 37

~

Galette with Tomato Sauce
page 124
Mushroom and Tofu Salad
page 148
Avocado and Kiwi Salad
page 144

~

Blackcurrant Yogurt
Ice Cream
page 163

~

Cheese Board with
Oatcakes
page 173

PREPARATION IN ADVANCE

★ **Galette:** make, assemble and freeze *or* make **pancakes** and **fillings** and store separately in refrigerator 1-2 days in advance.
★ **Blackcurrant and yogurt ice:** make and freeze.
★ **Oatcakes:** make and freeze

or store in an airtight container.
Vinaigrette: make and keep in a screwtop bottle in the refrigerator for 1-2 days.

EVENING BEFORE
Lemon sauce: make and refrigerate.
Thaw galette and oatcakes if frozen.

ON THE DAY
Prepare salad ingredients.
Assemble **mushroom and tofu salad,** toss in dressing and keep it cool.
Do not assemble the avocado and kiwi salad until the last moment.
One hour before serving boil and prepare **artichokes.**
Assemble the **galette** if not from the freezer.
Thirty minutes before serving preheat the oven to gas mark 4, 180°C (350°F) and put in the galette.
Reheat the lemon sauce for the artichokes.
Reheat the extra tomato sauce for the galette.
Assemble the **avocado and kiwi salad.**
Remove the ice from the freezer when you serve the first course.

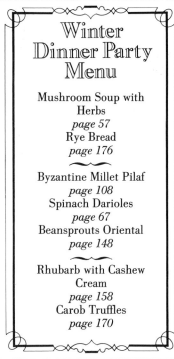

Winter Dinner Party Menu

Mushroom Soup with
Herbs
page 57
Rye Bread
page 176

~

Byzantine Millet Pilaf
page 108
Spinach Darioles
page 67
Beansprouts Oriental
page 148

~

Rhubarb with Cashew
Cream
page 158
Carob Truffles
page 170

PREPARATION IN ADVANCE

★ **Mushroom soup:** make and freeze *or* make 1-2 days in advance and refrigerate.
Beansprouts: Start a week in advance and grow beansprouts (see page 216). Store in refrigerator.

★ **Rye bread:** make and freeze *or* make 1-2 days in advance and refrigerate.

★ **Carob truffles:** freeze *or* make 3-4 days in advance and store in airtight container.

EVENING BEFORE
Thaw soup and bread if frozen. Make the **cashew cream** and refrigerate.

ON THE DAY
Make the **rhubarb dessert** and refrigerate.
Make the **beansprout salad** and refrigerate.
Make the **pilaf** and put in a baking dish. Prepare the **aubergines** for the topping. Prepare the **spinach darioles.** Take the dessert, cashew cream and truffles out of the refrigerator.
Forty minutes before serving preheat the oven to gas mark 4, 180°C (350°F) and put in the **darioles.**
Thirty minutes before serving cover the pilaf tightly with foil and put in the oven. Bake the aubergines.
Gently reheat the soup and the rhubarb dessert.

IMPROMPTU DINNER PARTY
This meal is based on ingredients you are likely to have in your store cupboard or refrigerator: pasta, potatoes, a fresh vegetable (although lentils could be used here instead of broccoli), salad and fruit. The only other assumption made is that you have some tomato sauce ready in the refrigerator, but even this too could be made in the time available.

Impromptu Dinner Party Menu

Spaghetti with Oil, Garlic and Chili Sauce
page 113

Broccoli Roulade
page 132
Tomato Sauce
page 72
Steamed Potatoes with Toasted Almonds
pages 217, 209
Mangetout and Mushroom Salad with Vinaigrette
page 191, 149

Marinaded Oranges
page 191

Two hours before serving prepare the broccoli and sauce for the **roulade base,** the **oranges,** and the vegetables for the **salad.**
Forty-five minutes before serving bring a pan of water to the boil and put the **potatoes** to steam. Preheat the oven to gas mark 5, 190°C (375°F).
Finish making the **roulade base** and put it in to bake.
Put on the water for the spaghetti. Assemble the salad. Heat the **tomato sauce.**
Fifteen minutes before serving fill the **roulade,** roll it up and put it back in the oven.
Put the **almonds** in to toast. Turn the heat down to gas mark 3, 170°C (325°F).
Throw the **spaghetti** into the boiling salted water. Make the **garlic and chili sauce.** As soon as the spaghetti is ready, drain, mix with the sauce and serve.

Christmas Menu 1

Cream of Cauliflower and Almond Soup
page 48

Mushroom Brioche
page 88
Cashew Sauce
page 153
Paprika Rice
page 100
Brussels Sprouts with Chestnuts
see overleaf
Glazed Carrots
see overleaf
Green Salad with Vinaigrette
pages 144, 149

Rich Fruit Pudding
page 158
Brandy Butter

Persimmon and Claret Water Ice
page 163

Rich Fruit Cake
page 167
Mince Pies
page 173

PREPARATION IN ADVANCE
★ **Mushroom filling for brioche:** make and freeze, *or* make and refrigerate the day before.
★ **Cashew sauce:** freeze *or* make the day before and refrigerate.
Vinaigrette: make and store in a screwtop jar in the refrigerator.
★ **Rich fruit pudding:** prepare the pudding, put it into a bowl and cover in readiness to cook. Cook and freeze *or* refrigerate, uncooked, for 1-2 days.

★ **Persimmon ice:** make and freeze.

Rich fruit cake: make well in advance, wrap in foil and store in an airtight tin.

★ **Mince pies:** make and freeze *or* store in an airtight tin 1-2 days in advance.

EVENING BEFORE

Mushroom brioche: prepare the dough, put in a bowl, cover and leave overnight in a cold place.

Paprika rice: prepare and cook the rice and refrigerate. If frozen take the pudding and brioche filling out of the freezer to thaw.

Put the **chestnuts** to soak in water overnight.

ON THE DAY

Thaw the cashew sauce and mince pies if frozen. Remove pudding from refrigerator if not frozen.

Make the **soup.**

Wash and prepare the **salad** ingredients, wrap in a tea towel and keep in refrigerator.

Take the rice out of refrigerator. Prepare **sprouts** and **carrots.**

Two hours before serving have water boiling in the steamer and put the **pudding** in to steam.

One hour before serving preheat the oven to gas mark 6, 200°C (400°F). Reheat the filling and assemble the **brioche.** Bake and when cooked set aside to cool slightly before serving.

Cook the **chestnuts** for 40 minutes and keep warm.

Thirty minutes before serving put the **rice** in a greased ovenproof dish, cover tightly with foil and heat through in the oven (or reheat in a steamer).

Take **persimmon ice** out of the freezer, scoop into individual bowls and put in refrigerator.

Gently reheat the soup and cashew sauce.

Steam the **carrots** for 15-20 minutes, season, toss in butter and keep warm in serving dish.

Steam **sprouts** for 6-10 minutes. Toss with **chestnuts,** a little butter and seasonings and keep them warm.

Toss salad in dressing.

Warm the mince pies a little.

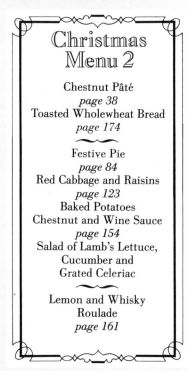

Christmas Menu 2

Chestnut Pâté
page 38
Toasted Wholewheat Bread
page 174

~~~

Festive Pie
page 84
Red Cabbage and Raisins
page 123
Baked Potatoes
Chestnut and Wine Sauce
page 154
Salad of Lamb's Lettuce,
Cucumber and
Grated Celeriac

~~~

Lemon and Whisky
Roulade
page 161

PREPARATION IN ADVANCE

★ **Chestnut pâté:** make and freeze *or* make a day in advance and refrigerate.

★ **Festive pie:** make the pastry and freeze *or* refrigerate (it will keep for 2-3 days).

★ **Red cabbage and raisins:** make and freeze *or* make 1-2 days in advance and refrigerate.

★ **Bread:** bake and freeze *or* refrigerate 1-2 days in advance.

★ **Lemon roulade:** make, decorate

and freeze *or* make the sponge the day before, roll it up and when cool keep in a airtight container.

EVENING BEFORE

Pâté: thaw if frozen

Festive pie: make filling and refrigerate.

Red cabbage: thaw if frozen.

Sauce for potatoes: make and refrigerate.

ON THE DAY

Assemble **pie** but do not bake. Defrost the roulade well in advance *or* if it is not frozen assemble it.

One hour before serving prepare the **salad** and refrigerate.

Gently heat the red cabbage.

Preheat the oven to gas mark 7, 220°C (425°F) and put potatoes and pie in to bake, potatoes at the top, pie at the bottom.

Gently reheat the sauce.

Thanksgiving Menu

Pumpkin Soup
page 56
Cornbread
page 179

~~~

Raised Pie
page 89
Tomato and Orange Sauce
page 154
Jacket Potatoes
page 217
Chicory, Orange and
Watercress Salad
page 144
Spinach, Apple and
Cauliflower Salad
page 142

~~~

Spiced Cranberry Soufflé
page 160

This is practicable only if you have a really large oven (or a double oven) or can share the preparation with a friend, as the pumpkin takes up rather a lot of space.

PREPARATION IN ADVANCE
★ **Filling for raised pie:** make and freeze *or* refrigerate for up to 3 days.
★ **Tomato and orange sauce:** make and freeze *or* refrigerate for 3-4 days.
★ **Cornbread:** make and freeze *or* make a day in advance and either keep chilled *or* wrap well and keep in an airtight container.

EVENING BEFORE
Pumpkin soup: scoop out the filling and make the soup. Refrigerate. Wrap the shell carefully in polythene film and keep cool.
Thaw pie filling, sauce and bread, if frozen.

ON THE DAY
Make **cranberry soufflé** and chill.
Prepare ingredients for **salads.**
Assemble and chill.
Make pastry for the **pie** and assemble.
An hour and a half before serving preheat the oven to gas mark 6, 200°C (400°F) and put in the pie.
Put in the **potatoes** to bake at the bottom of the oven.
Forty-five minutes before serving put the pumpkin shell with the soup in the oven.
Make the **sauce** for the soufflé.
With ten minutes to go warm the cornbread.
Gently reheat the tomato and orange sauce.

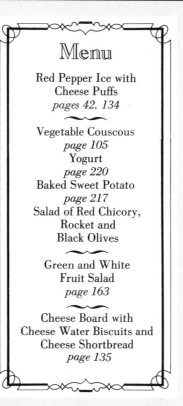

Menu

Red Pepper Ice with
Cheese Puffs
pages 42, 134

Vegetable Couscous
page 105
Yogurt
page 220
Baked Sweet Potato
page 217
Salad of Red Chicory,
Rocket and
Black Olives

Green and White
Fruit Salad
page 163

Cheese Board with
Cheese Water Biscuits and
Cheese Shortbread
page 135

PREPARATION IN ADVANCE
★ **Red pepper ice.**
★ **Water biscuits** and **Shortbread:** if not freezing, both will keep for 4-5 days in an airtight tin.
Vinaigrette: if you have none ready, make extra and keep it chilled.

ON THE DAY
Thaw biscuits and shortbread if necessary.
Prepare all vegetables for the **couscous** and the **green salad,** and the fruit for the **fruit salad.**
Make the **cheese puffs.**
They do not need a filling.
About one and a half hours before serving preheat the oven to gas mark 6, 200°C (400°F).
Put the **sweet potato** in to bake.
Make the **couscous.**
Assemble **chicory salad** and **fruit salad.**

Twenty minutes before serving scoop out red pepper ice into individual bowls and put in the refrigerator.

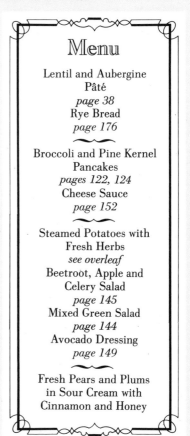

Menu

Lentil and Aubergine
Pâté
page 38
Rye Bread
page 176

Broccoli and Pine Kernel
Pancakes
pages 122, 124
Cheese Sauce
page 152

Steamed Potatoes with
Fresh Herbs
see overleaf
Beetroot, Apple and
Celery Salad
page 145
Mixed Green Salad
page 144
Avocado Dressing
page 149

Fresh Pears and Plums
in Sour Cream with
Cinnamon and Honey

PREPARATION IN ADVANCE
★ **Lentils:** cook and freeze *or* refrigerate for 1-2 days.
★ **Rye bread:** make and freeze *or* make 1-2 days in advance and store or chill.
★ **Pancakes:** make both pancakes and filling. If making the day before, chill pancakes and filling separately; if freezing, assemble and freeze.

EVENING BEFORE
Pâté: thaw lentils if frozen. Make pâté and refrigerate.
Cheese sauce: make and refrigerate.
Avocado dressing: make and chill.

ON THE DAY
Thaw out bread and pancakes if frozen; bring pâté to room temperature.
Prepare all vegetables for **salads** and fruit for **sweet;** chop **herbs** for potatoes.
Forty-five minutes before serving preheat the oven to gas mark 6, 200°C (400°F). Put in the pancakes, tightly covered.
Put the **potatoes** on to steam.
Assemble the **salads** and **sweet.**
Reheat the cheese sauce.
When the potatoes are ready, put them in a heated serving dish and keep warm.
Just before serving the potatoes, sprinkle with the chopped herbs.

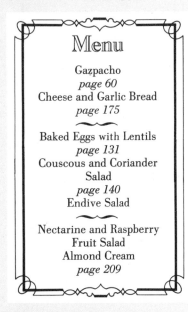

Menu

Gazpacho
page 60
Cheese and Garlic Bread
page 175

Baked Eggs with Lentils
page 131
Couscous and Coriander
Salad
page 140
Endive Salad

Nectarine and Raspberry
Fruit Salad
Almond Cream
page 209

PREPARATION IN ADVANCE
★ **Gazpacho:** make and freeze, *or* keep chilled for 1-2 days.

Cheese and garlic bread: make 1-2 days in advance and keep chilled.
★ **Chick peas (for couscous salad):** if not frozen soak overnight and cook.
★ **Almond cream:** make and freeze *or* keep chilled for 3-4 days.

EVENING BEFORE
Couscous salad: thaw chick peas if frozen, cook couscous and assemble salad. Chill.
Cook **lentils** for main course.
Vinaigrette: make and chill.

ON THE DAY
Thaw gazpacho, bread and almond cream if necessary.
Not more than 2 hours before serving, prepare the **endives** and mix the **raspberries and nectarines.**
Prepare the **baked eggs and lentils** and bake at gas mark 4, 180°C (350°F) for 20 minutes.
Toss the endives in the vinaigrette.

Menu

Strawberry and Hibiscus
Soup
page 62
Oatcakes
page 173

Blue Cheese and
Onion Quiche
page 130
Paprika Pasta Salad
page 142
Coleslaw with Fennel
in Mayonnaise
page 147

Prune and Brandy Mousse
page 161

PREPARATION IN ADVANCE
Soup: make and keep in refrigerator (it will keep for 3-4 days).
★ **Oatcakes:** make and freeze *or* store in an airtight tin.
★ **Pastry base for quiche:** make and bake blind (see page 92) and freeze, *or* prepare the day before and refrigerate.
Mayonnaise: make and keep in the refrigerator (it will keep for 3-4 days).
★ **Prunes:** soak, cook and purée. Freeze *or* keep in the refrigerator (4-5 days).

EVENING BEFORE
Prune Mousse: make the mousse and spoon into individual glasses. Keep chilled.

ON THE DAY
Take the oatcakes and pastry base out of the freezer well in advance to thaw.
Toast **almonds** for soup garnish.
Cook the **pasta,** drain and cool.
Toss pasta in dressing and set aside in a cool place.
Prepare the vegetables for the **coleslaw,** toss with the mayonnaise, put in a bowl and refrigerate.
Make the filling and assemble the **quiche.**
Forty-five minutes before serving preheat the oven to gas mark 6, 200°C (400°F) and put in the quiche. Set aside after cooking to cool slightly.
Ten minutes before serving reheat the **soup** just enough to warm it slightly.

Menu

Avgolemono with
Cheese Water Biscuits
pages 57, 135

Cauliflower Moussaka
page 72
Jacket Potatoes
page 217
Lentil and Mint Salad
in Yogurt
page 141
Celeriac and Courgette
Salad in Tahini and
Orange Dressing
page 145

Apricot Slice
page 172

Goat's Cheese with Celery

PREPARATION IN ADVANCE
Cheese water biscuits: make and store in an airtight container up to a week before.
Lentil salad: cook the lentils and refrigerate 1-2 days in advance.
★ **Apricot slice:** make and freeze *or* store in an airtight container for 2-3 days.

EVENING BEFORE
Avgolemono: make stages 1 and 2 of the recipe then strain and refrigerate.
Lentil salad: prepare, assemble and refrigerate.
Apricot slice: thaw if frozen.

ON THE DAY
Prepare, assemble and refrigerate the **celeriac and courgette salad.**
Prepare and assemble the **moussaka.**

Make the **tahini and orange dressing** and mix with the salad not too far in advance.

One and a quarter hours before serving preheat the oven to gas mark 5, 190°C (375°F) and put in the **potatoes.**
Thirty minutes before serving put the moussaka in the oven.
Fifteen minutes before serving finish making the **soup.**

Menu

Crudités with Caper and
Olive Dip
page 42

Mexican Croustade
page 94
Rice with
Red Pepper Sauce
pages 107, 206
Leafy Green Salad
with Vinaigrette
pages 144, 149

Salad of Fresh Figs
and Melon
Brownies
page 170

PREPARATION IN ADVANCE
Caper and olive dip: prepare and refrigerate 1-2 days in advance.
★ **Red kidney beans for croustade:** prepare and freeze *or* cook 2-3 days in advance and refrigerate.
★ **Brownies:** make and freeze *or* store in an airtight container for 2-3 days.
Vinaigrette: prepare and store in a screwtop jar in the refrigerator.

EVENING BEFORE
Croustade: make the crust and keep in an airtight tin or in the refrigerator.
Red pepper sauce: make and refrigerate.

ON THE DAY
Thaw **beans** and **brownies** if frozen.
Prepare the **fruit salad.**
Prepare the **green salad** but do not dress it until the last minute. Keep both salads chilled.
Cook and mash the **sweet potatoes** and assemble the croustade.
Take the caper and olive dip out of the refrigerator and leave to warm to room temperature.
Prepare the **crudités** and keep chilled.
Cook the **rice** and keep hot.
Thirty minutes before serving, preheat the oven to gas mark 5, 190°C (375°F). Cover the croustade lightly with foil and put in the oven to heat through. Gently reheat the red pepper sauce.

Menu

Carrot and Coriander Soup
with Lemon Croûtes
page 51

Baked Cabbage with
Chestnuts
page 66
Celery and Dill Sauce
page 155
Baked Onions
page 217
Spinach, Apple and
Potato Salad
page 142

Millet Pudding with
Apricots
page 157

PREPARATION IN ADVANCE
Chestnuts: soak and cook.

EVENING BEFORE
Carrot Soup: make and refrigerate.

Apricots: soak and cook; refrigerate.

ON THE DAY
Assemble the **cabbage.**
Make the **dill sauce.**
Lightly cook the **potato** and **spinach** and leave to get cold.
Assemble the **salad** and toss in its dressing.
Two hours before serving prepare the **millet pudding.** Preheat the oven to gas mark 4, 180°C (350°F) and bake the pudding.
One hour before serving put in the cabbage and **onions.**
Prepare the **lemon croûtes** for the soup.
Gently reheat the dill sauce and the apricots.
Reheat the soup and garnish just before serving.

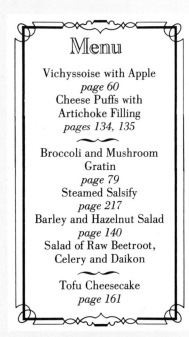

Menu

Vichyssoise with Apple
page 60
Cheese Puffs with
Artichoke Filling
pages 134, 135

Broccoli and Mushroom
Gratin
page 79
Steamed Salsify
page 217
Barley and Hazelnut Salad
page 140
Salad of Raw Beetroot,
Celery and Daikon

Tofu Cheesecake
page 161

PREPARATION IN ADVANCE
Barley salad: cook barley and refrigerate 2-3 days in advance.
★ **Vichyssoise:** freeze *or* make and refrigerate 1-2 days ahead.

★ **Tofu cheesecake:** freeze *or* make and refrigerate 1-2 days in advance.

EVENING BEFORE
Cheese puffs: make the filling and refrigerate.
Beetroot salad: prepare, assemble and refrigerate.

ON THE DAY
Make the **cheese puffs.** Take the filling for the puffs out of the refrigerator.
Prepare, assemble and refrigerate the **barley salad.**
Prepare the **raw salad** but do not assemble until just before serving.
One hour before serving steam the **salsify.**
Prepare and assemble the **gratin.**
Forty-five minutes before serving preheat the oven to gas mark 6, 200°C (400°F) and bake gratin.
Fill the **cheese puffs.**

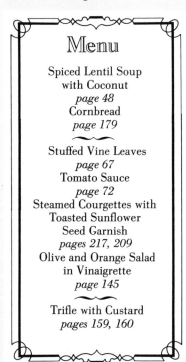

Menu

Spiced Lentil Soup
with Coconut
page 48
Cornbread
page 179

Stuffed Vine Leaves
page 67
Tomato Sauce
page 72
Steamed Courgettes with
Toasted Sunflower
Seed Garnish
pages 217, 209
Olive and Orange Salad
in Vinaigrette
page 145

Trifle with Custard
pages 159, 160

PREPARATION IN ADVANCE
★ **Soup:** make the soup up to the point of adding the coconut milk. Freeze for up to 2 weeks *or* keep in the refrigerator for up to 2 days.
★ **Cornbread:** make and freeze *or* make a day ahead and either keep chilled *or* wrap well and keep in an airtight container.
★ **Tomato sauce:** make and freeze *or* keep it in the refrigerator for 3-4 days.
★ **Vinaigrette:** make and store in a screwtop bottle in the refrigerator.
★ **Trifle:** make and freeze *or* make the sponge the day before and keep in an airtight container.
★ **Custard:** make and freeze *or* keep chilled for 2 days.

EVENING BEFORE
Stuffed vine leaves: cook the filling and refrigerate.
Trifle and **Custard:** thaw and refrigerate if frozen *or* make and refrigerate.

ON THE DAY
Thaw the **soup** if frozen and finish making it.
Stuff the **vine leaves** and put in baking dish.
Thaw the tomato sauce and cornbread if frozen.
Toast the **sunflower seeds** (see page 209).
One hour before serving prepare and dress the **salad** and prepare the **courgettes.**
Forty-five minutes before serving preheat the oven to gas mark 4, 180°C (350°F) and bake the **vine leaves.**
Fifteen minutes before serving, heat the soup and the tomato sauce and warm the cornbread.
Lightly steam the **courgettes,** sprinkle with the sunflower seeds and keep warm.

WEEKEND ENTERTAINING

Whether you're having people to stay or just catering for yourself and the family, there's no need to spend the whole time in the kitchen in order to provide interesting and nutritionally balanced meals. If you haven't a freezer it would help if you had a little time during the previous week to make some of the basics such as bread, cakes and biscuits and some of the more substantial dishes such as soups or casseroles. Friday supper is simple but tasty and filling; Saturday lunch is fairly light, but there is a substantial tea which can be made in advance; Saturday supper offers a choice of main dishes; and Sunday lunch would appeal to many a meat-eater.

Friday

Supper
Gumbo
page 57

Lentil and Spinach Quiche
page 92
Mixed Grain Salad on
Lettuce
page 138
Green Salad with
Avocado Dressing
pages 144, 149

Fruit Crumble
page 219

Saturday

Breakfast
Fruit Compote
page 159
Yogurt
page 220
Heaven's Rolls
page 179

Lunch
Khichhari
page 104
Chicory, Orange and
Watercress Salad
page 144

Fresh Fruit and Nuts

Tea
Rosemary and Walnut
Scones
page 184
Parkin
page 166
Malted Fruit Loaf
page 184
Sunflower Crunch
page 167

Supper
Cream of Cauliflower and
Almond Soup
page 48

Mushroom-stuffed
Aubergines
page 64
Lasagne with Leeks
and Lentils
page 117
Steamed Cucumber
with Chives
page 217

Cheese Board with Cheese
Shortbread
page 135

Apricot Slice (as a flan)
page 172

Sunday

Breakfast
Fruit Juice
Granola Muffins
page 182
Muesli
page 206

Lunch
Cream of Broccoli Soup
page 49

Hazelnut and
Courgette Bake
page 73
Red Pepper Sauce
page 107
Lentil and Mint Salad
in Yogurt
page 141
Steamed Carrots with
Sesame Seeds
page 217

Peach and Claret
Water Ice
page 163

PREPARATION IN ADVANCE

★ **Heaven's rolls, granola muffins, malted fruit loaf** and any **bread** you will need: if not frozen, can be made 3-4 days in advance and stored in tins.

★ **Parkin, sunflower crunch, cheese shortbread** and **apricot slice** can also be made 2-3 days ahead if not frozen. **Crumble topping** can be made 3-4 days ahead and kept in a screwtop jar.

★ **Gumbo, khichhari** and **lasagne** can be made a day or two ahead if not frozen. One or two days in advance, cook and refrigerate: **grains** for salad, **fruit compote** and the **red pepper sauce.**

★ Make and freeze **peach water ice.** You can also freeze **lentil and spinach quiche, broccoli soup, stuffed aubergines, rosemary and walnut scones, hazelnut and courgette bake** and **red pepper sauce.**

THURSDAY
EVENING

Quiche: if not frozen, make the pastry base, bake blind and refrigerate.

FRIDAY
MORNING

Thaw gumbo and quiche for tonight if frozen, or finish preparing quiche.
Broccoli soup for Sunday: if not from freezer, make and refrigerate but do not garnish.
Grain salad: assemble and chill.
Green salad: prepare ingredients and chill but toss in dressing at the last moment.
Fruit crumble: assemble.

EVENING

One hour before serving supper preheat the oven to gas mark 4, 180°C (350°F) and put in the crumble.
Forty-five minutes before serving put the quiche in the oven. Let it cool slightly before serving.
Fifteen minutes before serving reheat the gumbo gently.

Thaw the heaven's rolls and khichhari for tomorrow, if frozen.

SATURDAY
MORNING

If frozen, defrost the stuffed aubergines, lasagne, scones, parkin, fruit loaf, sunflower crunch, cheese shortbread and apricot slice.
Make the **scones** if not frozen.
Cauliflower soup: make and chill.
Lentil and mint salad: make and chill.

MIDDAY

Chicory, orange and watercress salad: prepare and refrigerate.
For dinner: prepare and stuff the **aubergines** if not frozen.

EVENING

Thirty minutes before dinner preheat the oven to gas mark 4, 180°C (350°F) and put in the aubergines and lasagne to bake and/or heat through.
Steam the **cucumber** and sprinkle with the chives.
Remember to thaw the granola muffins for Sunday breakfast and the broccoli soup, hazelnut and courgette bake and red pepper sauce for lunch, if frozen.

SUNDAY

If not frozen, prepare the **hazelnut and courgette bake.**
Forty minutes before lunch preheat the oven to gas mark 4, 180°C (350°F) and put in the dish to bake or heat through.
Prepare and steam the **carrots.**
Reheat the red pepper sauce.
Reheat the soup: steam the **broccoli florets** and add to the soup with the cream.
Take the water ice out of the freezer when the soup is served.

MEALS FOR A WEEK

Planning ahead a week at a time is sensible for the busy family cook to minimize the work and time spent in the kitchen. In these sample menus, as far as possible, the preparation for the day's meals is done the night before—it has not been assumed that the cook can spend the entire day in the kitchen. All the weekday lunch menus can be quickly prepared and are adaptable as packed lunches to take to work or school.

This sort of family cooking relies to a large extent on dishes that can be frozen or made in advance, and that are versatile even if left over—for example, grains make good bases for salads or croquettes; pasta can be added to salads or soups; beans, peas or lentils can be used for all of these or, mashed up, as sandwich spreads or refried beans. Although a freezer is a real asset, the preparation notes here do not assume that you will automatically have one.

If you do have a freezer, it makes sense to cook double batches of those dishes that can be frozen, and do double quantities of grains and beans for use as suggested above. Other ways to take advantage of a freezer include the following:
★ grate Cheddar cheese in quantity and freeze in 100 g (4 oz) packs for quick toppings, fillings and sauces;
★ make crumble topping in quantity and freeze for use in both savoury dishes and puddings;
★ purée fruit in season and freeze for ices, puddings and sauces;
★ keep a stock of bread, rolls, cakes and biscuits; cooked beans and

grains; croquettes and other made-up dishes; stocks, soups and sauces.

The sample menus suggested here are balanced, nutritious and tasty. They include a cross-section of nutrients: *grains* (whether whole, flaked, in bread, puddings or cakes): wheat, rye, rice, buckwheat, millet, oats and corn; *beans:* lima, red kidney and aduki; split peas and chick peas; *nuts and seeds:* walnuts, almonds, cashews, hazelnuts, sunflower and pumpkin seeds. Each day includes a salad and/or steamed or stir-fried vegetables, and fresh or dried fruit.

As an alternative to the cooked meals suggested here, a quickly prepared and nutritious offering could be chunks of tofu, cheese and nuts (the best of convenience foods), perhaps served with a simple salad and fresh fruit. A baked potato is another useful and filling standby.

SUNDAY
EVENING
★ Thaw **croquettes** *or* make and chill overnight.
★ Thaw bread or muffins if frozen. Put **muesli** to soak; also **dried fruit** for compote.
Make **granola** if not on hand.

MONDAY
MORNING
Cook **muffins** if not from freezer. Make **compote.**
★ Take double quantities lima beans and red kidney beans from freezer *or* put to soak (separately).

MIDDAY
Make **soda bread** if no bread already in freezer.

EVENING
Cook **red kidney beans** and **lima beans** separately. Use half the lima beans for the casserole and mix the rest with half the red kidney beans and the marinade for Tuesday's **many bean salad.** Refrigerate; freeze the rest of the kidney beans until Friday.
Make **broccoli and walnut bake.**
Steam double quantity **green beans;** use half tonight, cool and

Breakfast
(for all days)

Fruit/Fruit Juice

Fruit Compote
page 159
Muesli/Granola/
Hot Cereal
pages 182, 206

Bread/Muffins
pages 174 to 184

Yogurt

Tea/Coffee/Herb Teas

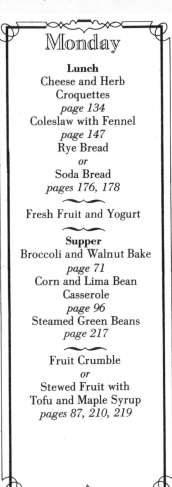

Monday

Lunch
Cheese and Herb
Croquettes
page 134
Coleslaw with Fennel
page 147
Rye Bread
or
Soda Bread
pages 176, 178

Fresh Fruit and Yogurt

Supper
Broccoli and Walnut Bake
page 71
Corn and Lima Bean
Casserole
page 96
Steamed Green Beans
page 217

Fruit Crumble
or
Stewed Fruit with
Tofu and Maple Syrup
pages 87, 210, 219

Tuesday

Lunch
Onion Soup
page 53

Wholewheat Sandwiches
with Tahini and Cucumber
or with
Peanut Butter and Cress
or
Pancakes with Beetroot
and Chive Filling
pages 122, 123
Many Bean Salad
page 142

Melon with Sunflower
and Pumpkin Seeds

Supper
Crudités with Almond Dip
pages 42, 43

Cauliflower Moussaka
page 72
Rice
page 206
Green Salad
page 144

Tofu Cheesecake
page 161

refrigerate other half for Tuesday's bean salad.

Prepare **crumble** or **stewed fruit**.
Make **onion soup** for Tuesday if not from freezer.

TUESDAY
MORNING
★ Thaw **onion soup** if frozen.
★ Thaw **pancakes** if frozen.
★ Thaw double batch of **chick peas** or put to soak.
★ Thaw **moussaka** if frozen.
Make **almond dip** and **tofu cheesecake**.

MIDDAY
Reheat soup and **pancakes** or make **pancakes** fresh.
Assemble **bean salad**.

EVENING
Make **moussaka** if not frozen.
Cook **chick peas** for Wednesday's **salad** and Thursday's **hummus**.

WEDNESDAY
MORNING
★ Thaw **shortbread** for lunch, **soup**, **bread** and **buckwheat** for supper if frozen.
Bake **bread** and make **shortbread** if not frozen.

MIDDAY
Cook **potatoes** and **spinach** for salad.
Make **jelly** and leave to set.

EVENING
If not frozen, cook **soup** and **buckwheat**.
Prepare **vegetables** to be **stir-fried**.
Assemble **buckwheat salad**.
★ Make **carob cake** for tomorrow or thaw overnight if frozen.

THURSDAY
MIDDAY
Make **hummus** and keep extra for a sandwich spread.

Wednesday

Lunch
Salad of Chick Peas
and Tomatoes
Spinach, Apple and
Potato Salad
page 142
Cheese Shortbread
page 135

~

Strained Yogurt with
Honey and Nuts

~

Supper
Miso Julienne
page 53
Wholewheat Bread with
Cheese and Onion
page 176

~

Stir-fried Vegetables
with Tofu
page 80
Marinaded Buckwheat
Salad
page 140

~

Fruit Jelly with Mangoes
page 158

Thursday

Lunch
Hummus with Pitta
Bread
page 43

~

Frittata Verde
page 130
Salad of Tomato,
Cucumber and Grapefruit

~

Carob Cake
page 166

Supper
Carrot and Coriander Soup
page 51

~

Macaroni with Yogurt and
French Beans
page 118
Steamed Courgettes
page 217

~

Peaches in White Wine

Friday

Lunch
Fresh Pea Soup with Mint
page 59

~

Rye Sandwich with
Mashed Kidney Bean,
Garlic and Tahini Filling
or
Pizza with Tomato
and Onion
page 120
Chicory, Orange and
Watercress Salad
page 144

~

Cheese Board

Supper
Aduki Beans in Wine
page 97
Steamed Carrots
and Celery
page 217
Green Salad
page 144

~

Millet Pudding with
Apricots
page 157

Make the **frittata**—instead of green herbs you could use any vegetables left from yesterday: tomato, spinach or potato, with onion.

★ Thaw **carrot and coriander soup** for supper if frozen. Marinade **peaches** (skinned if fresh—see page 218—or dried) in **white wine** for supper.

EVENING
If not from freezer, cook **carrot and coriander soup**. Make **macaroni with beans**. Steam **courgettes**.

★ Thaw **kidney beans** for sandwiches tomorrow.

FRIDAY
MORNING
★ Thaw **filling** for tomorrow's tortillas and double quantity **aduki beans** or put **beans** to soak, including those for **tortilla filling**.
★ Thaw **fresh pea soup** and **pizza** (or **pizza base**) if frozen.

MIDDAY
Make **fresh pea soup** if not from freezer.
Make **pizza** if not frozen. (If you made extra tomato sauce for

the moussaka on Tuesday, use this for the pizza.)

EVENING
Cook the **aduki beans in wine**. Make **millet pudding with apricots**. Steam **carrots** and **celery**. For tomorrow: make **brown sauce** and cook **beans** for **tortillas** if not from freezer.

SATURDAY
MORNING
★ Thaw (or make) for lunch: **croquettes; oaten rolls; banana cake**.
★ Thaw **brown sauce** if frozen.
★ Thaw **tofu dip** and **tortillas** (filled or unfilled) for supper.

EVENING
Make **tofu dip** if not from freezer; also **tortillas** and/or **filling** if not frozen.
★ Thaw/make **cashew cream**. Soak **prunes** for Sunday lunch.
★ Thaw **kasha ring** or put buckwheat to soak overnight.
★ Thaw **mustard sauce** if frozen.

SUNDAY
MORNING
★ Thaw **flageolet soup** if frozen or put **flageolets** to soak.
Make **gnocchi** and refrigerate.
Make **prune mousse** and chill.

MIDDAY
Make **kasha ring** and **sauce** if not from freezer.
★ Thaw **cornbread** if frozen.

EVENING
Make **flageolet soup** and **cornbread** if not from freezer. Steam **broccoli**.

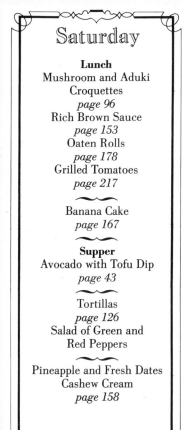

Saturday

Lunch
Mushroom and Aduki
Croquettes
page 96
Rich Brown Sauce
page 153
Oaten Rolls
page 178
Grilled Tomatoes
page 217

Banana Cake
page 167

Supper
Avocado with Tofu Dip
page 43

Tortillas
page 126
Salad of Green and
Red Peppers

Pineapple and Fresh Dates
Cashew Cream
page 158

Sunday

Lunch
Spinach Gnocchi
page 37

Kasha Ring with
Mustard Sauce
page 110
Roast Parsnips
page 217
Olive and Orange Salad
page 145

Prune and Brandy Mousse
page 161

Supper
Flageolet Soup with Juniper
page 46
Cornbread
page 179

Poached Eggs
Steamed Broccoli
pages 217

Fresh Fruit
Cheese Board

GRAINS

Wheat, rice, barley, oats, millet, rye and maize (corn) are the world's major food grains or cereals, and all belong to the immense family of grasses. The other grain of culinary interest, buckwheat, is the seed not of a grass but of a herbaceous plant.

For thousands of years cereals have been the staple foods that have kept people alive: wheat, rye, barley and oats in temperate climates; rice, maize and millet in the tropics and subtropics. Most of the world's populations still eat the staple that grows in their backyard, but in the affluent countries meat has pushed cereals out of their primary position, and grains have been refined and processed to the point where all the fibre and many of the nutrients have been lost, along with two other important ingredients: taste and texture.

Unrefined cereals (whole grains) still contain the germ, an important source of oils, proteins and minerals, and bran, a source of fibre. They may be bought whole or cracked, flaked, parboiled, steamed or toasted, all of which help to shorten cooking time and make them easier to digest.

Wheat

The most universally grown and the most important of all food grains, wheat is available in various forms from the whole berry to flour, and wheat flour is used more than any other for making bread, cakes, pastry and pasta. The whole grain or berry is by far the most nutrititious form. It retains its outer covering, or bran, which contains valuable vitamins, minerals and fat as well as fibre, and the germ, which is only 2 per cent of the grain but contains the bulk of the nutrients. The rest of the grain, some 70 per cent, is known as the endosperm and consists mainly of starch.

Flour is the form in which wheat is most easily available. Most of today's flour is produced by roller-milling, a process that involves high temperatures and consequent loss of vitamins and flavour. For this reason, stone-ground flour is generally considered preferable, although it is more expensive and slightly coarser.

Bread is the end product of most of the world's flour. Leavened bread is made mainly from wheat, the only grain high in gluten, a protein that stretches to form an impermeable skin over the thousands of bubbles of gas formed when yeast ferments. Bread made with strong or hard flour has a lighter consistency than bread made with soft flour. Whole-wheat flour gives a dense loaf, unbleached white flour one with a light texture and some percentage of the nutrients still intact. Wheatmeal flour is often considered a good compromise.

YEAST Fresh yeast, specified in all the recipes in this book, is usually the easiest for the beginner to work with. Try to buy it in one piece: it should be a pale beige colour, look smooth and have a pleasant, fresh smell. Yeast that smells stale or that is crumbly and beginning to dry out will not work as well as fresh yeast. Store it wrapped up, in the refrigerator, for up to 10 days (or freeze it—small pieces, separately wrapped, are convenient; to revive it, put it in tepid water for 15 minutes). It will also keep if submerged in cold water.

Dried yeast is usually sold as granules. It gives the same results as fresh yeast if used properly. Use only a third to a half as much as fresh yeast. To reactivate dried yeast, sprinkle it into a cup of hot water with a little sugar, stir well and leave in a warm place for 10-15 minutes. It will keep for up to a year if stored in airtight containers in a cool, dry place.

Rice

Rice can be divided into two main categories, long-grain and short-grain. Properly cooked long-grain rice has dry, separate grains, usually associated with curries or pilafs. Short-grain rice has a softer texture and is stickier when cooked. Brown (whole grain) rice has a chewy texture and nutty flavour that make white rice seem bland, stripped as it is of the outer layers and germ, and with them most of the nutrients.

Rice can also be found in the form of flakes and flour; the flour has a light consistency and small quantities are good in bread and cakes. The bran and germ removed when rice is milled are sold as rice polish, an excellent source of vitamin B as well as minerals and protein. Small quantities can be added to cakes, biscuits or crumble toppings.

Wild rice is not a rice at all, although it is a member of the grass family. It is often served on its own so as not to submerge its characteristic delicate, subtle flavour, a little like that of artichokes. It is also good mixed with brown rice.

Corn (maize)

This originated in Central America, where it was the staple grain of the Incas, Mayas and Aztecs. Its popularity has spread not only to North America but to Europe, where it is used for such national dishes as polenta in Italy and mamaliga in Rumania. Unlike other whole grains it is not usually dried but is eaten fresh. There are three main varieties: dent corn, which supplies commercial cornmeal; sweet corn, or corn on the cob, the form in which we know it as a fresh vegetable; and popcorn.

Cornmeal is available finely or coarsely ground. Stone-ground or water-ground is best, as the germ is not removed. It is too low in gluten to make leavened bread, but mixes well with wheat to give muffins and flat breakfast breads a distinctive taste and colour. Other important products of corn are cooking oil (see page 219) and corn syrup, used for sweetening (see page 212).

Barley

The whole grain is known as pot barley. Pearl barley has been polished and has lost most of the bran, germ and vitamin B. Low in gluten, barley flour will not make leavened bread (unless mixed with wheat flour), but the greyish flat bread made from it is sweet-tasting and delicious. Barley syrup, sometimes known as malt extract, is used as a sweetening agent.

Oats

Still a popular food in Scotland, northern England and Ireland, oats probably originated in northern Europe. They are made into oatcakes and parkin, or used for soups, as well as for the traditional porridge. They are higher in protein and fats than other grains and rich in B vitamins and iron.

Oats are most often found as flakes or meals, which cook quickly. Flakes can be used for porridge, granola, muesli and crumble toppings as well as for oatcakes, to which they add a crunchy texture. Oatmeal is used for porridge and oatcakes and as a crunchy coating for croquettes. It is often mixed with wheat flour to improve the taste of bread.

Rye

The groats can be treated like rice or wheat berries, or cracked to produce grits or flakes, which cook more quickly. Rye is a good source of B vitamins, especially B_2 and B_3 and the minerals potassium and magnesium. It also contains rutin, once known as vitamin P, which is good for circulatory complaints.

Millet

Richer than other grains nutritionally, millet is a particularly good source of iron and the B vitamins. Its delicate flavour can seem bland at first, but it amalgamates well with other flavours and makes an excellent alternative to rice in risottos or milk puddings.

Buckwheat

This is not a cereal grain at all but the seed of a herbaceous plant related to dock and rhubarb. It is high in iron and other minerals and in all the B vitamins, as well as containing rutin. Kasha, the porridge-like cooked cereal popular in Russia, is usually made from roasted buckwheat.

BUYING

Most healthfood and wholefood shops sell grains in all their forms from berries to flour, bread and pasta. Choose a shop where you can rely on the stock being fresh. Supermarkets often have a range, if not such a wide one. You may find "brown" flour and/or bread that is (or is made from) white flour treated with caramel or other colouring: it may have the nutrients that were milled out of it added back as synthetic vitamins and minerals. Do, therefore, read the labels and make sure you are getting the whole grain or its product, or that you know exactly what proportion of it you are buying. Also, if you care about organically grown food, check where the flour comes from. Most of the world's bread wheat comes from North America and is not organically grown. Organically grown flour is likely to be soft, giving a dense-textured but well-flavoured loaf.

STORING

Whole grains keep indefinitely in cool dry conditions in an airtight container, but the longer they are stored the longer they take to cook. Flakes and flours do not keep so long and are best used within 3-6 months as the oil contained in the germ eventually goes rancid, particularly in oats; wheatgerm itself should be used within 2-3 weeks.

COOKING

To cook whole grains, first rinse them to remove surface dust. Choose a pan with a close-fitting lid, or use a pressure cooker. Rub a little oil around the pan to prevent the grains from sticking—this will also make the pan easier to clean. One cup—250 ml (8 fl oz)—is enough for 2-3 people.

Put some water in the pan (see the table below for quantities) and bring to the boil. Put in the grains, bring to the boil again, then cover the pan and simmer very gently until the water is absorbed. Do not stir unnecessarily as this tends to make the grains sticky, and do not add salt until just before the end of the cooking time.

There are simple ways to vary the basic method. Sauté the grain lightly in a little oil or shoyu before adding boiling water (this is good with barley, buckwheat and millet in particular); add spices and vegetables for flavour, particularly saffron, ginger, coriander, garlic or onions. Mix different grains—rice with wheat or barley—for more texture and taste.

The softer grains—millet, rice and buckwheat—make excellent croquettes, Rice, barley and millet are good for sweet puddings, and buckwheat, wheat and oats for substantial breakfast porridges. Cracked grains absorb water more easily and cook quickly. Bulgar wheat, which is steamed, cracked and toasted, needs soaking but no further cooking.

Flakes and meals are used in breakfast cereals (muesli or granola) and as versatile toppings for either sweet or savoury dishes. For a crumble topping try the topping for the winter hotpot on page 76. You can vary the proportions of flakes to flour. Substitute granola (see recipe on page 182) for the flakes if you want a sweet crumble.

Muesli is generally a combination of various flakes, mainly oats, with seeds, nuts and dried fruit. I prefer a version nearer to the original Bircher-Benner muesli, with more emphasis on fresh fruit. For one person, soak 2 tablespoons rolled oats in 30 ml (2 tablespoons) water for 1-2 hours (or overnight). Just before eating, stir in the juice of an orange, a tablespoon of ground almonds and a whole unpeeled apple, grated.

Leftover cooked grains make excellent salads when mixed with beans or vegetables, or they can be added to soups or casseroles. Cooked grain keeps for two days in the refrigerator and can be successfully frozen. To reheat, first thaw, either overnight in the refrigerator or for several hours (the exact time depends on how large a portion you are thawing) at room temperature. Turn into an oiled dish, cover with foil and heat in a moderate oven (gas mark 4, 180°C, 350°F) for 15-20 minutes.

PREPARATION AND COOKING TIMES FOR WHOLE GRAINS

TYPE OF GRAIN	PREPARATION BEFORE COOKING	AMOUNT OF LIQUID PER CUP OF GRAIN	AVERAGE COOKING TIME	PRESSURE COOKING
Wheat	soak overnight (8-12 hours)	4 cups	50-60 minutes	20 minutes
Rice long-grain short-grain	can be toasted or lightly fried	1¾-2 cups 1¾-2 cups	25-30 minutes 20-25 minutes	10 minutes 8-10 minutes
Wild rice		3 cups	50-60 minutes	20 minutes
Corn		plenty of water	5-10 minutes	
Barley	toast	4 cups	50-60 minutes	20 minutes
Oats	can be toasted	3 cups	30-35 minutes	12 minutes
Rye	soak overnight (8-12 hours)	3 cups	50-60 minutes	20 minutes
Millet	can be toasted or lightly fried	2½-3 cups	20 minutes	8 minutes
Buckwheat	toast or lightly fry	2-2½ cups	20 minutes	8 minutes

BEANS, PEAS AND LENTILS

Sometimes collectively known as legumes or pulses, these have the advantage that they are cheap to buy, readily available (although some of the less common ones may not be so easy to find) and keep well. Most tend to be bland in taste, but cooked in combination with other ingredients they have a capacity for amalgamating with them, especially with stronger flavours, and enhancing them: chick peas with tahini (sesame seed paste), lentils with spices, butter or haricot beans with onions, tomatoes, peppers. Cooked dishes generally improve on being left for several hours or overnight for the full development of flavour before reheating. They may not be the answer if you need to prepare a meal or a snack in a hurry, but they are ideal if you prefer to do the preparation beforehand.

One common objection to legumes is that they tend to cause wind. The best way to counter this is to accustom yourself to eating them gradually, making sure they are thoroughly cooked. Lentils and smaller beans are sometimes found to be more easily digestible.

BUYING AND STORING

It is becoming easier nowadays to find good quality dried beans and peas. Buy from somewhere with a good turnover: although they do keep well, if they have spent a year sitting on a shelf they will take a very long time to cook. Choose beans or peas that look plump, brightly coloured and unwrinkled. They are worth buying in bulk as they will keep in good condition for up to six months.

Keep up to 6 months (1 month if in glass jars).

All legumes keep best in cool, dry, dark conditions in airtight containers. If you have a fairly rapid turnover—say within a month—they can be kept in glass jars, as long as they are not exposed to full sun, which impairs flavour and nutrients.

PREPARATION

You do need to pick them over (lentils especially) for stones and grit and give them a rinse to wash off the surface dust. Lentils and split peas can then be cooked straight away, but beans and whole peas should be soaked before cooking. Use plenty of water, remembering that pulses absorb water and will swell up to between two and three times their original bulk. There is a quick method, which is the equivalent of an overnight soak: bring to the boil in plenty of water, boil for 3-5 minutes and leave to stand in the water for an hour.

COOKING

After soaking, drain and rinse again. Some vitamins will be lost in the soaking water, but this is not crucial. Put in a saucepan, cover with plenty of fresh water and bring to the boil. Skim off any scum. Do not salt the water: salt toughens the outer skin and cooking will take longer. Vegetables, herbs, spices or flavourings can be added: onions, garlic, carrots, other root vegetables, black peppercorns, ginger or chili peppers. The addition of anise, dill, fennel or caraway seeds—1 teaspoon for 225 g (8 oz) legumes—or a strip of the sea vegetable kombu (see page 212) helps digestion. After the preliminary boiling (see note on chart), turn the heat down until they just simmer and cover the pan, but not too tightly. If you add a little oil this will prevent the beans or peas boiling over and also give them a smoother texture. The cooking time depends on the kind of legume, how long it has been stored, and whether you want it for a salad or a purée: those for salads should be just tender, while those for a purée need longer cooking. Use the times given in the chart above as a guide, and test for tenderness by pressing lightly.

An alternative cooking method is in a pressure cooker (see the chart overleaf for times). It cuts the cooking time by about two-thirds, and there is no need to worry about fast boiling as this happens automatically. Don't cook more than about half a kilo (1 lb) at a time, or they may froth up and block the safety valve. Even a little overcooking may result in a purée, so use an ordinary saucepan if you are making, say, a bean salad, where the appearance is important.

SERVING AND KEEPING

All beans, peas and lentils can be used as a basis for casseroles and can be served as a simple side dish, perhaps as a purée: aduki beans, flageolets or mung beans have a subtle taste and are particularly suitable. Haricots, lima or butter beans and the other kidney beans (see illustration on page 12) are often cooked with spices, herbs and vegetables for a contrast of flavour. For croquettes, the most suitable are aduki beans, lentils, mung beans and black-eyed beans. All of them can also be used in soups, and this is the most common use for peas, both split and whole. Almost all beans and lentils are good eaten cold in salad, with the exception of broad beans and soya beans.

Once cooked, beans, peas and lentils keep well: several days in a covered container in the refrigerator, or they can be frozen—they retain their flavour excellently. Cool and open freeze them, then pack in rigid containers and label. For soups, a handful or two can be removed and put straight into the soup near the end of the cooking time. For salads, allow to thaw for about an hour at room temperature, or overnight in the refrigerator, then mix with the other vegetables or herbs and the dressing. Croquettes, cooked or uncooked, also freeze very successfully: shape into patties, open freeze on trays and pack in boxes or bags with waxed paper between them. Thaw overnight in the refrigerator or for two hours at room temperature.

The cooking liquid is well worth keeping. Any toxins will have been destroyed, and it is excellent for soups, stews and sauces, particularly if flavoured with vegetables or spices. It will keep for 4-5 days in the refrigerator, and can be frozen.

SOAKING AND COOKING CHART FOR BEANS, PEAS AND LENTILS

TYPE OF BEAN	RECOMMENDED SOAK OVERNIGHT	AVERAGE COOKING TIME	PRESSURE COOKING
Aduki beans	yes	45 minutes	15 minutes
Black-eyed beans	yes	45-50 minutes	15 minutes
Black beans	yes	50-60 minutes	20 minutes
Broad beans	yes	1½ hours	40 minutes
Butter or lima beans	yes	60-90 minutes	25-30 minutes
Cannellini	yes	45-50 minutes	15 minutes
Flageolets	yes	45-50 minutes	15 minutes
Ful medames	yes	60 minutes	20 minutes
Haricot beans	yes	50-60 minutes	20 minutes
Mung beans	yes	30-45 minutes	15 minutes
Pinto beans	yes	60-90 minutes	25-30 minutes
Red kidney beans	yes	45-50 minutes	15 minutes
Soya beans	yes	2-2½ hours*	45-50 minutes
Chick peas	yes	60-90 minutes	25-30 minutes
Whole green peas	yes	60-90 minutes	25-30 minutes
Split peas	no	40-45 minutes	—
Whole lentils	no	30-45 minutes	12-15 minutes
Split lentils	no	15-30 minutes	—

"Overnight" here means approximately 8-12 hours. All times given are only a rough guide, as cooking times can vary considerably depending on the age and origin of the crop. The first ten minutes' cooking of all except lentils and split peas should be done at a fast boil, uncovered, to destroy any toxic elements on the outer skin, except *soya beans which should boil hard for the first hour. Although lentils and split peas need not be soaked overnight, they will cook faster if they are first steeped in boiling water for 15-30 minutes. Drain before cooking them.

NUTS AND SEEDS

Botanically, nuts and seeds are the same: both have kernels containing the whole future plant in embryo and are a concentrated source of food.

A combination of mixed nuts and cereals with green vegetables makes a nutritionally adequate main course, and nuts give taste and texture to salads, cooked vegetables and grains. By themselves, or with sunflower or pumpkin seeds, they make a good snack. Watermelon and pomegranate seeds are also edible.

BUYING

It is better to buy nuts in their shells: this protects the kernels and keeps them fresh. If you do want them shelled, buy loose nuts, preferably whole, as these tend to be of better quality. Avoid nuts that have been coated in fat and salted. Seeds should always be bought whole.

STORING

Store in a cool place. Unshelled nuts will keep up to six months. Keep seeds and shelled nuts in an airtight container; whole, they will stay in good condition for up to three months, unless kept in a warm place, when their high fat content means they are liable to go rancid quickly. Split, chopped or ready-ground nuts will go stale more quickly still and should be eaten within 4-6 weeks.

PREPARATION

Nuts can be blanched to remove the dark skin; roasted or toasted to improve their flavour (although there is a certain amount of nutrient loss); ground, which also makes them easier to digest; or, in the case of coconut, grated. Seeds, especially sunflower and sesame, are also good toasted.

To blanch nuts, except for hazelnuts, put them in a bowl, cover with boiling water and leave for a few minutes or until they can be popped out of their skins when gently pressed. If you are not using the skinned nuts immediately, drop them in cold water to keep them white. Hazelnuts should be baked in the oven (or toasted under the grill) for 5 or 6 minutes. If they are then rubbed in a cloth, the fibrous skin will come away.

To roast nuts or seeds in the oven, spread them out in a single layer on a shallow tray or baking tin. Sprinkle with a very little oil. Put in a moderate oven for about 10 minutes, and shake the tin two or three times to turn them and ensure even browning. You can also fry them. Use a heavy pan and just enough oil to grease the bottom lightly. Shake or stir the nuts or seeds over gentle heat until evenly browned. If you are prepared to watch them carefully, they will toast under a hot grill in 2 or 3 minutes but must be turned before they burn.

To skin sweet chestnuts, slash each one with a sharp knife (take care, as the skins can be tough), drop them in boiling water and leave them for about 10 minutes, by which time both the outer and inner skins should come away. Dried chestnuts do not need shelling.

Nuts are easily ground: use a small grater, a nut mill or a liquidizer. A coffee mill, kept specially for the purpose, is ideal. Nuts tend to grind unevenly and it is easier to do a few at a time. Walnuts and Brazil nuts have a tendency to be greasy, and you may need to scrape around the sides of the mill once or twice.

COOKING

As well as being eaten raw, nuts and seeds are used in roasts, bakes, croquettes and casseroles, in cereal mixtures and crumble toppings. Peanut butter is the best known nut butter, but cashews, hazelnuts and almonds also make good spreads and dips. Blend them with a little oil and salt to taste. Alternatively, mix equal quantities of nuts and water with a little oil and salt and blend. Nut butters will keep in the refrigerator for 4-6 weeks if made with only oil, for 3-4 days if made with water. They can also be frozen.

Nut creams and milks are easy to make and can form the basis for sauces or substitutes for cream to serve with puddings or cakes. Almond milk can be made by blending together 1½ tablespoons blanched ground almonds, 175 ml (6 fl oz) water and 5 ml (1 tsp) honey. There is a recipe for cashew cream on page 158. Both will keep in the refrigerator for up to 3-4 days.

COCONUT CREAM To make 300 ml (½ pint) coconut cream, grate 75-100 g (3-4 oz) of the creamed coconut block, cover with boiling water and leave for half an hour (or put in a blender for half a minute). Stir well and strain before using. For coconut milk, use twice the amount of water. Season with a little salt and use with curries and other rice dishes.

DRIED FRUIT

It takes up to six pounds of tree fruit (or two pounds of grapes) to produce a pound of dried fruit so the vitamin, mineral and sugar content is highly concentrated. Dried fruit should not be reconstituted in liquids with extra sugar added.

Sulphur is often added to preserve colour and maintain water content, thus keeping the fruit plumper. It also prevents fermentation and decay, and helps retain vitamins A and C (although it destroys B vitamins). There is no evidence that this is harmful—sulphur, in small quantities, is an essential mineral. Where possible healthfood shops will stock fruits that have not undergone unnecessary chemical treatment.

BUYING AND STORING

Choose plump unblemished fruit. No fruit, sun-dried or otherwise, should be rock-hard. It will keep for up to a year in airtight containers, although it is best within six months. A piece of orange or lemon peel in the container helps to keep the fruit moist. Alternatively, dried fruit can be frozen, and will keep for up to a year. Reconstituted dried fruit will keep frozen for 2-3 months.

PREPARATION

Much fruit sold these days is already cleaned but it is still wise to rinse again under running water to remove any traces of preservative. Drain well. If it is for a cake mix, where the fruit may sink if damp, clean it by sieving with some flour.

Sieving currants with flour   *Plumping raisins*

To plump raisins, currants and sultanas, soak them in hot liquid—water, fruit juice or wine— for 5 minutes. Drain, pat dry and use at once. Plumped vine fruits give a juicy texture to cakes and puddings. To reconstitute tree fruits, cover with liquid and leave to soak for 8-12 hours. You may need to add more liquid. A quicker method is to put the fruit in a pan, cover it with liquid and bring it to the boil; simmer, covered, for 10-15 minutes and leave for an hour. It may be eaten at this stage or cooked until soft, whichever you prefer.

COOKING

Stew or cook the fruit for 30-40 minutes or until tender: use the soaking liquid, which now contains valuable nutrients, for cooking. It will keep for 3-4 days in the refrigerator.

Cooked fruit can be eaten hot as fruit compote, puréed for use as a sweet pastry filling or in cakes, or it can be added to breakfast cereals, salads, stuffings and savoury dishes such as curries.

Apples are unusual in that they do not lose vitamin C in the drying process. They are mostly used in fruit compotes.

Apricots are sold whole, halved, or in pieces. The pieces are cheaper and are good for purées and jams. Hunza apricots, from the Himalayas, are small, unsulphured and pale beige in colour. They are sold whole and unpitted: the stone can be cracked and the delicious kernel, tasting rather like an almond, extracted.

Bananas have an excellent flavour. Good mixed with dates and figs for rich fruit purées to use in sauces or cakes, they can also be baked in rum or deep-fried.

Dates should be plump and moist with thin skins. Cooking dates are compressed into blocks; break them up before use to check for stones, as it is not uncommon to find some have been left in. These dates make splendid fruit purées.

Figs are high in calcium and potassium as well as sugar. They can be stuffed: soak them first to reconstitute them and use a cottage cheese stuffing or one based on almonds—figs and almonds are a traditional combination.

Peaches and **nectarines,** usually available halved, are used in the same way as apricots.

Pears keep their distinctive slightly gritty texture when dried, and are a good addition to compotes.

Prunes (dried plums) are lower in sugar and calories than dates or figs. Ready-made prune purée can also be bought; this is popular in France, where it is used in confectionery, pastries and cakes.

Raisins, currants and **sultanas** are all dried grapes, widely used for fruit cakes and mincemeats. Australian sultanas are unsulphured and are sprayed with vegetable rather than mineral oil, so it is worth trying to find them. Lexia raisins from Australia are large, sticky and very sweet and are sold with the seeds removed. Another sweet variety, the Muscatel from Spain, is not chemically treated.

SEASONINGS AND FLAVOURINGS

Any well-stocked vegetarian store cupboard should contain a wide range of flavourings and seasonings, from spices and vinegars, seaweeds and syrups, to flavourings made from nuts and vegetables and the indispensable soya products.

Soya bean products

The soya bean, difficult to digest when whole, is easily assimilated when fermented and provides nutrients as well as flavourings. The best known fermented products are **shoyu, tamari** and **miso.** The soya sauce familiar to many non-vegetarians is too often a synthetic reproduction.

Miso is a living food rather in the same way that yogurt is, and contains bacteria and enzymes which are destroyed by boiling. It is therefore usually added as a flavouring at the end of cooking, often mixed with a little warm water so it dissolves easily. The most commonly available is mugi miso, a combination of soya and barley with a warm, mellow flavour. Hatcho miso, made from soya beans alone, is denser and more strongly flavoured, while genmai miso, made with rice, is lighter and sweeter.

Tamari, shoyu and miso all keep well but should not undergo sudden changes of temperature. Miso may develop a white mould: this is a natural yeast and can simply be mixed back in.

Rock salt, held by some to have the finest taste, and **sea salt** are preferable to refined table salt, which may have additives. Both can be used for cooking and at the table. **Salt substitutes** often consist of potassium salts. One of the most successful combinations of salt with other flavourings is **gomashio**, or sesame salt, whose nutty flavour complements many vegetable and grain dishes. It will keep for up to two weeks.

Both the strong **English mustard powder** and the gentler, more aromatic made-up **French mustard** have their place in the kitchen. With mustard powder, make up only as much as you are going to need at any one time.

Horseradish sauce can be bought, but does not compare in flavour with sauces made from the freshly grated root, as the aroma is very volatile. Dried horseradish is the best substitute.

Nuts and seeds provide useful flavourings, from peanut butter to tahini, a beige paste of similar consistency made from sesame seeds.

Dried mushrooms add rich natural flavouring and are popular in Japan and China. They keep well in an airtight container and are reconstituted by soaking in warm water for at least half an hour.

Vegetable concentrates, stock cubes and **yeast extracts** are all quick ways of adding flavour. Yeast extracts in particular are rich in nutrients, but also in salt so should not be used too generously. They are sold in screwtop jars and will keep for at least six months.

Sea vegetables

Sea vegetables are an important source of minerals, particularly iodine, calcium, potassium and iron, and of vitamins, mainly the B group and including traces of B_{12}, which is rare in vegetable foods: they are also a good protein source. However, their main culinary use is probably as seasoning, and, in the case of agar and carrageen, as setting agents in place of animal gelatine. Much appreciated in Japan, they also have a long tradition of use in other parts of the world, especially around the North Atlantic.

BUYING AND STORING

It is usually best to buy from a healthfood shop, where sea vegetables are sold already cleaned, dried and packaged. Unopened, they will keep indefinitely; opened, up to 4 months in an airtight container.

PREPARATION

Dried nori, dulse, kombu, wakame and arame need a preliminary brief soaking for 5 minutes or so to soften them, although this is not necessary if they are to be added straightaway to a soup or stew.

The exception is dulse, which needs to be rinsed and then soaked again for 10 minutes. Nori need not be softened if it is to be crumbled over a salad. Carrageen may need rinsing before use.

Nori is traditionally toasted and wrapped around small rice balls which are then dipped in shoyu. After its preliminary soaking, it can be used to flavour soups or as a salad ingredient, when it should be rinsed and boiled for about 15 minutes.

Dulse can be eaten raw, or, if dried, simmered for 30 minutes after being soaked. It is a dark, leafy vegetable with a sweet, tangy taste and is particularly good with cooked cabbage.

Kombu can also be eaten raw as well as cooked. It has a sweet flavour and is good for stocks and soups.

Wakame should have the central vein cut out after soaking. It is then simmered for 10 minutes or cut into small pieces and served as salad. Of all the sea vegetables it is the one that comes closest in taste to green land vegetables.

Arame has a broad leaf and is usually shredded into hair-like threads. (Another sea vegetable, hijiki, looks similar but more matchstick-like. It can be used in the same way.) Arame can be lightly steamed, sautéed or eaten cold.

Agar is a vegetable gelatine, available in powder or flake form. The powder is easier to use and ensures better results. The main point to watch for when using it is to make sure that it is thoroughly dissolved in boiling water or liquid before use, otherwise it will not set. Use 2 teaspoons agar powder to 570 ml (1 pint) liquid for a delicate jelly.

Carrageen is most often used to make carrageen mould, or blancmange. Soak 10-15 g (½ oz) dried carrageen in water for 15 minutes. Drain, rinse and cover with 570 ml (1 pint) milk; bring to the boil and simmer, covered, for 20-30 minutes. Strain, cool slightly, sweeten to taste, pour into a wet mould and leave to set. This basic method can be adapted to fruit puddings or savoury moulds.

Sweetenings

Rather than substituting one kind of sugar for another, it is important to monitor your intake of sugar and cut down on the total. There is little difference nutritionally between white and brown sugar, but **brown sugar** does contain a little fibre.

A product of cane sugar, **molasses,** especially black-strap molasses, contains small amounts of minerals, including calcium and iron, and some B vitamins. Its strong flavour makes it suitable for fruit breads and ginger cakes. It will keep up to 6 months in an airtight jar.

Honey is twice as sweet as sugar, so you need use only half the amount of sugar given in a recipe (reduce the liquid elsewhere to allow for the water content of honey). Look for the word "pure" on the label: this indicates that the product has not been tampered with . Blended honey may contain sugars, syrups and possibly additives. A jar of clear honey may sometimes crystallize if stored at a low temperature. Simply warm gently and the honey will become clear again.

Maple syrup is not so sweet as honey but it does contain some minerals, especially calcium. Other syrups available include corn syrup, rice syrup, sorghum syrup and barley syrup, also known as malt extract.

Fruit juice concentrates are very useful flavourings and can be combined with other sweetenings, such as honey, to reduce the total amount of sweetening needed in cakes and pastries—on their own the taste is too strong. Add them to fruit salads, sauces and cereals. Once opened, store the bottle in the refrigerator for up to 3 weeks. Dried fruits, especially dates, are also good for sweetening.

Carob powder, or carob flour, made from the seeds of the Mediterranean carob tree, tastes very similar to chocolate. It is naturally sweeter than cocoa and has no caffeine, a lower fat content and also contains some vitamins. When substituting carob for cocoa, use about half the quantity suggested. It makes cakes and biscuits a very dark brown.

Herbs

BUYING AND STORING

Most herbs should be bought and used fresh whenever possible, although a few (principally oregano, marjoram, sage, bay leaf and dill) keep their aroma well when dried. Buy small amounts or dried herbs, if possible from a wholefood shop or somewhere where there is a high turnover.

To dry your own herbs, pick them when the leaves are dry, preferably just before flowering. Tie in bunches and hang upside down in a cool dark place.

HERB CHART

HERB	SOUPS	STEWS	SAUCES	SALADS	GARNISH	OTHER REMARKS
Basil	yes	—	yes	yes	yes	Goes particuarly well with tomatoes; an essential ingredient of pesto (see p.115).
Bay leaf	yes	yes	yes	—	—	A bay leaf, combined with a sprig of thyme and some parsley, makes a *bouquet garni*.
Chervil	yes	yes	yes	yes	yes	The mixture known as *fines herbes* is made of finely chopped chervil, parsley, tarragon and chives.
Chives	—	—	yes	yes	yes	Particularly good with potato salad.
Coriander leaves	yes	yes	yes	yes	yes	Use like parsley.
Dill leaves	—	—	yes	yes	yes	Good with potatoes and green vegetables.
Garlic	yes	yes	yes	—	—	Extremely versatile and enhances other flavours.
Lemon balm	yes	yes	—	—	—	Use to flavour summer drinks and tisanes.
Sweet marjoram	yes	yes	—	—	—	Goes well with nuts, eggs and tomatoes.
Mint	—	—	yes	yes	yes	Use to flavour young vegetables, especially peas and new potatoes, or add to yogurt or bean dishes. Also good with fruit and summer drinks.
Oregano	yes	yes	yes	—	—	Indispensable to many Greek and Italian dishes.
Parsley	yes	yes	yes	yes	yes	Use generously both as flavouring and as garnish. Combines well with other herbs.
Rosemary	yes	yes	—	—	—	Good with oily foods. Strong camphor-like flavour.
Sage	—	yes	—	—	—	Use sparingly; very pungent.
Savory	yes	yes	—	yes	yes	Use like thyme or marjoram; good with beans.
Tarragon	yes	yes	yes	—	yes	Particularly good with cheese, cream, eggs, sauces and mild-flavoured vegetables.
Thyme	yes	yes	—	—	—	Good with most vegetables, such as tomatoes, courgettes, aubergines and peppers.

When dry, crumble them and put in small jars.

Some herbs can also be frozen for use as flavouring rather than as a garnish: parsley, coriander leaves, chives, tarragon and chervil are all suitable. Blanch in boiling water for a few seconds (otherwise they will lose their colour and look unappetizing). Blanching also helps to retain flavour and aroma. Drain them, leave in sprigs and open freeze. Wrap in polythene bags and keep for not more than 3-4 months. Keep dried herbs away from light or heat, in airtight containers.

USING

To get the best flavour from fresh herbs, tear or snip them rather than chop them, except parsley. Dried herbs are more pungent than fresh, so use only one teaspoon of the dried herb where you would use 2-3 teaspoons of the fresh one.

Spices

Even a small amount of spice, judiciously used, alters the whole character of a dish. The term generally refers to the dried roots, bark, pods, berries or seeds of aromatic plants. Most spices come from the East, but allspice, chili peppers and vanilla originated in the New World.

BUYING AND STORING

Buy spices whole whenever possible as they keep their flavour and freshness much better. Turmeric and chili peppers (including cayenne and paprika) are generally sold ready ground. Keep in airtight containers, in a cool dark place.

PREPARATION

Some spices can be crushed in a pestle and mortar: they include allspice, cardamom, cloves, coriander, cumin, dill and fennel seed, juniper, black peppercorns and saffron. Poppy seeds are tough and need a proper nut mill, which can of course also be used for other spices. Aniseeds, capers, caraway, celery, dill and fennel seeds are generally used whole. Green peppercorns are not strictly speaking a spice, as they are not dried. They are easily crushed or mashed. Nutmeg needs grating: a cheese grater does perfectly well. Ginger can also be grated, especially when fresh, or it can be sliced thinly or chopped. Always prepare spices just before they are to be cooked.

Chili peppers can be chopped (remove the seeds unless you are quite sure you like the chili hot),

or kept in a jar of oil to impart their flavour. Keep topping up with oil as you use it—you will need only a few drops at a time. This is an excellent standby for the spaghetti with garlic, oil and chili on page 113. Saffron threads are often mixed with a little warm water, when they will expand and give out their colour and flavouring more easily. They may also be lightly crushed and put in a warm oven for a few minutes.

Chili peppers in oil

Saffron threads

USING

Many spices benefit from being lightly fried in a little oil before being added to the dish they are to flavour. This seems to bring out and reinforce their aroma, removing any suspicion of rankness or coarseness, and applies particularly to coriander, cumin, cardamom, ginger and fenugreek.

Cinnamon and mace, being difficult to grind, are often used whole to flavour liquids—sauces or drinks—from which they can be easily extracted once they have yielded their aroma. In the same way, a vanilla pod can be used to flavour drinks, syrups or custards.

Coriander, cumin, cardamom, peppercorns, turmeric, cloves, ginger and chili peppers are the most important spices for curry. Some recipes call for "garam masala", a combination of spices. This can be bought, or you can make your own: there is no standard recipe (the name means "hot mixture"). It is a starting mixture rather than a complete curry powder. A possible mixture might be 4 parts coriander, 1 part cumin, 1 part chili, all lightly roasted or fried and added to 1 part ground black peppercorns.

VEGETABLES

Organically grown vegetables (a phrase used to describe produce that has been grown without the aid of artificial fertilizers, pesticides or other sprays) are usually more expensive than intensively farmed vegetables, because it costs more to produce them. They tend to be smaller and more irregularly shaped than supermarket produce grown for eye appeal. Still, many people consider this is a small price to pay for vegetables uncontaminated by chemicals and which have a finer flavour and better keeping qualities. They contain minerals and fibre and are excellent sources of vitamins, particularly vitamin C. Root vegetables supply starch and natural sugars for energy. They complement beans, grains and nuts, providing taste and colour, palatability and texture, as well as the vitamins and minerals we need.

BUYING

Freshness is all-important, and being wrapped in polythene does nothing for a vegetable's flavour, so wherever possible buy from a reputable greengrocer. Look for plumpness and fresh, bright colour: avoid damaged, shrunken or wrinkled, faded or limp vegetables.

STORING

The following should be eaten as soon as possible: saladings and those to be eaten raw; green vegetables; pods; fruit vegetables such as courgettes, peppers and aubergines (but tomatoes are often picked unripe and allowed to continue to ripen); shoots; mushrooms; and above all sweet corn. If any of these vegetables do have to wait, remove any polythene wrappings and keep them in a cool, dark place as light and heat destroy crispness and nutrients, particularly vitamins B_2 and C. Greens can lose up to 50 per cent of their vitamin C in one day if kept at room temperature.

If kept in cool, well-ventilated conditions, carrots and onions will keep longer—several weeks—and potatoes will keep for several months but will lose much of their vitamin C content.

Some fresh vegetables are suitable for freezing and this causes very little loss of nutrients. Sweet corn, spinach, seakale beet, broccoli, carrots, peas and beans (runner and broad) are all good.

To freeze, prepare the vegetables as directed below and blanch them by plunging into boiling water for a minute; do about 450 g (1 lb) at a time, so that the water does not cool down too much. This destroys the enzyme that causes deterioration. Drain them and plunge immediately into cold water to prevent further cooking. Drain again, using a salad spinner or dryer. Freeze on a tray in a single layer, covered with a plastic bag. Pack in boxes or bags. They will keep for up to a year. Use straight from frozen and do not thaw first, or the vitamin content will be reduced.

PREPARATION

Many vegetables are best eaten raw, for both flavour and nutrition. If you have any suspicion that your vegetables may have been contaminated by chemicals, it is advisable to wash or scrub them.

Raw saladings should be rinsed thoroughly and put in a polythene bag in the refrigerator until just before use, when they should be prepared, dressed and eaten immediately. **Root vegetables** and **tubers** should be scrubbed and cooked in their skins. In general, do not peel first: scrubbing removes most pesticides, and much of the goodness of root vegetables is contained in or near the skin. Potatoes can lose up to 25 per cent of their protein if peeled too coarsely.

Celeriac is the exception that does need peeling before cooking. Peel others (except potatoes) after cooking and chop, slice or dice them. Jerusalem artichokes, small turnips, especially the young white French ones, and small kohlrabi can also be left whole, and all can be mashed or puréed.

Some vegetables (Jerusalem artichokes, celeriac, potatoes) go brown when cut: to prevent this, drop them in water, preferably lightly acidulated by adding 3-4 teaspoons of lemon juice or vinegar to each litre (2 pints) of water, or rub with lemon juice. **Aubergines** also go brown, but this does not matter as when cooked it will not show. I do not find it necessary to salt them to draw out their bitter liquid, as many books recommend.

With **okra,** cut off the conical cap at the stalk end, salt them and leave for an hour, then rinse carefully and dry. Cut **fennel** in thin slices across, discarding the stems and, if tough, the bottom.

Spinach and **other leaf vegetables** should be well washed and drained before cooking. Do not discard the outer leaves: they are often the most nutritious, but must of course be well washed to remove any pesticides.

COOKING

When choosing vegetables for a meal, calculate about 225 g (8 oz) per person for a main dish, less for a side dish (see also page 78).

Of the many different ways of cooking vegetables, boiling is one of the most popular. It is also one of the least desirable, as up to 45 per cent of the minerals and 50 per cent of the vitamin C may be lost. If you must boil vegetables, use the minimum amount of water and make sure it is boiling when you add the vegetables. Never add bicarbonate of soda: it may keep the colour in, but it destroys vitamin C. For green vegetables, 1 cm (½ in) water should be enough. If spinach has been thoroughly rinsed and not too well drained, it will need no further liquid. Root vegetables should be barely covered. Keep the pan tightly covered—this will help prevent vitamin loss—and cook as shown opposite.

Steaming is a good method, as vitamins are not lost in the cooking liquid. Put the vegetables in a basket over a pan of fast-boiling water. Don't pack them too tightly, and cover with a well-fitting lid.

Baking or roasting is particularly suited to root vegetables and potatoes. Prick the skins first to prevent them bursting. I have also successfully baked green vegetables, particularly Brussels sprouts, first brushing both the sprouts and the cooking dish with a little oil. This produces a crisp cooked vegetable, the leaves on the outside well cooked and the inside tender.

To braise vegetables, brown them lightly in a little oil and bake in the oven, adding a little hot liquid, in a covered dish.

Asparagus is best cooked with the stems in boiling water but the tops out of it, so that the tender tips cook in the steam.

Sprouts

Easy and quick to grow at home, sprouts provide fresh, uncontaminated green vegetables of outstanding nutritional value: they contain valuable amounts of protein as well as vitamins A, B complex, C and E, minerals and enzymes.

The changes that take place as the seed grows are incredible. The total vitamin content can increase by up to 800 per cent within a few days.

BUYING

Buy untreated seeds from a healthfood shop or a firm specializing in organically grown produce, as almost all seeds sold for planting will have been treated with fungicides and pesticides. Split beans or seeds will not sprout.

GROWING

If you don't have proper tiered sprouting trays, fine sieves or mesh trays, or a wide-necked jar with a cover of muslin or other porous substance, will do very well. Pick over the seeds carefully, removing any tiny stems and stones.

Put 2 tablespoons of seeds in a jar and soak them in plenty of lukewarm water overnight, to encourage them to germinate more quickly. Next day, drain off the water. Put the seeds on a suitable tray or leave them in the jar. Put in a warm place but not in direct sun (the airing cupboard is ideal). They need good ventilation and a constant temperature of 13-21°C (55-70°F). Remember to allow enough space in the container for growth—they will increase in volume by 4 to 6 times.

Every night and morning pour warm water over the seeds. Turn the jar, if you are using one, upside down so the water can drain away completely. If not properly drained the sprouts can go mouldy, but be careful not to rinse them so vigorously that you damage the delicate shoots. Grain sprouts take 2-3 days, beans and lentils 5-7 days to be at their best. When ready, give them a final rinse.

STORING

Sprouts keep in the refrigerator for up to 4 days. Use an airtight container with a double layer of kitchen paper or muslin at the bottom, to absorb excess moisture and retard deterioration.

USING

All sprouts can be eaten raw in salads. The delicate green leaves of mustard and cress and alfalfa look particularly pretty and can also be used to garnish. Aduki bean sprouts have a distinct flavour of peanuts; mung beans taste a little like delicate peapods, but if grown for too long will develop too intense a flavour and lose some of their nutritive value. Fenugreek sprouts taste spicy.

The best known and easiest to sprout are mustard and cress, mung beans and alfalfa; aduki beans are also easy, and so are whole lentils.

Sprouts are good as an addition to bread: use wheat sprouts, or alfalfa sprouts grown to only 0.5 cm (¼ in).

COOKING TIMES AND METHODS FOR DIFFERENT VEGETABLES

VEGETABLE	STEAM	BOIL	BAKE (WHOLE)	BRAISE	STIR FRY
Potatoes	25-30 minutes	20 minutes	1-1½ hours	15-20 minutes	
Carrots	20 minutes	10-15 minutes	45-60 minutes	15-20 minutes	yes
Turnips	25-30 minutes	10-15 minutes		15-20 minutes	yes
Swedes	25-30 minutes	20 minutes		15-20 minutes	yes
Parsnips		15-20 minutes	45-60 minutes	15-20 minutes	
Celeriac & kohlrabi	20 minutes	10-15 minutes		15-20 minutes	yes
Salsify & scorzonera	30-40 minutes	20-30 minutes			
Sweet potato	25-30 minutes	20 minutes	1-1½ hours		
Jerusalem artichokes		15-20 minutes			
Radish/daikon					yes
Beetroot		40-60 minutes			
Asparagus		10-15 minutes			
Fennel	12-15 minutes	10-12 minutes		15-20 minutes	yes
Onions			45-60 minutes		
Leeks	15-20 minutes	10-15 minutes		8-10 minutes	
Celery	12-15 minutes	8-10 minutes		10-12 minutes	yes
Globe artichokes		30-40 minutes			
French beans	4-8 minutes				yes
Broad beans		10-15 minutes			
Peas		8-12 minutes			yes
Mangetout peas	6-8 minutes				yes
Okra		15-20 minutes			
Mushrooms					yes
Sweet corn		8-15 minutes			yes
Cabbage	4-6 minutes				yes
Red cabbage				45-60 minutes	
Brussels sprouts	6-10 minutes		25-30 minutes		yes
Cauliflower	4-8 minutes				
Broccoli	4-8 minutes				yes
Spinach		*6-8 minutes			
Pak choi	4-8 minutes				yes
Spinach beet	10-12 minutes				
Chard (seakale beet)	10-12 minutes				
Endive				10-12 minutes	
Chicory					yes
Chinese leaves	4 minutes				yes
Courgettes	4-8 minutes				yes
Marrow	10-20 minutes		45-60 minutes		yes
Peppers					yes
Cucumbers	5-10 minutes				

Aubergines are usually sautéed and/or baked, often with a stuffing: see specific recipes for directions.
Tomatoes can be grilled for 3-4 minutes. No times have been given for frying or sautéing as these will be found in specific recipes.

*Spinach is not strictly speaking boiled, but cooked in the water still adhering to it after a final rinsing.
All the above times give *very lightly cooked* vegetables, many with a crisp, crunchy texture. If you prefer vegetables softer, you will need to increase the cooking time.

FRUIT

Fresh fruit, preferably eaten raw, is part of any healthy diet. Most fruits contain vitamin C (which cannot be stored in the body). They also contain a high proportion of natural sugars (fructose), carbohydrates and fibre as well as minerals and other vitamins.

BUYING

Buy fresh, firm, plump fruit that is not shrunken or damaged. Stone fruit, such as peaches, plums and cherries, should be yielding, neither rock-hard nor too squashy. Melons should be heavy, yielding at the stalk end and smell ripe. Pineapples too should smell ripe and the leaves should come away without too much effort.

Kiwi fruit can be bought when still hard and will ripen at home. Papayas will also go on ripening at home until soft enough to eat. Mangoes should be soft and yielding, figs soft but not squashy—the skin should feel as if it is just at bursting point but not beyond it. When buying persimmons, check with your greengrocer: some can be eaten straight away, some are far too bitter and must be kept until squashy. Passion fruit have wrinkled skins when ripe. Guavas turn light yellow and are very fragrant and soft. Lychees turn to a vivid rosy red.

STORING

Pears in particular have only a day or so when they are at their best, and strawberries, raspberries and other soft fruits are best eaten as soon as possible after picking. Ripe figs and persimmons should also be eaten quickly. Melons, pineapples, mangoes, papayas and guavas should all be eaten within a few days of ripening; so should grapes and stone fruit.

Apples, however, store well, especially if kept without touching one another in a cool, dry, well-ventilated place. Other fruits that keep well are all the citrus family, kiwi fruit and bananas. Lychees keep up to three months in the refrigerator.

PREPARATION

Scrub fruit if you think it needs it, but try not to peel unnecessarily. Citrus fruit are often sprayed to give them a healthy shine. This should not affect the fruit inside, but if you are going to use the zest (or eat them whole, as you can with tiny kumquats, the smallest of the family) they will need a scrub.

If making a fruit salad, slice or section the fruit well ahead of time and leave the salad in a cool place for the flavours to develop and mingle. Brush sliced apples and pears with lemon juice so that they will not discolour. Apricots and peaches (and tomatoes) are easy to skin if you pour boiling water over them and leave for 1 minute.

Section oranges and grapefruit by cutting down on either side of the membranes to get skinless segments. For zesting, use a special zester if you have one; otherwise use a potato peeler or a small sharp knife, but as the strips of peel will be a little thicker than true zest, they can be simmered in water for 5-6 minutes to soften them.

A cherry stoner can also be used for olives. Grapes can be halved and the pips hooked out with a hairpin or paperclip. (See also page 223).

Melons are usually halved or cut into segments, and pineapples can be halved lengthways, when the flesh can be removed easily. Alternatively, slice pineapples across and remove the peel and core.

Kiwi fruit look prettiest when sliced across. Figs can be halved or sliced. Lychees should be peeled. Persimmons look attractive when sliced across, or (if the kind that must be allowed to ripen) can have their tops sliced off and the insides scooped out; passion fruit can have the same treatment.

Soft fruit need to be picked over carefully and any mouldy specimens removed; hull, or top and tail, them as necessary. This can be done a few hours in advance and they should then be kept cool.

SLICING FRUIT

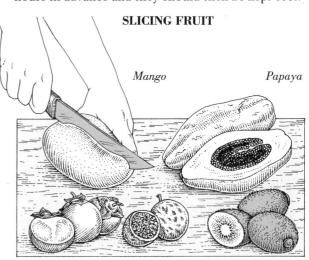

Mango   *Papaya*

Persimmons   *Passion fruit*   *Kiwi fruit*

Papayas can be eaten like melons. They are particularly good with a sprinkling of lime juice. Guavas are usually peeled and the seeds discarded.

Mangoes are not the most accommodating of fruit to prepare. Remember that the stone is flat and oblong, and examine the fruit to work out how the stone is lying. Cut down on either side and close to it: you will have two shallow"cheeks", which are easy to deal with—the flesh can be scooped out and chopped or diced—and the stone, with a strip of flesh round it that will yield a few more cubes.

USING

It is hard to improve on the refreshing flavour of raw fruit, and most of the best ways of cooking it are simple so as to keep as much of the taste and goodness as possible. Apple crumble is a basic recipe, and can be varied by using different fruit. Stew peeled, sliced apples in a little water for 5 minutes or until soft with sugar, honey or dried dates to taste. Sprinkle with one of the crumble toppings suggested on page 206 and bake at gas mark 4, 180°C (350°F) for 40 minutes.

OILS, FATS, DAIRY PRODUCTS AND ALTERNATIVES

Oils

Oils are used mainly as a cooking medium for frying and sautéing, as a condiment and also sometimes as shortening in baking bread, cakes or biscuits. Fats are fundamentally the same as oils, but are solid at room temperature (see also page 229). They are a principal source of energy and, when unrefined, of nutrients as they contain vitamins and minerals, especially vitamin E. There are three main types of oil obtained from seeds, beans and nuts.

Cold pressed oil is still extracted using the ancient method of hydraulic pressing. Much of the oil remains in the pulp, but that which is extracted is high quality and full of flavour. Unfortunately true cold pressed oil is very expensive.

Semi-refined oil requires greater pressure and higher temperatures. The extraction rate is higher, but the vitamin content suffers.

Refined oil, confusingly labelled "pure", is produced by a method called solvent extraction, which removes most of the goodness as well as bleaching and deodorizing the oil. Many of the vitamins are then added back artificially along with preservatives to prevent the oil going rancid. This is generally the cheapest type available.

BUYING

It depends what you want your oil for: dressing salads, frying vegetables and grains, or baking. For eating raw, as a salad dressing, use cold-pressed or unrefined oil: it tastes much the best to most palates and is nutritionally the most valuable.

Olive oil has a rich flavour, but one that varies widely depending on the country of origin. "Virgin oil" means oil from the first pressing, the best quality of oil and recommended for salad dressings.

Safflower oil is pale in colour, with a delicate flavour, high in linoleic acid and low in cholesterol (see page 229), which justifies its high price.

Sunflower oil is perhaps the best all-purpose oil. It is high in linoleic acid, second only to safflower oil and slightly cheaper.

Sesame oil does not go rancid quickly, and food containing it will not go stale, which makes it a good oil for baking.

Corn oil is cheap to produce, almost tasteless and popular as a cooking oil. It is also widely used as an ingredient in margarine.

Peanut oil is another very popular oil. It is particularly good for frying as it can be heated to very high temperatures without burning.

Soya oil is also cheap and popular.

Walnut oil has a strong, nutty taste and is very expensive, so it is used chiefly for dressing salads.

STORING

Cold pressed oils, apart from sesame oil, do not keep well. They are not heat-treated or otherwise stabilized and may go rancid, so buy comparatively small quantities (enough for a month or two) and keep in a cool, dark place. If it is too cold and the oil congeals, do not worry—the oil will liquefy very quickly when brought to room temperature. Semi-refined oils will keep up to three months.

Fats

Butter is high in saturated animal fats (see page 229) and as such should not be overindulged in, but current medical thinking is that animal fats do not have an adverse effect on cholesterol levels if eaten in conjunction with twice the amount of polyunsaturated fats (see page 229). Since most of us could do with reducing our total fat intake, this leaves a comparatively small amount of butter available, but still an appreciable one, and for its addicts there is no real substitute, either for taste or quality. So unless you need to keep to a low-cholesterol diet use butter (preferably unsalted) for cooking whenever it will make a difference.

Margarine is often presented as the healthy alternative to butter. In fact many margarines are highly refined and contain additives. Soft margarines contain about 30 per cent polyunsaturated fat. In hard margarines the original polyunsaturated fats have been hydrogenated, so they are not much better for you than butter from the point of view of fat content. If you do not eat any animal product, then you will want a vegetable-based margarine; if you do eat butter but want to cut down on cholesterol, an excellent compromise is to mix equal parts of butter and good quality oil (safflower or sunflower). This will keep for several days in a covered container in the refrigerator.

Ghee is clarified butter, popular in cooking because any impurities have been removed and it can be heated to a much higher temperature than ordinary butter without burning. To make your own, simply melt butter and filter it through muslin. Vegetable ghee is also available. This is oil that has been hydrogenated to make it solid at room temperature. So has **solid vegetable fat,** which is hard enough to grate. Neither will do anything to lower your cholesterol level, but they should not contain unwelcome additives.

Milk products

Milk provides protein, vitamins and minerals, particularly calcium and phosphorus, as well as the essential B_{12}, which is lacking in a strictly non-animal diet. However, it also contains saturated fat. Skimmed milk has had most of the fat content removed and in the process has also lost vitamins A, D and E (but not B). Goat's milk is often tolerated by those who cannot drink cow's milk.

Yogurt is a living food, in which bacteria act on the milk sugars to produce lactic acid, a job normally done by our digestive juices. It is easy to assimilate, being in a sense pre-digested, and eating it regularly helps the digestion. Many commercial yogurts contain additives, preservatives and colouring agents, so it is worth making your own. Yogurt-makers are available which maintain the milk at exactly the right temperature while it ferments, thus cutting out the guesswork and giving a consistent product.

MAKING YOGURT IN A VACUUM FLASK OR BOWL
Bring 570 ml (1 pt) of milk to the boil, then let it cool to approximately blood heat (37°C, 98.6°F) or until you can keep your finger in it comfortably for a count of ten. Add a generous tablespoon of good live plain yogurt, mix thoroughly, pour into a vacuum flask and stopper tightly. If you have no vacuum flask, pour the mixture into a bowl, cover it with a plate or polythene film, wrap it well in a towel or blanket and leave in a warm place, free of draughts, such as an airing-cupboard. It will be ready after 8-12 hours (do not leave it too long or it may turn sour). Store in the refrigerator where it will keep for up to a week. Save a tablespoon or so for a "starter" for your next batch. If your batches of yogurt become progressively weaker, you may need to buy fresh "starter".

Buttermilk If properly made, this is another easily digestible milk product. It has a similar protein and mineral content to whole milk but has less vitamin A and hardly any fat.

Soya bean products

Over more than a thousand years, the Chinese have evolved many ways of preparing the soya bean. One is **soya milk,** an easily digested substitute for dairy milk and recommended to sufferers from allergies. To make it, soak soya beans in water overnight (one cup of beans will produce about 8 cups soya milk). In the morning, strain them and grind them to a meal with the same volume of water (each cup will have roughly doubled in size, so add two cups of water for each original cup of beans). Put this in a large pan and add the same quantity of water (another four cups for each original cup). Bring to the boil and boil for 20 minutes, uncovered. It should be at a fairly fast boil to ensure all toxins are destroyed and you'll find that the water froths up considerably —sprinkling cold water on top will help to settle it. Strain before use. It makes an excellent substitute for milk in custards, puddings and milk shakes.

Tofu is soya bean curd, another way of utilizing the soya bean. Its high protein content (it is also rich in iron, calcium and B vitamins while containing few calories and saturated fats and no cholesterol) makes it a nutritious substitute not only for meat and fish but also for dairy products —the Chinese hardly use milk. In Chinese and Japanese cooking it is a most versatile ingredient, whether marinated, stir-fried or deep-fried, beaten into dressings and sauces, or added to soups, burger mixes, even puddings. Surprisingly, this easily digested "miracle" food is taking time (rather as yogurt did) to become popular in the West. Perhaps our taste buds needs a while to get used to its consistency and flavour, or lack of it. It is bland, with a hint of an aftertaste which some might find sickly, others dry, due to the low fat content —this can be counteracted by adding a little oil. It blends beautifully with other flavours, for example in mixed vegetable dishes, binding them together and adding texture and consistency.

It is available in various forms. Silken tofu is the softest, a mixture of some curds and whey, with a consistency like firm junket. It is best for mashing or blending for dips, dressings and sauces. It is usually sold in a carton or tetrapak, which will keep unopened and unrefrigerated for six months. Once opened, it should be used within two days.

Firm tofu is a heavily pressed version, with a dense texture like firm cheese; it can be cubed, sliced and marinated. When sold loose, you will usually find it refrigerated, submerged in deep buckets of water. It will keep fresh for a week, in water in the refrigerator, with the water changed daily. It is also sold in vacuum packs, which keep unopened for 3-4 weeks. Once opened, keep it under water and treat it just like loose tofu, otherwise it will develop a fresh skin. Soft tofu, with a texture between firm and silken, can be treated like firm tofu.

Tofu can be frozen, which drastically changes its look and texture. Squeeze out thawed tofu to get rid of excess water. It will then resemble a spongy lattice-work, with a chewy texture that soaks up sauces and marinades with ease.

Cheese

Strict vegetarians eat only cheese made with non-animal rennet. These can be found in healthfood shops and include Cheddar and other hard cheeses, as well as the soft cheeses such as cottage cheese, ricotta and feta, some varieties of which do not use rennet anyway. Although a good source of protein, cheese made from whole milk is high in fat and cholesterol, so use it sparingly and substitute low fat cheese wherever possible.

Eggs

It is hard to ignore the horrors of battery farming. Vegetarians will prefer to buy humanely produced free-range eggs, which are generally considered to have a superior taste although nutritionally there is little difference.

Eggs, particularly the yolks, are an excellent source of protein and contain all the essential amino acids. They are also high in fat and cholesterol, which is why many people are advised to limit their consumption of eggs.

STORAGE
Store eggs in a cool place. There is no need to keep them in the refrigerator. If the shell is soiled, wipe it with a dry cloth; washing removes the protective film. Avoid shiny shells as this is an indication of age. When cracked open, the yolk of a fresh egg remains firm and round.

SUBSTITUTES FOR EGGS
Eggs in cooking can be replaced in a number of ways. All the following variations will alter the texture and flavour to a certain extent but it's certainly worth experimenting if you want to cut down on cholesterol or have allergy problems.

Where eggs are used to enrich a dish such as pastry or bread dough, use soya flour instead. One to two tablespoons mixed with 225 g (8 oz) flour give a richer pastry; 50 g (2 oz) soya flour in 450 g (1 lb) flour gives a rich bread dough. Soya flour mixed to a cream with water can be used instead of an egg-wash, or glaze. One to two tablespoons of soya flour can be added to savoury bakes as a substitute for an egg, but will not bind the mixture in the same way. Tahini (see page 19) can be used instead of an egg as a binding agent. In a nut roast, for example, instead of 2 eggs, use 30 ml (2 tbsp) tahini and add extra stock or water.

GARNISHES

Whether you're preparing everyday meals for yourself or your family or giving a dinner party, spend a little extra time ensuring that the food looks good. Even a sprinkling of chopped herbs or nuts makes such a difference to the look of the dish and takes only a moment to do. Carefully arranged julienne strips of carrot, fluted mushroom caps or melon balls, for example, take a little longer but are well worth the extra effort.

A garnish should contrast visually or in taste or texture—a sprinkling of bright colour, crunchy seeds or nuts, or spicy poppy or sesame seeds. It should not overpower the dish or mask its flavour at all. Here are some suggestions.

Chopped herbs: as well as parsley and chives, use mint, coriander, chervil, dill and fennel leaves, lemon balm, savory and tarragon. Basil leaves are traditionally torn rather than cut, as this is supposed to retain the flavour better. Watercress leaves are usually left whole.

Spices: pepper of all kinds—coarsely ground black peppercorns, crushed green peppercorns, chili powder, cayenne, paprika (you can be generous with this as it is so mild); capers; powdered cinnamon—this goes particularly well with chocolate-flavoured dishes.

Seeds: anise, caraway, celery, dill, fennel, mustard, poppy and sesame.

Nuts: almonds, walnuts, cashews and hazelnuts can be blanched (see page 209), chopped or left whole. Use the tip of a sharp knife to split almonds in half or flake them thinly. Put pistachios in boiling water for a minute with a pinch of bicarbonate of soda to enhance their bright green colour.

Chopped hard-boiled egg: use both yolk and white.

Vegetables and fruit: these offer a lot of scope for decoration. Some —onions, kiwi fruit, pineapple—can be simply sliced across, while others lend themselves to more elaborate treatment (see illustrations). Apples, mushrooms and celeriac discolour on peeling and need to be kept in water to which a little lemon juice or vinegar has been added, or else brushed with lemon juice.

CARROT

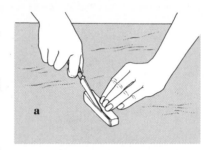

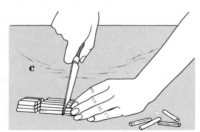

Carrots can be grated, diced or cut into julienne strips. For julienne strips, first trim off the top, base and sides to get a neat squared-off shape. Cut this into thin slices (*a*) and cut the slices lengthways into matchstick-sized strips (*b*). These can then be cut across into short lengths (*c*) or into dice. Other root vegetables—celeriac, kohlrabi, swedes and turnips—as well as peppers, courgettes, mushrooms, cucumber and celery are also suitable for cutting into julienne strips or dicing.

CELERY

To make tassels from celery or spring onions, cut into short pieces and slice these down into thin strips almost but not quite as far as the end (*top*). Put in cold water to open out. For celery crescents (*above*), cut slices across or on the diagonal.

CUCUMBER

A ridged effect with contrasting colours is achieved by scoring cucumber peel lengthways with a fork.

GRAPES

Using the rounded end of a hairpin makes it easy to remove grape pips.

LEMON

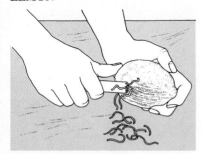

Grate the rind of lemons or oranges, or use a zester for professional-looking fine strips (*above*). Lemon quarters or wedges can be dusted with paprika.

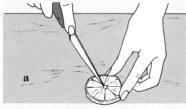

For lemon or orange twists, make a cut to the centre with a sharp knife (*a*). Hold the slice on either side of the cut and twist in opposite directions (*b*). Cucumber slices can be treated in the same way.

MELON

A special scoop is used to produce small balls of melon or cucumber.

MUSHROOMS

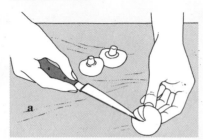

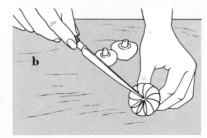

To flute mushroom caps, use the tip of a sharp knife, held at an angle to make a series of curved cuts from the centre outwards (*a*). Reversing the angle, make another series of cuts in the other direction (*b*). Remove the skin from between the cuts (*c*).

PEPPERS

Cut peppers downwards or across into thin rings.

RADISHES

For radish roses, slice downwards from the base almost to the stalk. Put them in cold water and they will open out.

TOMATOES

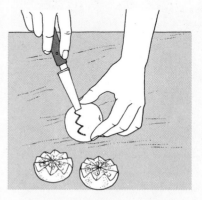

To cut tomato halves in a zigzag pattern, insert the point of a sharp knife into the centre and make a series of V-shaped cuts all around the tomato until you can pull the halves apart. Leave cherry tomatoes whole.

EQUIPMENT

Vegetarian cookery doesn't really call for any special equipment, so don't feel you have to buy a whole new batterie de cuisine. Here are a few suggestions and guidelines for buying and using a selection of the most useful kitchen tools.

Knives
Choose knives carefully as they are going to be in constant use. An 18 cm (7 in) chef's knife is a good all-purpose knife. With a long blade you can chop more ingredients at the same time, and, because of the depth of the blade it is less likely to slip. A small serrated knife is ideal for slicing citrus fruit or tomatoes and a short-bladed paring knife is useful for peeling vegetables and fruit. Work with the ingredients close to the handle where the blade is

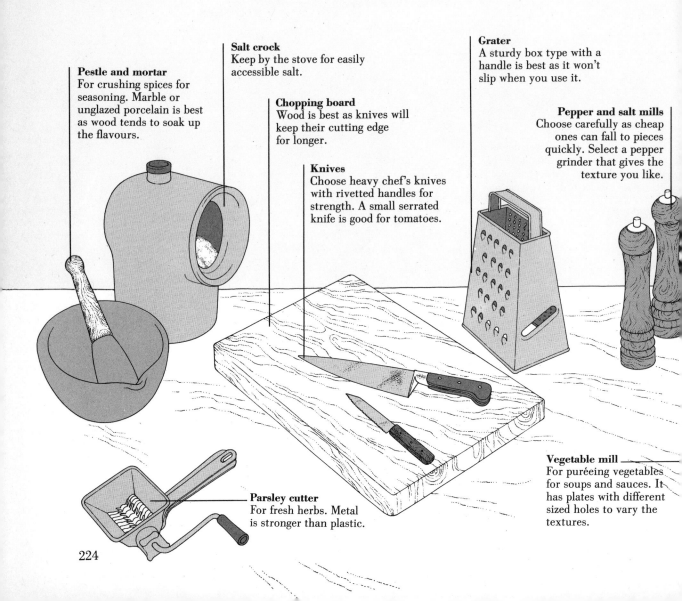

Pestle and mortar
For crushing spices for seasoning. Marble or unglazed porcelain is best as wood tends to soak up the flavours.

Salt crock
Keep by the stove for easily accessible salt.

Chopping board
Wood is best as knives will keep their cutting edge for longer.

Knives
Choose heavy chef's knives with rivetted handles for strength. A small serrated knife is good for tomatoes.

Grater
A sturdy box type with a handle is best as it won't slip when you use it.

Pepper and salt mills
Choose carefully as cheap ones can fall to pieces quickly. Select a pepper grinder that gives the texture you like.

Parsley cutter
For fresh herbs. Metal is stronger than plastic.

Vegetable mill
For puréeing vegetables for soups and sauces. It has plates with different sized holes to vary the textures.

deepest. Carbon steel knives sharpen more easily than stainless steel knives but the latter tend to keep their edges longer. Carbon steel also reacts with the acids in certain foods, especially fruits. It is very important to keep your knives sharp. If a blade is dull it is more likely to slip and you will have to use more effort.

Pans
A good pan should have a close-fitting lid and strong, secure handles. Ideally both the handles and

the knob on the lid should be made of a different heat-resistant material.

I prefer a good-quality stainless steel pan and look for not only a thick heavy base but thickness round the sides as well. Try not to scratch stainless steel as small amounts of metallic compounds then dissolve into the food. If you burn a pan, cover the burn with plenty of salt and a little water, leave overnight and it should clean easily the next day. Enamelled cast iron pans are also excellent. Glass, ceramic and thin enamel cookware can heat unevenly causing

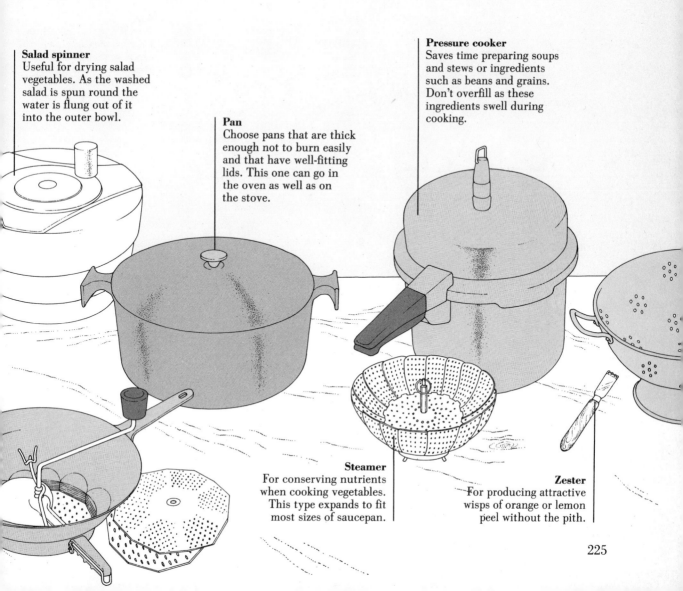

Salad spinner
Useful for drying salad vegetables. As the washed salad is spun round the water is flung out of it into the outer bowl.

Pan
Choose pans that are thick enough not to burn easily and that have well-fitting lids. This one can go in the oven as well as on the stove.

Pressure cooker
Saves time preparing soups and stews or ingredients such as beans and grains. Don't overfill as these ingredients swell during cooking.

Steamer
For conserving nutrients when cooking vegetables. This type expands to fit most sizes of saucepan.

Zester
For producing attractive wisps of orange or lemon peel without the pith.

foods to stick or burn. Aluminium oxides will dissolve into food cooked in aluminium utensils and certain foods, such as eggs, will discolour. For cooking foods with the minimum of water or oil it is advisable to use non-stick pans.

Other useful pans are a pressure cooker and a slow cooker. By trapping the steam and increasing the pressure, a pressure cooker raises the temperature to above the boiling point of water, so the food cooks more quickly. A slow cooker is excellent for casseroles, soups, dried fruit and grains.

Electrical equipment
A blender is essential if you want to avoid hours of chopping and sieving. It blends liquids better and faster than a food processor. In addition it is very useful to have a mixer or food processor. Both are available with a variety of attachments for mincing, grating, shredding, making pastry or dough. One advantage of the shredding gadgets on a mixer is that you can continue shredding until you have enough without having to stop from time to time to empty the container.

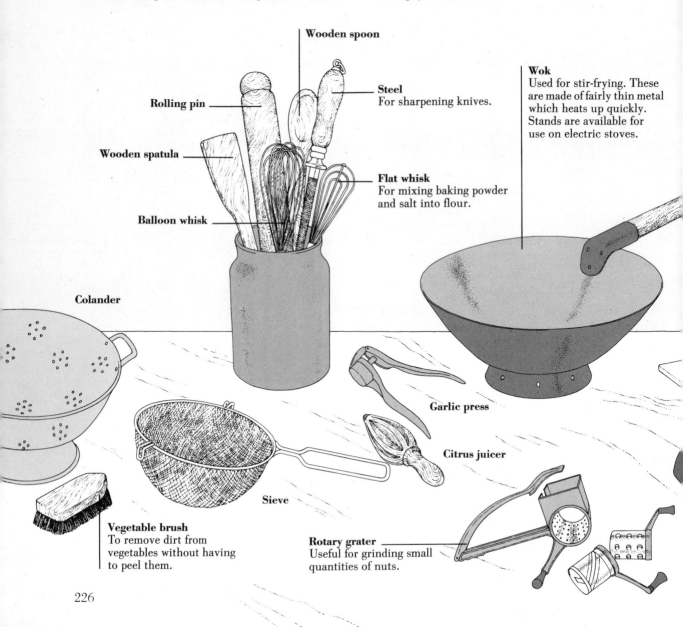

Wooden spoon

Steel
For sharpening knives.

Rolling pin

Wooden spatula

Balloon whisk

Flat whisk
For mixing baking powder and salt into flour.

Wok
Used for stir-frying. These are made of fairly thin metal which heats up quickly. Stands are available for use on electric stoves.

Colander

Garlic press

Citrus juicer

Sieve

Vegetable brush
To remove dirt from vegetables without having to peel them.

Rotary grater
Useful for grinding small quantities of nuts.

With a food processor, choose one that grates, shreds and slices as well as mixes and purées. Don't rely on it to chop everything for you though because it is just as important to have a variety of shapes and sizes in a dish as it is to vary texture. Processors cannot grind small quantities as finely as a nut mill.

Other useful items
There are many other tools which are useful to have in your kitchen, for example a pestle and mortar for grinding spices (see page 224), a nut mill or small rotary grater for grinding small quantities of nuts or cheese finely, a garlic press and a citrus juicer.

Blender
For soups, sauces breadcrumbs and drinks. Choose one that holds at least a litre and which has a strong motor and a tight-fitting lid. Do not fill to more than two-thirds capacity as the contents will swirl up when the machine is turned on.

Shredder

Food mixer
For batters, cake mixtures and whisking eggs and cream. The most useful attachments for vegetarian cookery are the **shredder** for vegetables and cheese and the **dough hook** for making bread and pastry.

Kitchen scales
The most accurate way to measure dry ingredients is to use kitchen scales. These balance scales are the easiest to use.

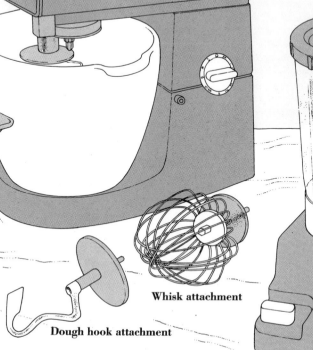

Dough hook attachment

Whisk attachment

227

DAILY NEEDS

Proteins, fats, carbohydrates, vitamins and minerals are all essential to life. This part of the book explains why they are so necessary, which foods supply them (including complementary proteins) and which are the best sources, and the recommended daily allowance of each one. Also included is a section describing the nutritional profiles of some of the commoner foods.

A common fear about giving up meat and fish is that it will lead to an unbalanced diet, particularly with regard to protein. In fact, a vegetarian diet is likely to supply more than adequate amounts of protein, for both adults and children, even if dairy products are not eaten.

A wholefood diet is of course not necessarily the same as a vegetarian one, but the two are often combined. Unrefined cereals, unprocessed beans and lentils, and untreated dried fruits and nuts are far better than canned, bottled and packaged foods with their hidden salt, sugar and additive content. A balanced wholefood vegetarian diet embodies the principles of healthy eating: plenty of protein, fibre, vitamins and minerals while cutting down on fat, sugar and salt.

What we need for health are the nutrients (proteins, fats, carbohydrates, vitamins and minerals) as well as water and fibre —these are not nutrients as such, but without them metabolism cannot take place, nutrients are not digested and absorbed, and waste matter is not eliminated.

Protein

We need protein to build new cells and repair damaged tissues. The importance of the protein in the food we eat is determined by the percentage of that protein which can be used by the body. This in turn depends on the pattern of amino acids present. Amino acids are the constituents of protein: about half of them must be supplied in our food, while the rest can be synthesized from these basic nine, which are known as essential amino acids. They can be fully utilized only if present in a particular pattern or proportion, and if one of them is in short supply the others are affected proportionately. The three most likely to be in short supply, especially in a vegetarian diet, are lysine, methionine and tryptophan. It is important therefore to try to ensure that the intake of these three is well balanced.

Some foods have a natural amino acid pattern close to the ideal, and their protein is therefore almost fully used by the body. Milk, eggs, fish, cheese and meat are good examples. Such foods are known as "complete" proteins and, in the past, misleadingly, as "first class" proteins. Since, apart from soya beans, most plant proteins are incomplete, the implication has been that a vegetarian diet must be inferior.

This might be so if we were to get our vegetable protein from a single source. Our natural instinct, however, is to vary our diet, which both makes it more palatable and is more likely to provide a complete range of protein. In India, for example, rice and lentils are generally eaten together. Since rice, like most grains, is low in lysine but high in methionine, while lentils, like most legumes, are the other way round, they complement each other to provide a complete protein, which can be superior to protein from a single source such as meat. The diagram (right) shows which foods can be eaten together to provide high quality protein. Many are popular combinations such as beans on toast, cereal with milk, tortillas with refried beans, pasta with beans, hummus (chick peas with sesame seeds), corn and lima beans, or bread and cheese.

COMPLEMENTARY PROTEINS

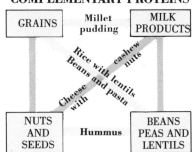

☐ Generally complement one another
▨ Sometimes complement one another

GOOD SOURCES OF PROTEIN

**Recommended daily intake:
65-75 g (men); 58-63 g (women)**

	g per 100 g
Yeast extract	39.7
*Soya flour	36.8
*Parmesan	35.1
Wheatgerm	26.5
*Cheddar & similar cheeses	26.0
Peanuts	24.3
*Brie & similar cheeses	22.8
Black walnuts	20.5
Pistachio nuts	19.3
Almonds	16.9
Bran	14.1
*Cottage cheese	13.6
Wholewheat flour	13.2
Oatmeal	12.4
*Eggs	12.3
Brazil nuts	12.0
Rye flour	8.2
Chick peas (cooked)	8.0
Lentils (cooked)	7.6

*Foods asterisked are complete proteins.

Fats

Although fats are necessary to health, we need only small amounts and are far more likely to eat more than we need, especially in a diet rich in hidden fats in meat, cheese, milk and many convenience foods. On a vegetarian diet the staple foods of grains, beans, peas and lentils are all low in fat.

Fats may be saturated or unsaturated. The former are found mainly in animal products, including butter, cream and cheese, which also contain cholesterol, a fatlike substance which (although necessary for health) can, if present to excess in the blood, build up a deposit on the artery walls and eventually clog them. Although research has not yet supplied the details, it is generally agreed that a high level of blood cholesterol is linked with susceptibility to heart disease, and saturated fats should therefore be eaten in moderation.

Monounsaturated fats, found in olive oil and other vegetable oils, seem not to affect the blood cholesterol level, while polyunsaturated fats such as linoleic acid, also found in vegetable oils, appear to lower it. In the Mediterranean, where oil consumption is high, incidence of heart disease is low.

Remember, though, that when oils or liquid fats are hydrogenated in order to make them solid (for example solid vegetable fat, vegetable ghee) the oils have been artificially saturated and behave just like saturated fats.

Carbohydrates

Our main source of energy is provided by carbohydrates occurring as sugars and starches (in fruits, milk, grains, legumes and vegetables as well as the more obvious sugar, honey and syrup). Refined carbohydrates, for example, cakes and biscuits containing white flour and sugar, provide a lot of calories but few nutrients, and their consumption has been linked with not only tooth decay but also heart disease, high blood pressure and diabetes. Again, a wholefood and vegetarian diet will help to guard against these diseases and is also rich in fibre, another form of carbohydrate, which although indigestible is important to our diet as it is essential for the elimination of toxins.

FATTY ACIDS
g per 100 g

VEGETABLE OILS	SATURATED	MONO-UNSATURATED	POLY-UNSATURATED
Corn (maize)	17.2	30.7	51.6
Olive	14.7	73.0	11.7
Peanut	19.7	50.1	29.8
Safflower	10.7	13.2	75.5
Soya bean	14.7	25.4	59.4
Sunflower	13.7	33.3	52.3
NUTS	SATURATED	MONO-UNSATURATED	POLY-UNSATURATED
Almonds	8.3	71.6	19.6
Brazils	26.7	34.3	39.0
Chestnuts	18.2	39.2	41.9
Hazelnuts	7.5	81.1	10.9
Coconut	83.0	7.0	1.8
Peanuts	15.2	50.1	29.8
Walnuts, English	11.4	16.3	71.4

GOOD SOURCES OF FIBRE

	g per 100 g
Bran	44.0
Dried apricots	24.0
Desiccated coconut	23.5
Dried figs	18.5
Prunes	16.1
Dried peaches	14.3
Almonds	14.3
Soya flour	11.9
Wholewheat flour	9.6
Parsley	9.1
Brazil nuts	9.0
Dates	8.7
Wholewheat bread	8.5
Peanuts	8.1
Haricot beans (cooked)	7.4
Raspberries	7.4
Oatmeal	7.0

Vitamins

Essential for growth, tissue repair and regulating the metabolism, most vitamins cannot be made in the body so it is important to ensure that we get enough in our food.

VITAMIN A (retinol) Needed for healthy skin and mucous membranes, and for vision in dim light. Found as such only in animal products, but can be made in the body from a substance called carotene, present in many brightly coloured orange or green vegetables ($6\mu g$ carotene $= 1 \mu g$ retinol or retinol equivalent). If massive doses taken over a period, excess can build up to toxic levels, but this is unlikely.

Deficiency Can cause eye fatigue or irritation and night blindness in the early stages, but quickly corrected by prompt treatment.

GOOD SOURCES OF VITAMIN A

Recommended daily intake: 750 μg

	retinol equivalents in μg per 100 g
Dandelion greens	2,333
Sorrel	2,150
Carrots	2,000
Parsley	1,166
Spinach (cooked)	1,000
*Butter	985
Sweet potatoes (cooked)	667
Dried apricots	600
Watercress	500
Broccoli (cooked)	417
*Cheddar & similar cheeses	410
Endive	334
Melon (cantaloupe)	334
Mango	200
*Eggs	140
*Milk	40
*Contains retinol	

B VITAMINS Usually treated as a group since tend to occur together. Main functions: to convert food into energy and ensure proper formation of red blood cells. Work best when all present in a balanced ratio; excess of one can create deficiency of others. If taking a supplement of one in particular, ensure adequate supplies of the others. Try to take as food rather than tablets.

VITAMIN B_1 (thiamin) Needed chiefly to metabolize carbohydrates: the more carbohydrates you eat, the more B_1 you need. Easily lost through cooking and storage.

Deficiency If other B vitamins in short supply and carbohydrate intake high, results in beri-beri.

VITAMIN B_2 (riboflavin) Easily destroyed by light. Milk, a primary source, can lose up to 70 per cent of B_2 content if left in direct sunlight for two hours.

Deficiency Common, especially in people who do not drink milk. Can show itself as bloodshot eyes and sore or cracked lips.

VITAMIN B_3 (niacin or nicotinic acid) Can be converted in the body from the amino acid tryptophan, found chiefly in milk and eggs.

Deficiency Can cause irritability, nervousness and eventually severe depression and pellagra, a potentially fatal skin disease associated with mental problems.

VITAMIN B_6 (pyridoxine) Needed in particular by women who are pregnant, on oral contraceptives or suffering from pre-menstrual tension. High alcohol consumption also increases need. Works best in conjunction with B_2 and magnesium. Easily destroyed by heat and during food processing.

Deficiency Symptoms include anaemia, fatigue, depression, nervous disorders and migraine.

VITAMIN B_{12} Found mainly in animal products, although sea vegetables contain traces. Unless eggs and dairy produce are eaten, a supplement must be taken. Easily destroyed by light and heat.

Deficiency Can lead to paralysis; deficiency of both B_{12} and folic acid (see below) results in pernicious anaemia.

FOLIC ACID Another B vitamin, found as name suggests in leaves. If plenty of raw leaf salads eaten, deficiency unlikely. Vegetables lose much of their folic acid in cooking.

Deficiency Found in some women who are pregnant or on oral contraceptives; leads to large-cell anaemia involving exhaustion and depression. May lead to neural tube defects such as spina bifida in foetus.

VITAMIN C (ascorbic acid) Needed to maintain connective tissue protecting and supporting all body cells, and for proper absorption of iron. Important in preventing disease and aiding recovery from illness, especially after an operation. Large amounts required by people under stress or taking drugs, including antibiotics, tranquillizers, alcohol, nicotine and coffee. Not known to be toxic even in massive doses, since excess will be eliminated in urine.

Quickly and easily lost in cooking, whenever cut surfaces are exposed to air, and destroyed by heat.

Deficiency and consequent weakening of connective tissue leads to bleeding, especially in gums, lowers resistance to infection and slows down healing. Deficiency likely unless a fair amount of fruit and vegetables are eaten raw and those that are cooked are treated carefully.

GOOD SOURCES OF VITAMIN B_1

Recommended daily intake: 0.9-1.2 mg

	mg per 100 g
Yeast extract	3.10
Wheatgerm	1.45
Brazil nuts	1.00
Peanuts	0.90
Bran	0.89
Soya flour	0.75
Millet	0.73
Oatmeal	0.50
Wholewheat flour	0.46
Rye flour	0.40
Hazelnuts	0.40
English walnuts	0.30
Wholewheat bread	0.26
Peas (cooked)	0.25

GOOD SOURCES OF VITAMIN B_3

Recommended daily intake: 15 mg-18 mg

	mg per 100 g
Yeast extract	58.0
Bran	29.6
Peanuts	16.0
Yeast	11.0
Wheatgerm	5.8
Wholewheat flour	5.6
Dried peaches	5.3
Mushrooms	4.0
Wholewheat bread	3.9
Dried apricots	3.0
Broad beans (cooked)	3.0
Millet	2.3
Soya flour	2.0
Dates	2.0

GOOD SOURCES OF VITAMIN B_{12}

Recommended daily intake: 1-2 μg

	μg per 100 g
Egg yolk	4.9
Eggs	1.7
Cheddar & similar cheeses	1.5
Parmesan	1.5
Brie & similar cheeses	1.2
Yeast extract	0.5
Cottage cheese	0.5
Milk	0.3
Single cream	0.2
Double cream	0.1
Yogurt	trace
Butter	trace
Sea vegetables	trace

GOOD SOURCES OF VITAMIN B_2

Recommended daily intake: 1.5-1.7 mg

	mg per 100 g
Almonds	0.92
Wheatgerm	0.61
Brie & similar cheeses	0.60
Cheddar & similar cheeses	0.50
Parmesan	0.50
Eggs	0.47
Mushrooms	0.40
Millet	0.38
Bran	0.36
Soya flour	0.31
Parsley	0.30
Yogurt	0.26
Dandelion greens	0.26
Rye flour	0.22
Milk	0.20
Broccoli (cooked)	0.20

GOOD SOURCES OF VITAMIN B_6

Recommended daily intake: 2.0 mg

	mg per 100 g
Bran	1.38
Yeast extract	1.30
Wheatgerm	0.93
English walnuts	0.73
Soya flour	0.57
Hazelnuts	0.55
Bananas	0.51
Wholewheat flour	0.50
Peanuts	0.50
Avocado pear	0.42
Rye flour	0.35
Currants, etc.	0.30
Brussels sprouts (raw)	0.28
Prunes	0.24
Cauliflower (raw)	0.20
Brie & similar cheeses	0.20

GOOD SOURCES OF FOLIC ACID

Recommended daily intake: 200 μg

	μg per 100 g
Yeast	1,250
Yeast extract	1,010
Wheatgerm	330
Endive	330
Bran	260
Spinach (cooked)	140
Sweet potatoes (cooked)	140
Broccoli (cooked)	110
Peanuts	110
Brussels sprouts (raw)	110
Almonds	96
Cabbage (raw)	90
Rye flour	78
Peas (cooked)	78
Hazelnuts	72
Avocado pear	66

GOOD SOURCES OF VITAMIN C

Recommended daily intake: 30 mg

	mg per 100 g
Red pepper	204
Blackcurrants	200
Parsley	150
Sorrel	119
Green pepper	100
Lemons	80
Watercress	60
Cabbage (raw)	60
Strawberries	60
Cauliflower (raw)	60
Oranges	50
Grapefruit	40
Lychees	40
Broccoli (cooked)	34
Mangoes	30
Radishes	25
Raspberries	25
Spinach (cooked)	25

VITAMIN D Needed for absorption of calcium and phosphorus. Formed by action of sunlight on oils in skin: most people who get a reasonable amount of sun need little if any extra in their diet, except for children and pregnant or lactating women.

Best dietary sources are dairy products. Free-range eggs provide a little and margarine is often fortified with it. Can be stored in liver, so excess possible but most unlikely when the vitamin has been produced by natural means.

Deficiency Can cause rickets and weakened or porous bones.

VITAMIN E Needed for formation and maintenance of body cells; helps wounds to heal without formation of scar tissue; thought to have rejuvenating effect. Widely available in foods, chiefly cold pressed vegetable oils, cereal products (wheatgerm and bread made from stone-ground wholemeal flour), eggs and nuts.

Deficiency Rare, but can cause tiredness and anaemia.

VITAMIN K Helps blood to clot. Can be synthesized in body. Widely available in food (in vegetables, cereals, sea vegetables).

Deficiency Unlikely.

Minerals

Like vitamins, needed to ensure that the body functions properly and for growth and repair of cells. Some (chiefly calcium, iron, potassium and magnesium) needed in appreciable quantities; others (zinc and iodine the most important) needed only in very small amounts and known as trace elements.

CALCIUM Needed for healthy bones, teeth and nerves. Vitamin D must also be present.

Deficiency Can lead to nervous exhaustion, irritability, leg cramps and insomnia (hence efficacy of hot milk nightcap). In children can mean stunted growth and rickets.

IRON Needed to carry oxygen around body and for formation of red blood corpuscles. Absorption greatly helped by vitamin C.

Deficiency Leads to tiredness and anaemia; can arise after loss of blood and iron supplements may be necessary—as these tend to destroy vitamin E, take supplement of this too.

GOOD SOURCES OF CALCIUM

Recommended daily intake: 500 mg

	mg per 100 g
Parmesan	1,220
Cheddar & similar cheeses	800
Spinach (cooked)	600
Brie & similar cheeses	380
Parsley	330
Dried figs	280
Almonds	250
Watercress	220
Soya flour	210
Brazil nuts	180
Yogurt	180
Egg yolk	130
Skimmed milk	130
Goat's milk	130
Cow's milk	120
Lemons	110

GOOD SOURCES OF IRON

Recommended daily intake: 10-12 mg

	mg per 100 g
Blackstrap molasses	16.1
Bran	12.9
Wheatgerm	10.0
Parsley	8.0
Soya flour	6.9
Dried peaches	6.8
Millet	6.8
Egg yolk	6.1
Yeast	5.0
Dried figs	4.2
Oatmeal	4.1
Dried apricots	4.1
Spinach (cooked)	4.0
Wholewheat flour	4.0
Yeast extract	3.7

SODIUM and **POTASSIUM** Often treated together, since balance between them is important. Act together to regulate body fluids and amount of water retained.

Sodium deficiency Rarely seen except in cases such as heatstroke involving salt loss through perspiration. For most people sodium is adequately supplied even without table salt. Excess more common, leading to high blood pressure with attendant risk of strokes and heart attacks; also prevents absorption of potassium in the body.

Potassium deficiency Serious, can lead to heart attacks. Associated with high sodium levels and hypoglycaemia (low blood sugar). Although potassium found in wide range of foods, deficiency can occur easily when vegetables overboiled, little raw fruit eaten and diet high in salt and refined foods.

GOOD SOURCES OF POTASSIUM

Recommended daily intake: 3,000 mg

	mg per 100 g
Blackstrap molasses	2,927
Yeast extract	2,600
Dried apricots	1,880
Soya flour	1,660
Bran	1,160
Dried peaches	1,100
Parsley	1,080
Dried figs	1,010
Wheatgerm	1,000
Sultanas	860
Prunes	860
Almonds	860
Raisins	860
Brazil nuts	760

MAGNESIUM Needed to retain potassium in cells and for proper functioning of vitamin B_6. Should be taken in proportion to calcium (about half as much magnesium as calcium).

Deficiency Common in diets rich in refined foods, soft drinks, alcohol and confectionery. Symptoms can be muscle cramps (often causing insomnia), nervous depression and convulsions. Excess, causing lethargy, less common but can occur if too many indigestion remedies containing magnesium taken.

GOOD SOURCES OF MAGNESIUM

Recommended daily intake: 340 mg

	mg per 100 g
Bran	520
Brazil nuts	410
Wheatgerm	300
Almonds	260
Soya flour	240
Black walnuts	190
Peanuts	180
Millet	162
Wholewheat flour	140
English walnuts	130
Oatmeal	110
Wholewheat bread	93
Chick peas (cooked)	67
Haricot beans (cooked)	65
Dried apricots	65
Spinach (cooked)	59

PHOSPHORUS Vital for bones and teeth. If more than twice as much phosphorus as calcium taken, calcium and zinc deficiency can arise.

Deficiency Virtually unknown as phosphorus widely available. Excess more dangerous.

ZINC Exact role not yet fully understood. Although present in many foods, not always fully absorbed, especially if phytic acid present (as in whole grains). Zinc content of crops depends largely on soil—chemical fertilizers can neutralize zinc in soil. As far as is known, even the prolonged taking of supplements is non-toxic.

Deficiency Can cause infertility and stunting and slow down healing of wounds.

GOOD SOURCES OF ZINC

Recommended daily intake: 15 mg

	mg per 100 g
Bran	16.2
Brazil nuts	4.2
Parmesan	4.0
Cheddar & similar cheeses	4.0
Almonds	3.1
Peanuts	3.0
English walnuts	3.0
Wholewheat flour	3.0
Oatmeal	3.0
Brie & similar cheeses	3.0
Rye flour	2.8
Hazelnuts	2.4
Wholewheat bread	2.0

IODINE Essential for correct functioning of thyroid. Only minute quantities needed. Most reliable sources are sea vegetables. Land vegetables (particularly onions and watercress) will contain iodine if present in soil. Nuts and unrefined oils also contain iodine.

Deficiency Even slight deficiency can lead to thyroid disease and high level of blood cholesterol and affect mental and physical development.

FOOD PROFILES

Listed below are some of the most common ingredients of the vegetarian store cupboard. Their protein, carbohydrate, fibre and fat content is given in grams per 100 grams. Vitamins and minerals are listed where significant quantities occur.

Grains

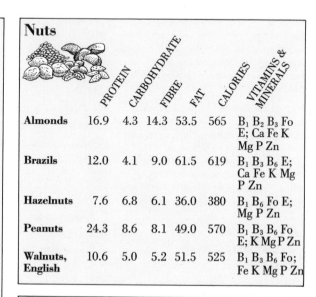

	PROTEIN	CARBOHYDRATE	FIBRE	FAT	CALORIES	VITAMINS & MINERALS
Bran	14.1	26.8	44.0	5.5	206	$B_1 B_2 B_3 B_6$ Fo E; Ca Fe K Mg P Zn
Wholewheat bread	8.8	41.8	8.5	2.7	216	$B_1 B_3$ Fo; Fe Na Mg P Zn
Wholewheat flour	13.2	65.8	9.6	2.0	318	$B_1 B_3 B_6$ Fo E; Fe Mg P Zn
Millet	9.9	72.9	3.2	2.9	327	$B_1 B_2 B_3$; Fe K Mg P
Oatmeal	12.4	72.8	7.0	8.7	401	$B_1 B_3$ Fo; Fe Mg P Zn
Brown rice (cooked)	2.5	25.5	0.3	0.6	119	B_3; Na
Rye flour	8.2	75.9	—	2.0	335	$B_1 B_2 B_3 B_6$ Fo; Fe K Mg P Zn
Wheatgerm	26.5	44.7	—	8.1	347	$B_1 B_2 B_3 B_6$ Fo E; Fe K Mg P

Beans and lentils

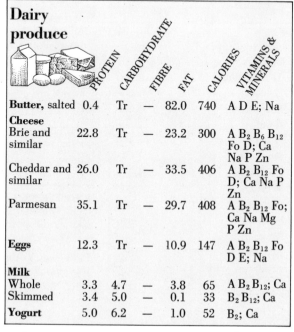

	PROTEIN	CARBOHYDRATE	FIBRE	FAT	CALORIES	VITAMINS & MINERALS
Broad beans	4.1	7.1	4.2	0.6	48	B_3
Butter beans	7.1	17.1	5.1	0.3	95	K Zn
Haricot beans	6.6	16.6	7.4	0.5	93	Fe Mg Zn
Red kidney beans	7.8	21.4	—	0.5	118	Fe
Lentils	7.6	17.0	3.7	0.5	99	B_6; Fe
Soya flour	36.8	23.5	11.9	23.5	447	$B_1 B_2 B_3 B_6$; Ca Fe K Mg P

Nuts

	PROTEIN	CARBOHYDRATE	FIBRE	FAT	CALORIES	VITAMINS & MINERALS
Almonds	16.9	4.3	14.3	53.5	565	$B_1 B_2 B_3$ E; Ca Fe K Mg P Zn
Brazils	12.0	4.1	9.0	61.5	619	$B_1 B_3 B_6$ E; Ca Fe K Mg P Zn
Hazelnuts	7.6	6.8	6.1	36.0	380	$B_1 B_6$ Fo E; Mg P Zn
Peanuts	24.3	8.6	8.1	49.0	570	$B_1 B_3 B_6$ Fo E; K Mg P Zn
Walnuts, English	10.6	5.0	5.2	51.5	525	$B_1 B_3 B_6$ Fo; Fe K Mg P Zn

Dairy produce

	PROTEIN	CARBOHYDRATE	FIBRE	FAT	CALORIES	VITAMINS & MINERALS
Butter, salted	0.4	Tr	—	82.0	740	A D E; Na
Cheese						
Brie and similar	22.8	Tr	—	23.2	300	A $B_2 B_6 B_{12}$ Fo D; Ca Na P Zn
Cheddar and similar	26.0	Tr	—	33.5	406	A $B_2 B_{12}$ Fo D; Ca Na P Zn
Parmesan	35.1	Tr	—	29.7	408	A $B_2 B_{12}$ Fo; Ca Na Mg P Zn
Eggs	12.3	Tr	—	10.9	147	A $B_2 B_{12}$ Fo D E; Na
Milk						
Whole	3.3	4.7	—	3.8	65	A $B_2 B_{12}$; Ca
Skimmed	3.4	5.0	—	0.1	33	$B_2 B_{12}$; Ca
Yogurt	5.0	6.2	—	1.0	52	B_2; Ca

Vegetables

	PROTEIN	CARBOHYDRATE	FIBRE	FAT	CALORIES	VITAMINS & MINERALS
Artichoke, globe (cooked)	1.1	2.7	—	Tr	15	Fo
Asparagus (cooked)	3.4	1.1	1.5	Tr	18	A Fo E
Avocado pear	4.2	1.8	2.0	22.2	223	B$_6$ Fo E
Beetroot (cooked)	1.8	9.9	2.5	Tr	44	Fo; Na
Broccoli (cooked)	3.1	1.6	4.1	Tr	18	A B$_2$ Fo C
Brussels sprouts (cooked)	2.8	1.7	2.9	Tr	18	A B$_6$ Fo C
Cabbage, Savoy (raw)	3.3	3.3	3.1	Tr	26	A B$_6$ Fo C
Carrots (raw)	0.7	5.4	2.9	Tr	23	A B$_6$; Na
Cauliflower	1.6	0.8	1.8	Tr	9	B$_3$ Fo C
Celery	0.9	1.3	4.9	Tr	8	Na
Courgettes (cooked)	1.0	2.5	0.6	0.1	12	
Cucumber	0.6	1.8	0.4	0.1	10	
French beans (cooked)	0.8	1.1	3.2	Tr	7	A Fo
Leeks (cooked)	1.8	4.6	3.9	Tr	24	B$_6$; Fe
Lettuce	1.0	1.2	1.5	0.4	12	A Fo
Mushrooms	1.8	0	2.5	0.6	13	B$_2$ B$_3$ Fo; K
Mustard & Cress	1.6	0.9	3.7	Tr	10	A C
Onions	0.9	5.2	1.3	Tr	23	
Parsley	5.2	Tr	9.1	Tr	21	A B$_2$ B$_6$ C; Ca Fe K
Peas (cooked)	5.0	7.7	5.2	0.4	52	A B$_1$ B$_3$ Fo
Peppers, green	0.9	2.2	0.9	0.4	15	A B$_6$ C
Potatoes (baked)	2.6	25.0	2.5	0.1	105	B$_3$ B$_6$
Potatoes (boiled)	1.4	19.7	1.0	0.1	80	B$_6$
Spinach (cooked)	5.1	1.4	6.3	0.5	30	A B$_2$ B$_6$ Fo C E; Ca Fe Na K Mg
Sweet Potatoes (cooked)	1.1	20.1	2.3	0.6	85	A B$_6$ Fo E
Tomatoes	0.9	2.8	1.5	Tr	14	Fo C
Watercress	2.9	0.7	3.3	Tr	14	A Fo C; Ca Na

Fruit

	PROTEIN	CARBOHYDRATE	FIBRE	FAT	CALORIES	VITAMINS & MINERALS
Apples	0.3	11.9	2.0	Tr	46	
Bananas	1.1	19.2	3.4	0.3	79	B$_6$ Fo
Cherries	0.6	11.9	1.7	Tr	47	
Figs	1.3	9.5	2.5	Tr	41	A
Grapes, black	0.6	15.5	0.4	Tr	61	
Grapefruit	0.6	5.3	0.6	Tr	22	C
Lemons	0.8	3.2	5.2	Tr	15	C; Ca
Mangoes	0.5	15.3	1.5	Tr	59	A C
Melon, cantaloupe	1.0	5.3	1.0	Tr	24	A Fo
Oranges	0.8	8.5	2.0	Tr	35	C Fo
Peaches	0.6	9.1	1.4	Tr	37	A B$_3$
Pears	0.3	10.6	2.3	Tr	41	
Plums	0.6	9.6	2.1	Tr	38	B$_3$
Pineapple	0.5	11.6	1.2	Tr	46	C
Raspberries	0.9	5.6	7.4	Tr	25	C
Strawberries	0.6	6.2	2.2	Tr	26	Fo C
Watermelon	0.4	5.3	—	Tr	21	

Dried fruit

	PROTEIN	CARBOHYDRATE	FIBRE	FAT	CALORIES	VITAMINS & MINERALS
Apricots	4.8	43.4	24.0	Tr	182	A B$_2$ B$_3$ B$_6$; Ca Fe Na K Mg
Currants	1.7	63.1	6.5	Tr	243	B$_6$; K
Dates	2.0	63.9	8.7	Tr	248	B$_3$ B$_6$ Fo; Mg
Figs	3.6	52.9	18.5	Tr	213	B$_3$ B$_6$; Ca Fe Na K Mg
Peaches	3.4	53.0	14.3	Tr	212	A B$_2$ B$_3$; Fe K
Prunes	2.4	40.3	16.1	Tr	161	A B$_2$ B$_3$ B$_6$; K
Raisins	1.1	64.4	6.8	Tr	246	B$_6$; Na K Mg
Sultanas	1.8	64.7	7.0	Tr	250	B$_6$; Na K

INDEX

ACKNOWLEDGMENTS

Author's acknowledgment
I would like to thank my friends and staff at both "Sarah Brown's", Scarborough, England and the Vegetarian Society U.K. for all their help with this book. Grateful thanks too to Jill Dunwoody for additional information and research on foods and nutrients; Jane O'Brien for preparing and testing recipes; Sue Buckley for typing the original draft; Joanne Edmonds of Show Space, York; and Pauline Ashley, Chris Glazebrook, David Sulkin and Fiona Elliott for their encouragement and support.
Sarah Brown

Dorling Kindersley would like to thank the following for their cooperation and help in the production of this book: Rachel Grenfell, Jemima Dunne and Joanna Godfrey Wood for their editorial assistance; Fred and Kathie Gill for proof reading; Anne Fisher for her design assistance; Sloane Square Tiles, The Cocktail Shop, The Reject China Shop, The Craftsmen Potters Association, Covent Garden Kitchen Supplies, David Mellor, The Copper Shop, Divertimenti and The Swiss Centre for supplying photographic props; Cornucopia of Ealing and Petty Wood and Co for supplying ingredients and for their helpful

advice; Andy Butler, assistant to Philip Dowell; Hilary and Richard Bird for the index; and Roger Hillier, Jean Coombes and Anne Burnham.

Photography
Philip Dowell
Peter Myers (pages 112, 113, 117, 119, 121, 162, 165 and 171)

Food for photography prepared by Valerie Barrett (except page 119)
Stylist
Carolyn Russell (except pages 119, 162, 165 and 171)

Illustrators
Rodney Shackell
Russell Barnett
Lindsay Blow

Typesetting
Modern Text Typesetting

Reproduction
A. Mondadori, Verona

The information in the nutritional tables is taken from **The Composition of Foods** (4th edition), McCance and Widdowson, H.M.S.O., London 1978, and **Composition of Foods**, Watt and Merrill, United States Department of Agriculture, 1963.